1
OHIO
CRIMINAL CODE

For Offenses Committed On or After July 1, 1996

Handbook for Law Enforcement Officers

With Selected Traffic and Miscellaneous Offenses

Including Laws Filed Through 1996

Sixteenth Edition

CJ Criminal Justice Studies
Anderson Publishing Co. / Cincinnati, Ohio

1997 OHIO CRIMINAL CODE
(ON OR AFTER JULY 1, 1996)
SIXTEENTH EDITION

© 1997 by Anderson Publishing Co.
2035 Reading Road / Cincinnati, Ohio 45202

Telephone: 800 582-7295
Fax: 513 562-8110
E-Mail: andpubco@aol.com
World Wide Web: http://www.legalpubs.com

All rights reserved.

No part of this book may be reproduced in any form or by any electronic or mechanical means including information storage and retrieval systems without permission in writing from the publisher.

ISBN: 0-87084-467-9

Other Anderson Criminal Justice Publications

- Ohio Criminal Law Handbook, 17th
- Legal Guide for Police: Constitutional Issues, 4th
- Community Policing: How to Get Started
- Community Policing: A Contemporary Perspective
- Issues in Community Policing
- Community Policing in a Rural Setting
- Crisis Negotiations: Managing Critical Incidents and Hostage Situations in Law Enforcement and Corrections
- Police Operations: Analysis and Evaluation
- Crime and Law Enforcement in the Global Village
- Criminal Evidence, 6th
- Effective Police Supervision, 2d (Study Guide Available)
- The Police Manager, 4th
- Police Administration, 3d
- Managing Police Organizations
- Managing Police Personnel
- Report Writing for Criminal Justice Professionals
- Briefs of Leading Cases in Law Enforcement
- Criminal Investigation: A Method for Reconstructing the Past, 2d

Call 1-800-582-7295 • Visit us at www.andersonpublishing.com

INTRODUCTION TO SIXTEENTH EDITION

For Offenses Committed On or After July 1, 1996

Like its predecessors, this edition of the Ohio Criminal Code Handbook focuses on the critical daily concerns of law enforcement officers, and its organization and contents reflect this emphasis.

Part I contains the elements of crimes. As in previous editions, it sets forth the elements of crimes in precise, straightforward outline form. Included are the elements of major traffic offenses and other miscellaneous offenses, in addition to all crimes established by the Criminal Code. It also contains a Penalty Table which lists the basic penalties for most offenses.

Part II, Law Enforcement Procedures, contains an up-to-date list of the miscellaneous sections of the Criminal Code which are most likely to affect the officer's daily work. The condensed time table and the synopsis, in outline form, of search and seizure principles, have been retained.

Part III contains selected Criminal Rules.

Part IV, the Glossary/Index, has been updated.

The search and seizure outline illustrates a cardinal principle of this handbook. The law governing search and seizure can be one of the most complex and confusing areas of American law. No outline of this length could cover all the issues involved. Similarly, the Criminal Code is a lengthy and complex body of law, and no handbook such as this could cover all its provisions. This book and each of its parts have been designed for use by law enforcement professionals who have a thorough familiarity with the Criminal Code and Rules of Criminal Procedure, and for use by educators and students in the criminal justice sciences. They are tools, and like all tools their value and effectiveness will be determined largely by the ability and diligence of those who use them.

This sixteenth edition applies to all crimes committed **on or after** July 1, 1996. For crimes committed **prior to** July 1, 1996, please consult the first volume of the 1996 Ohio Criminal Code Handbook Fifteenth Edition available from Anderson Publishing Co. at 1-800-582-7295.

The comments and suggestions of users are always welcome.

TABLE OF CONTENTS

	Page
INTRODUCTION	v
PART I—ELEMENTS OF CRIMES	1
Chapter 2901—General Provisions	2
In General	
Jurisdiction, Venue, and Limitation of Prosecutions	
Criminal Liability	
Missing Children	2
Chapter 2903—Homicide and Assault	4
Homicide	5
Assault	9
Functionally Impaired Persons	12
Menacing and Stalking	13
Hazing	14
Patients	15
Chapter 2905—Kidnapping and Extortion	18
Kidnapping and Related Offenses	18
Extortion	21
Chapter 2907—Sex Offenses	24
In General	
Sexual Assaults	25
Prostitution	31
Obscenity	34
Chapter 2909—Arson and Related Offenses	43
Chapter 2911—Robbery, Burglary, Trespass and Safecracking	51
Robbery	51
Burglary	52
Trespass	54
Safecracking	56
Chapter 2913—Theft and Fraud	57
In General	
Theft	58
Passing Bad Checks	61
Misuse of Credit Card	61
Forgery	63
Frauds	67
Receiving	74
Chapter 2915—Gambling	75

Bingo	78
Chapter 2917—Offenses Against the Public Peace	85
Inciting, Riot, and Related Offenses	85
Disorderly Conduct	88
Harassment	90
False Alarms	92
Crowd Safety	93
Block Parent Symbol	96
Chapter 2919—Offenses Against the Family	97
Bigamy	97
Abortion	98
Nonsupport and Related Offenses	104
Domestic Violence	111
Chapter 2921—Offenses Against Justice and Public Administration	113
In General	
Bribery and Intimidation	114
Perjury	117
Compounding	121
Obstructing and Escape	125
Peculation and Dereliction	132
Impersonating Peace Officer	137
Using Sham Legal Process	138
Chapter 2923—Conspiracy, Attempt, and Complicity; Weapons Control; Corrupt Activity	140
Conspiracy, Attempt, and Complicity	141
Weapons Control	144
Corrupt Activity	157
Chapter 2925—Drug Offenses	160
Corrupting; Trafficking	160
Drug Abuse	172
Drug Theft	180
Harmful Intoxicants	182
Drug Samples	186
Chapter 2927—Miscellaneous Criminal Code Offenses	188
Chapter 2929—Penalties and Sentencing	196
In General	
Penalties for Murder	
Penalties for Felony	
Penalties for Misdemeanor	
Imprisonment	
Reimbursement by Arsonist	

Organizational Penalties
Multiple Sentences
Modification of Sentence
Offenses Prior to January 1, 1974
Chapter 2933—Search Warrants 199
Selected Miscellaneous and Traffic Offenses 205
PART II—LAW ENFORCEMENT PROCEDURES 215
PART III—CRIMINAL RULES 223
  Crim. R. 3—Complaint 223
  Crim. R. 4—Warrant or Summons: Arrest 223
  Crim. R. 4.1—Optional Procedure in Minor
                Misdemeanor Cases 228
  Crim. R. 41—Search and Seizure 229
  Crim. R. 46—Bail 231
PART IV—GLOSSARY/INDEX 237

PART I

ELEMENTS OF CRIMES

The basic "elements" required to prove every substantive crime defined by the Ohio Criminal Code (Title 29 of the Ohio Revised Code) are listed in this section. In addition, the penalties for each are explained. The section follows the same numerical arrangement as the Criminal Code. The elements of selected traffic and miscellaneous offenses follow those of the Criminal Code.

Venue is not listed in any of the outlines, but must be proven to obtain a conviction.

Some of the penalty sections herein indicate that the presence of one or more additional elements increases the seriousness of the offense. As Section 2945.75 states, "When the presence of one or more additional elements makes an offense one of more serious degree: (1) The affidavit, complaint, indictment, or information either shall state the degree of the offense which the accused is alleged to have committed, or shall allege such additional element or elements. Otherwise such affidavit, complaint, indictment, or information is effective to charge only the least degree of the offense." Therefore, it is important to examine not only the outlines, but the penalty sections, as well.

The elements as listed will suffice where the "attempted offense" rather than the offense itself is to be charged. It should be remembered that an attempt must be committed either purposely or knowingly, and that where the offense attempted must be committed purposely, so must an attempt to commit that offense. Thus, for example, a charge of attempted murder might read, "John Doe did purposely engage in conduct which, if successful, would constitute or result in a violation of R.C. § 2903.02. . . ."

CHAPTER 2901

GENERAL PROVISIONS

IN GENERAL

2901.01	Definitions
2901.02	Classification of Offenses
2901.03	Common Law Offenses Abrogated
2901.04	Rules of Construction
2901.05	Burden and Degree of Proof

JURISDICTION, VENUE, AND LIMITATION OF PROSECUTIONS

2901.11	Criminal Law Jurisdiction
2901.12	Venue
2901.13	Limitation of Criminal Prosecutions

CRIMINAL LIABILITY

2901.21	Requirements for Criminal Liability
2901.22	Culpable Mental States
2901.23	Organizational Criminal Liability
2901.24	Personal Accountability for Organizational Conduct

MISSING CHILDREN

2901.32	Improper Solicitation of Contributions for Missing Children

MISSING CHILDREN

2901.32 Improper Solicitation of Contributions for Missing Children

Elements:

Division (A):

(1) Being an organization
(2) Solicit contributions
(3) For purpose of distributing materials containing information relating to missing children
(4) Unless
   (a) For period of two years prior to time of such solicitation

GENERAL PROVISIONS 2901.32

  (i) Incorporated under R.C. Chapter 1702 or nonprofit corporation law of another state
  (*and*)
  (ii) Exempt from federal income taxation under I.R.C. § 501(a) and described in I.R.C. § 501(c)(3), 501(c)(4), 501(c)(8), 501(c)(10) or 501(c)(19)
  (*and*)
 (b) Does not use fund-raising counsel, professional solicitors, commercial co-venturers, or other charitable organizations as defined in R.C. § 1716.01 to solicit such contributions

Division (B):
(1) Being an organization
(2) Solicit contributions for purpose of distributing materials containing information relating to missing children
(3) Expressly stating or implying in any way that it is affiliated with or soliciting contributions on behalf of an organization established to assist in the location of missing children
(4) Without the express written consent of that organization

Penalty:
A misdemeanor of the third degree.

CHAPTER 2903

HOMICIDE AND ASSAULT

HOMICIDE

2903.01	Aggravated Murder
2903.02	Murder
2903.03	Voluntary Manslaughter
2903.04	Involuntary Manslaughter
2903.05	Negligent Homicide
2903.06	Aggravated Vehicular Homicide
2903.07	Vehicular Homicide
2903.08	Aggravated Vehicular Assault

ASSAULT

2903.11	Felonious Assault
2903.12	Aggravated Assault
2903.13	Assault
2903.14	Negligent Assault

FUNCTIONALLY IMPAIRED PERSONS

2903.16	Failing to Provide for a Functionally Impaired Person

MENACING AND STALKING

2903.21	Aggravated Menacing
2903.21.1	Menacing by Stalking
2903.22	Menacing

HAZING

2903.31	Hazing

PATIENTS

2903.34	Patient Abuse and Neglect
2903.35	Filing a False Patient Abuse or Neglect Complaint

HOMICIDE

2903.01 Aggravated Murder

Elements:

Division (A):

(1) Purposely
(2) With prior calculation and design
(3) (a) Cause another's death
   (*or*)
   (b) the unlawful termination of another's pregnancy

Division (B):

(1) Purposely
(2) (a) Cause another's death
   (*or*)
   (b) the unlawful termination of another's pregnancy
(3) While committing, attempting to commit, fleeing immediately after committing or attempting to commit
(4) Kidnapping, rape, aggravated arson, arson, aggravated robbery, robbery, aggravated burglary, burglary, or escape

Penalty:

Death, life without parole, or life with parole as determined under Sections 2929.02.2, 2929.03, and 2929.04. In addition, offender may be fined not more than $25,000.

The death penalty may not be imposed unless the indictment contains a specification of an aggravating circumstance as set forth in 2929.04.

Note:

Attempted aggravated murder is the same as attempted murder under 2923.02 and is a felony of the first degree.

2903.02 Murder

Elements:

(1) Purposely
(2) (a) Cause another's death
   (*or*)
   (b) the unlawful termination of another's pregnancy

Penalty:
Indefinite term of 15 years to life (see Section 2929.02). In addition, the offender may be fined not more than $15,000.

2903.03 Voluntary Manslaughter

Elements:

(1) Knowingly
(2) (a) Cause another's death
    (*or*)
   (b) the unlawful termination of another's pregnancy
(3) While under the influence of sudden passion or in a sudden fit of rage
(4) Brought on by serious provocation occasioned by the victim
(5) Reasonably sufficient to incite the offender
(6) To use deadly force

Penalty:
Felony of the first degree.

2903.04 Involuntary Manslaughter

Elements:

Division (A):
(1) (a) Cause another's death
    (*or*)
   (b) the unlawful termination of another's pregnancy
(2) As proximate result of committing or attempting to commit a felony

Division (B):
(1) Cause another's death
(2) As proximate result of committing or attempting to commit a misdemeanor of the first, second, third, or fourth degree or a minor misdemeanor

Penalty:
(A) Felony of the first degree.
(B) Felony of the third degree.

If offense that proximately resulted in death of victim and that is basis of violation included as an element the offender's operation or participation in the operation of a motor vehicle, motorcycle, snowmobile, locomotive, watercraft, or aircraft while under the influence of alcohol, drug of abuse, or both, driver's license shall be permanently revoked.

2903.05 Negligent Homicide

Elements:

(1) Negligently
(2) (a) Cause another's death
   (*or*)
   (b) the unlawful termination of another's pregnancy
(3) By means of a deadly weapon or dangerous ordnance

Penalty:
  Misdemeanor of the first degree.

2903.06 Aggravated Vehicular Homicide

Elements:

(1) Recklessly
(2) (a) Cause another's death
   (*or*)
   (b) the unlawful termination of another's pregnancy
(3) While operating or participating in operation of
(4) A motor vehicle, motorcycle, snowmobile, locomotive, watercraft, or aircraft

Penalty:
  Felony of the third degree.
  If a previous conviction of 2903.04 (involving certain conditions), 2903.06, 2903.07, or 2903.08 then a felony of the second degree.

2903.07 Vehicular Homicide

Elements:

(1) Negligently
(2) (a) Cause another's death
   (*or*)
   (b) the unlawful termination of another's pregnancy

(3) By operating or participating in operation of
(4) Motor vehicle, motorcycle, snowmobile, locomotive, watercraft, or aircraft

Penalty:

Misdemeanor of the first degree.

If a previous conviction of 2903.04 (involving certain conditions), 2903.06, 2903.07, or 2903.08 then a felony of the fourth degree.

Note:

An attempt must be committed purposely or knowingly. Therefore, an attempt under 2903.04 (involuntary manslaughter), 2903.05 (negligent homicide), 2903.06 (aggravated vehicular homicide), or 2903.07 (vehicular homicide) necessarily constitutes attempted murder or attempted voluntary manslaughter.

2903.08 Aggravated Vehicular Assault

Elements:

(1) (a) While operating
  (*or*)
  (b) While participating in the operation of
(2) A motor vehicle, motorcycle, snowmobile, locomotive, watercraft, or aircraft
(3) Recklessly cause
(4) Serious physical harm
(5) (a) To another person
  (*or*)
  (b) Another's unborn

Penalty:

A felony of the fourth degree. If the offender has been previously convicted under 2903.04 (involving certain conditions), 2903.06, 2903.07, or 2903.08, a felony of the third degree.

If trier of fact finds offender was under influence of alcohol, drug of abuse, or both, at time of offense—permanent revocation of license.

Note:

As used in this section, "serious physical harm" means any

physical harm which carries a substantial risk of death, or which involves acute pain of such duration as to result in substantial suffering, or which involves any degree of prolonged or intractable pain.

ASSAULT

2903.11 Felonious Assault

Elements:

(1) Knowingly
(2) (a) Cause serious physical harm to another or to another's unborn
    (*or*)
   (b) Cause or attempt to cause physical harm to another or to another's unborn by use of deadly weapon or dangerous ordnance

Penalty:

Felony of the second degree. If the victim is a peace officer, a felony of the first degree.

2903.12 Aggravated Assault

Elements:

(1) While under
    (a) the influence of sudden passion or in a sudden fit of rage
       (*or*)
    (b) extreme emotional stress
(2) Brought on by serious provocation occasioned by the victim reasonably sufficient to incite the person into using deadly force
(3) Knowingly
    (a) Cause serious physical harm to another or to another's unborn
       (*or*)
    (b) Cause or attempt to cause physical harm to another or to another's unborn by means of deadly weapon or dangerous ordnance

Penalty:
Felony of the fourth degree. If the victim is a peace officer, a felony of the third degree.

2903.13 Assault

Elements:

Division (A):
(1) Knowingly
(2) Cause or attempt to cause
(3) Physical harm to another or to another's unborn

Division (B):
(1) Recklessly
(2) Cause serious physical harm to another or to another's unborn

Penalty:
Misdemeanor of the first degree. If committed by a caretaker against a functionally impaired person under the caretaker's care, a felony of the fourth degree. If committed by a caretaker against a functionally impaired person under the caretaker's care, and if the offender has been previously convicted under 2903.11, 2903.13, or 2903.16, and if the previous offense was against a functionally impaired person under the care of the offender, who was acting as a caretaker, a felony of the third degree.

If committed (a) in or on the grounds of a state correctional institution or an institution of the Department of Youth Services, the victim is an employee of the Department of Rehabilitation and Correction, the Department of Youth Services, or a probation department or is on the premises of the particular institution for business purposes or as a visitor, and the offense is committed by a person incarcerated in the state correctional institution, a person institutionalized in the Department of Youth Services institution pursuant to a commitment to the Department of Youth Services, or a probationer, furloughee, or parolee; or (b) in or on the grounds of a local correctional facility, the victim is an employee of the local correctional facility or a probation department or is on the premises of the facility for business purposes or as a visitor, and the offense is committed by a person who is under custody in the facility subsequent to the person's arrest for any crime or delinquent act, subsequent to the person's being charged with or convicted of any crime, or subsequent to the person's being alleged to be or adjudicated a delinquent child; or (c) off the grounds of a state correctional institution and off the grounds of an institution of the Department of Youth Services, the victim is an employee of the Department of Rehabilitation and Correction, the Department of Youth Services, or a probation department, the offense occurs during the employee's official work hours and while the employee is engaged in official work responsibilities, and the offense is committed by a person incarcerated in a state correctional institution or institutionalized in the Department of Youth Services who temporarily is outside of the institution for any purpose or by a probationer, parolee, or furloughee; or (d) off the grounds of a local correctional facility, the victim is an employee of the local correctional facility or a probation department, the offense occurs during the employee's official work hours and while the employee is engaged in official work responsibilities, and the offense is committed by a person who is under custody in the facility subsequent to the person's arrest for any crime or delinquent act, subsequent to the person being charged with or convicted of any crime, or subsequent to the person being alleged to be or adjudicated a delinquent child and who temporarily is outside of the facility for any purpose or by a probationer, parolee, or furloughee, a felony of the fifth degree.

If the victim of the offense is a peace officer, a fire fighter, or person performing emergency medical service, while in the performance of their official duties, felony of the fourth degree.

2903.14 Negligent Assault

Elements:

(1) Negligently
(2) By means of a deadly weapon or dangerous ordnance
(3) Cause physical harm to another or to another's unborn

Penalty:
Misdemeanor of the third degree.

FUNCTIONALLY IMPAIRED PERSONS

2903.16 Failing to Provide for a Functionally Impaired Person

Elements:

Division (A): Knowingly Failing to Provide for a Functionally Impaired Person
(1) Being a caretaker
(2) Knowingly
(3) Fail to provide
(4) To a functionally impaired person under the caretaker's care
(5) Any treatment, care, goods, or service
(6) Necessary to maintain the health or safety of the functionally impaired person
(7) When the failure results in physical harm or serious physical harm to the functionally impaired person

Penalty:

A misdemeanor of the first degree. If the functionally impaired person under the offender's care suffers serious physical harm as a result of the violation, a felony of the fourth degree.

Division (B) Recklessly Failing to Provide for a Functionally Impaired Person
(1) Being a caretaker
(2) Recklessly
(3) Fail to provide
(4) To a functionally impaired person under the caretaker's care
(5) Any treatment, care, goods, or service
(6) Necessary to maintain the health or safety of the functionally impaired person
(7) When the failure results in serious physical harm to the functionally impaired person

Penalty:

A misdemeanor of the second degree. If the functionally impaired person under the offender's care suffers serious physical harm as a result of the violation, a felony of the fourth degree.

Note:
See R.C. § 2903.34 for similar offenses involving residents or patients of care facilities.

MENACING AND STALKING

2903.21 Aggravated Menacing

Elements:

(1) Knowingly
(2) Cause another to believe
(3) That the offender will cause serious physical harm to the person or property of such other person, such other person's unborn, or member of his immediate family

Penalty:
Misdemeanor of the first degree.

2903.21.1 Menacing by Stalking

Elements:

(1) By engaging in a pattern of conduct
(2) Knowingly
(3) (a) Cause another to believe that the offender will cause physical harm to the other person
    (*or*)
    (b) Cause mental distress to the other person

Penalty:
Misdemeanor of the first degree. If prior conviction under this statute involving same victim, a felony of the fifth degree.

Note:
See R.C. § 2903.21.2 for special provisions concerning repeat offenders and offenders violating prior anti-stalking orders. See R.C. § 2903.21.2 for special provisions concerning bail. See R.C. § 2903.21.3 for special provisions concerning anti-stalking protection orders. See R.C. § 2919.26 for special provisions concerning protection orders. See R.C. § 2925.03 for special provisions concerning arrest and detention.

"Pattern of conduct" means two or more actions or incidents closely related in time, regardless of whether there has been a prior conviction based on any of those actions or incidents, R.C. § 2903.21.1.

"Mental distress" means any mental illness or condition that involves some temporary substantial incapacity or mental illness or condition that would normally require psychiatric treatment, R.C. § 2903.21.1.

2903.22 Menacing

Elements:

(1) Knowingly
(2) Cause another to believe
(3) That the offender will cause physical harm to the person or property of such other person, such other person's unborn, or member of his immediate family

Penalty:
Misdemeanor of the fourth degree.

HAZING

2903.31 Hazing

Elements:

Division (B)(1):
(1) Recklessly
(2) Participate in hazing
(3) Another

Division (B)(2):
(1) Being an administrator, employee, or faculty member
(2) Of a public or private primary, secondary, post-secondary school, or other educational institution
(3) Recklessly
(4) Permit hazing
(5) Any person

PATIENTS

2903.34 Patient Abuse and Neglect

Elements:

(A) Patient Abuse
(1) While owning, operating, administering, or an agent or employee of a care facility
(2) (a) Knowingly cause physical harm
      (*or*)
   (b) Recklessly cause serious physical harm
(3) To a resident or patient of the facility
(4) (a) By physical contact with the person
      (*or*)
   (b) By the inappropriate use of physical or chemical restraint, medication, or isolation on the person (i.e., use as punishment, for staff convenience, excessively, as substitute for treatment, or in quantities which preclude habilitation or treatment)

Penalty:
   A felony of the fourth degree. If the offender has previously been convicted under this section, then a felony of the third degree.

(B) Gross Patient Neglect
(1) While owning, operating, administering, or an agent or employee of a care facility
(2) Knowingly
(3) Fail to provide
(4) To a resident or patient of the facility
(5) Any treatment, care, goods, or service
(6) Necessary to maintain the health or safety of the person
(7) When the failure results in physical harm or serious physical harm to the person

Penalty:
   A misdemeanor of the first degree. If the offender has pre-

viously been convicted under this section, then a felony of the fifth degree.

(C) Patient Neglect
(1) While owning, operating, administering, or an agent or employee of a care facility
(2) Recklessly
(3) Fail to provide
(4) To a resident or patient of the facility
(5) Any treatment, care, goods, or service
(6) Necessary to maintain the health or safety of the person
(7) When the failure results in serious physical harm to the person

Penalty:

A misdemeanor of the second degree. If the offender has previously been convicted under this section, then a felony of the fifth degree.

Note:

Any individual convicted of felony violation of this statute who is required to be licensed under Ohio law shall have license revoked. R.C. § 2903.37.

Affirmative defense to charge of neglect or gross neglect that conduct in good faith solely because ordered by person with supervisory authority. See R.C. § 2903.34(B)(2).

Person who relies on treatment by spiritual means through prayer alone under tenets of recognized denomination not to be considered neglected under (D) above for that reason alone. See R.C. § 2903.34(B)(1).

Discharge, discrimination, and retaliation for filing complaint, etc. prohibited, see R.C. § 2903.36.

See also R.C. §§ 2903.11, 2903.13, 2903.16 for similar offenses involving functionally impaired persons.

2903.35 Filing a False Patient Abuse or Neglect Complaint

Elements:

(1) Knowingly
(2) (a) Make a false statement
   (*or*)

(b) Swear or affirm the truth of a false statement previously made

(3) Alleging a violation of R.C. § 2903.34

(4) When statement made with purpose to incriminate another

Penalty:
A misdemeanor of the first degree.

CHAPTER 2905

KIDNAPPING AND EXTORTION

KIDNAPPING AND RELATED OFFENSES

2905.01	Kidnapping
2905.02	Abduction
2905.03	Unlawful Restraint
2905.05	Criminal Child Enticement

EXTORTION

2905.11	Extortion
2905.12	Coercion
2905.22	Extortionate Extension of Credit; Criminal Usury

KIDNAPPING AND RELATED OFFENSES

2905.01 Kidnapping

Elements:

Division (A):
(1) (a) By force, threat, or deception
  (*or*)
  (b) By any means where victim is under 13 or mentally incompetent
(2) (a) Remove person from the place the other person is found
  (*or*)
  (b) Restrain another person of the other person's liberty
(3) With a purpose to:
  (a) Hold for ransom, or as a shield or hostage
  (b) Facilitate commission of any felony or flight thereafter
  (c) Terrorize or inflict serious physical harm on the victim or another
  (d) Engage in sexual activity (R.C. § 2907.01) with the victim against the victim's will
  (e) Hinder, impede, or obstruct a function of government, or to force any action or concession on the part of governmental authority

KIDNAPPING AND EXTORTION 2905.02

Division (B):
(1) (a) By force, threat, or deception
   (*or*)
   (b) By any means where victim is under 13 or mentally incompetent
(2) Knowingly
(3) Under circumstances creating a substantial risk of serious physical harm to the victim, or in the case of a minor victim, under circumstances that either create a substantial risk of serious physical harm to the victim or cause physical harm to the victim
(4) (a) Remove another from the place the other person is found
   (*or*)
   (b) Restrain another of the other person's liberty
   (*or*)
   (c) Hold another in a condition of involuntary servitude

Penalty:
Felony of the first degree. If the victim is released in a safe place, unharmed, a felony of the second degree.

2905.02 Abduction

Elements:

(1) Knowingly
(2) (a) Remove another by force or threat from the place where the other person is found
   (*or*)
   (b) Restrain the liberty of another person by force or threat under circumstances creating a risk of physical harm to the victim or by placing the other person in fear
   (*or*)
   (c) Hold another in a condition of involuntary servitude
(3) Without privilege to do so

Penalty:
Felony of the third degree.

2905.03 Unlawful Restraint

Elements:

(1) Knowingly
(2) Restrain another of his liberty
(3) Without privilege to do so

Penalty:
Misdemeanor of the third degree.

2905.05 Criminal Child Enticement

Elements:

(1) Knowingly
(2) By any means
(3) Without privilege to do so
(4) Solicit, coax, entice, or lure
(5) Any child under 14 years of age (regardless of actor's ignorance of child's age)
(6) To enter into any vehicle as defined in R.C. § 4501.01
(7) If actor does not have express or implied consent of child's parent, guardian, or other legal custodian
(8) (a) Where actor is not either of the following
    (i) A law enforcement officer, medic, firefighter, or other person regularly providing emergency services
    (or)
    (ii) An employee or agent of, or volunteer acting under the direction of, any board of education
    (or)
  (b) Where actor is a person described in (a)(i) or (ii) who at the time is not acting within the scope of the actor's lawful duties in that capacity

Penalty:
A misdemeanor of the first degree. If the offender has previously been convicted of an offense under 2905.05, 2907.02, 2907.03, 2907.12, 2905.01 or 2907.05 when the victim was under 17, then a felony of the fifth degree.

Note:
It is an affirmative defense that the actor undertook the activity

KIDNAPPING AND EXTORTION

in response to a bona fide emergency situation, or in a reasonable belief that it was necessary to preserve the health, safety, or welfare of the child.

EXTORTION

2905.11 Extortion

Elements:

(1) With a purpose to:
   (a) Obtain anything of value or valuable benefit
      (*or*)
   (b) To induce another to do any unlawful act
(2) (a) Threaten to commit a felony
      (*or*)
   (b) Threaten to commit an offense of violence
      (*or*)
   (c) Violate R.C. §§ 2903.21 or 2903.22
      (*or*)
   (d) Utter or threaten any calumny against any person
      (*or*)
   (e) Expose or threaten to expose any matter that tends to:
      (i) Subject any person to hatred, contempt, or ridicule
         (*or*)
      (ii) Damage any person's personal or business reputation
         (*or*)
      (iii) Impair any person's credit

Penalty:
   Felony of the third degree.

Note:
   As used in this section, "threat" includes a direct threat and a threat by innuendo.

2905.12 Coercion

Elements:

(1) With purpose to coerce another into taking or refraining from action concerning which he has a legal freedom of choice

(2) (a) Threaten to commit any offense
   (*or*)
   (b) Utter or threaten any calumny against any person
   (*or*)
   (c) Expose or threaten to expose any matter tending to:
      (i) Subject any person to hatred, contempt, or ridicule
      (*or*)
      (ii) Damage his personal or business repute
      (*or*)
      (iii) Impair his credit
   (*or*)
   (d) Institute or threaten criminal proceedings against any person
   (*or*)
   (e) Take or withhold, or threaten to take or to withhold official action, or cause or threaten to cause official action to be taken or withheld

Penalty:
A misdemeanor of the second degree.

Note:
As used in this section, "threat" includes a direct threat and a threat by innuendo.

2905.22 Extortionate Extension of Credit; Criminal Usury

Elements:

Divisions (A)(1) or (2):
(1) Knowingly
(2) Make or participate in an extortionate extension of credit
    (*or*)
(3) Engage in criminal usury

Division (A)(3):
(1) Possess
(2) Any writing, paper, instrument or article used to record criminally usurious transactions
(3) Knowing that the contents record a criminally usurious transaction

Penalty:
    (A)(1) or (2) Felony of the fourth degree.
    (A)(3) Misdemeanor of the first degree.

Note:
    For standard of proof see R.C. § 2905.23. For evidence as to proof of an implicit threat see R.C. § 2905.24.
    For definitions, see R.C. § 2905.21.

CHAPTER 2907

SEX OFFENSES

IN GENERAL

2907.01	Definitions

SEXUAL ASSAULTS

2907.02	Rape
2907.03	Sexual Battery
2907.04	Corruption of a Minor
2907.05	Gross Sexual Imposition
2907.06	Sexual Imposition
2907.07	Importuning
2907.08	Voyeurism
2907.09	Public Indecency
2907.11	Suppress Information Upon Request

PROSTITUTION

2907.21	Compelling Prostitution
2907.22	Promoting Prostitution
2907.23	Procuring
2907.24	Soliciting; After Positive HIV Test
2907.24.1	Loitering to Engage in Solicitation; Solicitation After Positive HIV Test
2907.25	Prostitution; After Positive HIV Test
2907.26	Rules of Evidence in Prostitution Cases
2907.27	Examination and Treatment for Venereal Disease
2907.28	Cost Incurred in Medical Examination
2907.29	Hospital Emergency Services for Victims

OBSCENITY

2907.31	Disseminating Matter Harmful to Juveniles
2907.31.1	Displaying Matter Harmful to Juveniles
2907.32	Pandering Obscenity
2907.32.1	Pandering Obscenity Involving a Minor
2907.32.2	Pandering Sexually Oriented Matter Involving a Minor
2907.32.3	Illegal Use of Minor in Nudity-Oriented Material or Performance
2907.33	Deception to Obtain Matter Harmful to Juveniles
2907.34	Compelling Acceptance of Objectionable Materials
2907.35	Presumptions; Notice

2907.36 Declaratory Judgment
2907.37 Injunction

SEXUAL ASSAULTS

2907.02 Rape

Elements:

(1) Engage in sexual conduct
(2) (a) With another by purposely compelling submission by force or threat of force
   (or)
   (b) With another not offender's spouse or with offender's spouse if living separate and apart, if:
      (i) For purpose of preventing resistance, offender substantially impairs victim's judgment or control by administering any drug/intoxicant surreptitiously or by force, threat of force, or deception
      (or)
      (ii) Victim under 13, regardless of offender's knowledge of age
      (or)
      (iii) Victim's ability to resist or consent is substantially impaired because of a mental or physical condition or because of advanced age and the offender knows or has reasonable cause to believe that the victim's ability to resist or consent is substantially impaired by such condition or advanced age

Penalty:

Felony of the first degree, unless both elements 2(a) and 2(b)(ii) apply, then the penalty is life imprisonment.

Note:

Victim need not prove physical resistance.

2907.03 Sexual Battery

Elements:

(1) Engage in sexual conduct

(2) With a person not the spouse of the offender when the offender:
   (a) Knowingly coerced the other person to submit by any means that would prevent resistance by a person of ordinary resolution
   (or)
   (b) Knows that the other's ability to appraise the nature of or control his or her conduct is substantially impaired
   (or)
   (c) Knows the other person submits because unaware that the act is being committed
   (or)
   (d) Knows the other person submits because the other person mistakenly identifies the offender as his or her spouse
   (or)
   (e) Is the other person's natural/adoptive parent, stepparent, guardian, custodian, or person in loco parentis
   (or)
   (f) Has supervisory or disciplinary authority over the other person and such person is in legal custody or a patient in a hospital or other institution
   (or)
   (g) Is a teacher, administrator, coach, or other person in authority in a school for which the state board of education prescribes minimum standards in which the other person is enrolled or attends that school and the offender is not enrolled and does not attend that school
   (or)
   (h) The other person is a minor, the offender is a teacher, administrator, coach, or other person in authority employed by or serving in an institution of higher education and the other person is enrolled in that institution
   (or)
   (i) The other person is a minor, and the offender is the other person's athletic or other type of coach, is the other person's instructor, is the leader of a scouting troop of which the other person is a member, or is a person with temporary or occasional disciplinary control over the other person

Penalty:

For a violation of divisions (a), (e), (f), (g), (h), or (i), a felony of the third degree. For a violation of divisions (b), (c), or (d), a felony of the fourth degree.

2907.04 Corruption of a Minor

Elements:

(1) Being 18 or older
(2) Engage in sexual conduct
(3) With another who is not the offender's spouse when:
   (a) Offender knows the other person is 13 years of age or older, but less than 16 years of age
   (or)
   (b) Offender is reckless in this regard

Penalty:

(1) Felony of the fourth degree.
(2) If the offender is less than four (4) years older than the victim, then a misdemeanor of the first degree.

2907.05 Gross Sexual Imposition

Elements:

(1) (a) Have sexual contact with another, not the spouse of the offender
   (or)
   (b) Cause another, not the spouse of the offender, to have sexual contact with the offender
   (or)
   (c) Cause two or more other persons to have sexual contact
(2) (a) By purposely compelling the other, or one of the others, to submit by force or threat of force
   (or)
   (b) For the purpose of preventing resistance, the offender substantially impairs the judgment or control of the other person, or one of the other persons, by administering a drug or intoxicant to the other person surreptitiously or by force, threat of force, or deception

(or)
(c) The offender knows that the judgment or control of the other person, or of one of the other persons is substantially impaired as a result of the influence of any drug or intoxicant administered to the other person with his consent for the purpose of any kind of medical or dental examination, treatment, or surgery

(or)

(d) The other person, or one of the other persons, is under 13, regardless of offender's knowledge of age[.]

(or)

(e) The ability of the other person to resist or consent or the ability of one of the other persons to resist or consent is substantially impaired because of a mental or physical condition or because of advanced age, and the offender knows or has reasonable cause to believe that the ability of the other person or one of the other persons is substantially impaired because of a mental or physical condition or because of advanced age

Penalty:

A felony of the fourth degree unless element (2)(d) applies, then a felony of the third degree.

Note:

Victim need not prove physical resistance.

2907.06 Sexual Imposition

Elements:

(1) (a) Have sexual contact with another, not the spouse of the offender

(or)

(b) Cause another, not the spouse of the offender, to have sexual contact with the offender

(or)

(c) Cause two or more other persons to have sexual contact

(2) (a) The offender knows that the sexual contact is offensive to the other person, or one of the other persons, or is reckless in that regard

(or)
- (b) The offender knows that the other person's, or one of the other persons', ability to appraise the nature of or control the offender's or the touching person's conduct is substantially impaired

  (or)
- (c) The offender knows that the other person, or one of the other persons, submits because of being unaware of the sexual contact

  (or)
- (d) The other person, or one of the other persons, is 13 years of age or older but less than 16 years of age, regardless of the offender's knowledge of this, and the offender is at least 18 and 4 or more years older than such other person.

Penalty:

Misdemeanor of the third degree. If prior conviction under this section or R.C. §§ 2907.02, 2907.03, 2907.04, 2907.05, or 2907.12, a misdemeanor of the first degree.

Note:

The testimony of the victim unsupported by other evidence is not enough for a conviction under this section.

2907.07 Importuning

Elements:

Division (A):
(1) Solicit a person under 13
(2) To engage in sexual activity with the offender
(3) Whether or not offender knows age of such person

Division (B):
(1) Solicit person of same sex
(2) To engage in sexual activity
(3) Knowing such solicitation is offensive to the other person, or being reckless in this regard

Division (C):
(1) Solicit another person, not the spouse of offender
(2) To engage in sexual conduct with the offender

(3) When offender is 18 or older and 4 or more years older than other person, and other person is over 12 years but not over 15 years

(4) Whether or not offender knows age of such person

Penalty:
A violation of (A) or (B) is a misdemeanor of the first degree. A violation of (C) is a misdemeanor of the fourth degree.

2907.08 Voyeurism

Elements:

(1) Trespass or otherwise surreptitiously invade privacy of another
(2) To spy or eavesdrop upon another
(3) With purpose of sexually arousing or gratifying self

Penalty:
A misdemeanor of the third degree.

2907.09 Public Indecency

Elements:

(1) Recklessly
(2) Under circumstances likely to be viewed by and affront others not members of his or her household
(3) (a) Expose his or her private parts, or masturbate
   (*or*)
   (b) Engage in sexual conduct
   (*or*)
   (c) Engage in conduct appearing to ordinary observer to be sexual conduct or masturbation

Penalty:
A misdemeanor of the fourth degree. If the offender previously has been convicted of one violation of this section, a misdemeanor of the third degree. If two prior violations, a misdemeanor of the second degree. If three or more prior violations, a misdemeanor of the first degree.

PROSTITUTION

2907.21 Compelling Prostitution

Elements:

(1) Knowingly
(2) (a) Compel another to engage in sexual activity for hire
      (*or*)
   (b) Induce, procure, encourage, solicit, request, or otherwise facilitate a minor under 16 to engage in sexual activity for hire, whether or not there is actual knowledge as to minor's age
      (*or*)
   (c) Pay or agree to pay a minor, directly or through the minor's agent, so that the minor will engage in sexual activity, whether or not there is actual knowledge of the minor's age
      (*or*)
   (d) Pay a minor, directly or through the minor's agent, for the minor having engaged in sexual activity pursuant to a prior agreement, whether or not there is actual knowledge of the minor's age
      (*or*)
   (e) Allow a minor to engage in sexual activity for hire if the person allowing the child to engage in sexual activity for hire is the parent, guardian, custodian, or person having custody or control, or person in loco parentis of the minor

Penalty:
   A felony of the third degree. If the offender commits a violation of Division (2)(a) and the person compelled to engage in sexual activity for hire is less than 16, a felony of the second degree.

Note:
   Sentences of imprisonment for violations under 2(b), (c), and (d) above are to be served consecutively to any other sentence of imprisonment.

2907.22 Promoting Prostitution

Elements:

(1) Knowingly

(2) (a) Establish, maintain, operate, manage, supervise, control, or have an interest in a brothel
(*or*)
  (b) Supervise, manage or control activities of a prostitute in engaging in sexual activity for hire
(*or*)
  (c) (i) Transport, or cause another to be transported
   (ii) Across the boundary of Ohio or any county in Ohio
   (iii) To facilitate the other person's engaging in sexual activity for hire
(*or*)
  (d) (i) Induce or procure another to engage in sexual activity for hire
   (ii) For the purpose of violating or facilitating a violation of this section

Penalty:

A felony of the fourth degree. However, if the prostitute, or person transported, induced or procured is a minor under 16 (whether or not the offender knows the age), then a felony of the third degree.

Note:

Any sentence of imprisonment imposed for a second-degree felony conviction is to be served consecutively to any other term of imprisonment.

2907.23 Procuring

Elements:

Division (A):

(1) Knowingly
(2) For gain
(3) (a) Entice or solicit another to patronize a prostitute or brothel
(*or*)
  (b) Procure a prostitute for another to patronize
(*or*)
  (c) Take or direct another person to place for the purpose of patronizing a prostitute as requested by such other person

Division (B):
(1) While having authority/responsibility over premises
(2) Knowingly
(3) Permit the premises to be used
(4) For the purpose of engaging in sexual activity for hire

Penalty:
A misdemeanor of the first degree.

2907.24 Soliciting; After Positive HIV Test

Elements:

Division (A):
(1) Solicit another
(2) To engage in sexual activity for hire

Division (B):
(1) Engage in conduct in violation of Division (A)
(2) With knowledge that he or she has tested positive as a carrier of a virus that causes AIDS

Penalty:
Division (A): A misdemeanor of the third degree.
Division (B): A felony of the third degree.

2907.24.1 Loitering To Engage in Solicitation; Solicitation After A Positive HIV Test

Division (A):
(1) (a) Beckon to, stop, or attempt to stop another
(*or*)
(b) Engage, or attempt to engage another in conversation
(*or*)
(c) Stop or attempt to stop the operator of a vehicle or approach a stationary vehicle
(*or*)
(d) If the offender is the operator of or a passenger in a vehicle, stop, attempt to stop, beckon to, attempt to beckon to, or entice another to approach or enter the vehicle of which the offender is the operator or passenger
(*or*)

(e) Interfere with the passage of another
(2) While in or near a public place
(3) With purpose to solicit another to engage in sexual activity for hire

Division (B):
(1) Engage in conduct in violation of Division (A)
(2) With knowledge that he or she has tested positive as a carrier of a virus that causes AIDS

Penalty:
   Division (A): A misdemeanor of the third degree.
   Division (B): A felony of the fifth degree.

2907.25 Prostitution; After Positive HIV Test

Elements:

Division (A):
(1) Engage in sexual activity
(2) For hire

Division (B):
(1) Engage in sexual activity
(2) For hire
(3) With knowledge that he or she has tested positive as a carrier of a virus that causes AIDS

Penalty:
   Division (A): A misdemeanor of the third degree.
   Division (B): A felony of the third degree.

OBSCENITY

2907.31 Disseminating Matter Harmful to Juveniles

Elements:

(1) Recklessly
(2) With knowledge of its character or content
(3) (a) Sell, deliver, furnish, disseminate, provide, exhibit, rent, or present to a juvenile any material or performance that

is obscene or harmful to juveniles
(*or*)
(b) Offer or agree to sell, deliver, furnish, disseminate, provide, exhibit, rent, or present to a juvenile any material or performance that is obscene or harmful to juveniles
(*or*)
(c) Allow any juvenile to review or peruse any material or view any live performance that is harmful to juveniles.

Penalty:

If the material or performance is harmful to juveniles but not obscene, a misdemeanor of the first degree. If the material or performance is obscene and the juvenile is thirteen years of age or older, a felony of the fifth degree. If the material or performance is obscene and the juvenile is under thirteen years of age, a felony of the fourth degree.

Note:

See R.C. § 2907.31 for affirmative defenses.

2907.31.1 Displaying Matter Harmful to Juveniles

Elements:

(1) Having custody, control, or supervision of a commercial establishment
(2) With knowledge of the character or content of the material involved
(3) Display at the establishment
(4) Any material that is
 (a) Harmful to juveniles
 (*and*)
 (b) Open to view by juveniles as part of the invited general public

Penalty:

A misdemeanor of the first degree.

Note:

Each day of violation is a separate offense.

See R.C. § 2907.31.1 for provisions regarding "blinder racks," placing material behind counter, etc.

2907.32 Pandering Obscenity

Elements:

(1) Knowing the character of the material or performance involved
(2) (a) (i) Create, reproduce or publish obscene material
    (ii) Knowing that the material is to be used for commercial exploitation or will be publicly disseminated or displayed, or is reckless in that regard
    (or)
  (b) (i) Promote or advertise for sale, delivery or dissemination or sell, deliver, or publicly disseminate, display, exhibit, rent, provide, or offer to do any of the foregoing
    (ii) Obscene material
    (or)
  (c) (i) Create, direct or produce
    (ii) An obscene performance
    (iii) Knowing it is to be commercially exploited or publicly presented, or being reckless in that regard
    (or)
  (d) (i) Advertise or promote an obscene performance for presentation
    (ii) Present or participate in an obscene performance
    (iii) Which is presented publicly, or when admission is charged
    (or)
  (e) (i) Buy, procure, possess or control obscene material
    (ii) With purpose to violate (2) (b) or (2) (d) above

Penalty:

A felony of the fifth degree. If the offender has previously been convicted of an offense under 2907.31 or 2907.32, then a felony of the fourth degree.

2907.32.1 Pandering Obscenity Involving a Minor

Elements:

(1) With knowledge of the character of the material or performance
(2) (a) Create, reproduce, or publish

SEX OFFENSES **2907.32.1**

- (i) Any obscene material
- (ii) That has a minor as one of its participants or portrayed observers
- (iii) When the offender knows that it will be used for commercial exploitation or will be publicly disseminated or displayed, or is reckless in that regard

  (*or*)

(b) Promote or advertise for sale or dissemination, sell, deliver, disseminate, display, exhibit, present, rent, or provide, or offer to do any of the foregoing
  - (i) Any obscene material
  - (ii) That has a minor as one of its participants or portrayed observers

    (*or*)

(c) Create, direct, or produce
  - (i) An obscene performance
  - (ii) That has a minor as one of its participants
  - (iii) When the offender knows that it will be used for commercial exploitation or will be publicly presented, or is reckless in that regard

    (*or*)

(d) Advertise or promote for presentation, present, or participate in presenting
  - (i) An obscene performance
  - (ii) That has a minor as one of its participants
  - (iii) When the performance is presented publicly or admission is charged

    (*or*)

(e) Buy, procure, possess or control
  - (i) Any obscene material
  - (ii) That has a minor as one of its participants

    (*or*)

(f) Bring or cause to be brought into this state
  - (i) Any obscene material
  - (ii) That has a minor as one of its participants or portrayed observers

Penalty:

A felony of the second degree, except Division (2)(e) which

is a felony of the fourth degree unless the offender has previously been convicted or pleaded guilty under R.C. §§ 2907.32.1-2907.32.3, in which case it is a felony of the third degree.

Note:

This section does not apply to any material or performance that is sold, disseminated, displayed, possessed, controlled, brought or caused to be brought into this state, or presented for a bona fide medical, scientific, educational, religious, governmental, judicial, or other proper purpose, by or to a physician, psychologist, sociologist, scientist, teacher, person pursuing bona fide studies or research, librarian, clergyman, prosecutor, judge, or other person having a proper interest in the material or performance.

Mistake of age is not a defense.

A sentence of imprisonment is to be served consecutively to any other sentence of imprisonment.

2907.32.2 Pandering Sexually Oriented Matter Involving a Minor

Elements:

(1) With knowledge of the character of the material or performance involved

(2) (a) Create, record, photograph, film, develop, reproduce, or publish any material that shows
   (or)
   (b) Advertise for sale or dissemination, sell, distribute, transport, disseminate, exhibit or display any material that shows
   (or)
   (c) Create, direct, or produce a performance that shows
   (or)
   (d) Advertise for presentation, present, or participate in presenting a performance that shows
   (or)
   (e) Solicit, receive, purchase, exchange, possess or control any material that shows
   (or)

- (f) Bring or cause to be brought into this state any material

   (*or*)
- (g) Bring, cause to be brought, or finance the bringing of a minor into or across this state, with the intent that

   (*or*)
- (h) Bring, cause to be brought, or finance the bringing of a minor into or across this state, for the purpose of producing material containing or representation depicting

(3) A minor

(4) Participating or engaging in sexual activity, masturbation, or bestiality

Penalty:

A felony of the second degree, except Division (2)(e) which is a felony of the fifth degree unless the offender has previously been convicted or pleaded guilty under R.C. §§ 2907.32.1-2907.32.3, then a felony of the fourth degree.

Note:

This section does not apply to materials or performances used for a proper purpose by persons having a proper interest therein. Proper purposes include bona fide medical, scientific, educational, religious, governmental, judicial, and other proper purposes; persons having a proper interest include physicians, psychologists, sociologists, scientists, teachers, persons pursuing bona fide studies or research, librarians, clergymen, prosecutors, judges, or other persons having a proper interest in the material or performance.

Mistake of age is not a defense.

A sentence of imprisonment is to be served consecutively to any other sentence of imprisonment.

2907.32.3 Illegal Use of Minor in Nudity-Oriented Material or Performance

Elements:

[A](1) (a) Photograph

   (*or*)

   (b) Create, direct, produce, or transfer any material or performance showing

2907.32.3

(2) A minor who is not the actor's child or ward
(3) In a state of nudity
(4) Unless
   (a) The material or performance is or is to be sold, disseminated, displayed, possessed, controlled, brought or caused to be brought into this state
      (i) For a proper purpose
      (ii) By or to a person having a proper interest
        (*and*)
   (b) The minor's parents, guardian, or custodian consents in writing to the photographing of the minor, to the use of the minor in the material or performance, or to the transfer of the material and to the specific manner in which the material or performance is to be used

[B](1) (a) Photograph
     (*or*)
   (b) Consent to
      (i) Photographing of
        (*or*)
      (ii) Use in any material or performance of
        (*or*)
   (c) Use or transfer of any material or performance using
(2) The actor's minor child or ward
(3) In a state of nudity
(4) Unless the material or performance is sold, disseminated, displayed, possessed, controlled, brought or caused to be brought into this state
     (i) For a proper purpose
     (ii) By or to a person having a proper interest

[C](1) (a) Possess
     (*or*)
   (b) View
(2) Any material or performance showing
(3) A minor who is not the actor's child or ward
(4) In a state of nudity
(5) Unless
   (a) The material or performance is sold, disseminated, displayed, possessed, controlled, brought or caused

      to be brought into this state
   (i) For a proper purpose
   (ii) By or to a person having a proper interest
      (*or*)
(b) The actor knows that the child's parents, guardian, or custodian has consented in writing to the photographing or use of the minor in a state of nudity, and to the manner in which the material or performance is used or transferred

Penalty:

A felony of the second degree, except [C] which is a felony of the fifth degree unless the offender has previously been convicted or pleaded guilty under R.C. §§ 2907.32.1-2907.32.3, then a felony of the fourth degree.

Note:

Under this section, a proper purpose is a bona fide artistic, medical, scientific, educational, religious, governmental, judicial, or other proper purpose; a person having a proper interest includes a physician, psychologist, sociologist, scientist, teacher, person pursuing bona fide studies or research, librarian, clergyman, prosecutor, judge, or other person having a proper interest in the material or performance.

2907.33 Deception to Obtain Matter Harmful to Juveniles

Elements:

Division (A):

(1) With purpose to enable a juvenile to obtain material, or gain admission to a performance, harmful to juveniles
(2) (a) Falsely represent that he is the juvenile's parent, guardian, or spouse
   (*or*)
   (b) Furnish the juvenile with identification or documents purporting to show the juvenile is 18 or over, or married

Division (B):

(1) Being a juvenile
(2) For purpose of obtaining material, or gaining admission to a

performance, harmful to juveniles
- (3) (a) Falsely represent the juvenile is 18 or over or married
    (*or*)
  - (b) Exhibit identification or documents purporting to show the juvenile is 18 or over or married

Penalty:

A misdemeanor of the second degree for an adult. A juvenile is to be judged an unruly child with appropriate disposition pursuant to Chapter 2151. of the Code.

2907.34 Compelling Acceptance of Objectionable Materials

Elements:

Division (A):
- (1) As a precondition to the sale, allocation, consignment, or delivery of any material or goods
- (2) Over objections of the purchaser/consignee
- (3) Require such purchaser/consignee
- (4) To accept other material reasonably believed to be obscene, or which, if furnished/presented to a juvenile, would violate R.C. § 2907.31

Division (B):
- (1) (a) Deny or threaten to deny any franchise to
    (*or*)
  - (b) Impose or threaten to impose any financial penalty upon
- (2) Any purchaser or consignee
- (3) (a) Because he failed or refused to accept any material reasonably believed to be obscene as a condition to the sale, allocation, consignment or delivery of any material or goods
    (*or*)
  - (b) Because he returned any material believed to be obscene which he initially accepted.

Penalty:

A felony of the fifth degree.

CHAPTER 2909

ARSON AND RELATED OFFENSES

2909.01	Definitions
2909.02	Aggravated Arson
2909.03	Arson
2909.04	Disrupting Public Services
2909.05	Vandalism
2909.06	Criminal Damaging or Endangering
2909.07	Criminal Mischief
2909.08	Endangering Aircraft or Airport Operations
2909.11	Determining Property Value or Amount of Physical Harm

2909.02 Aggravated Arson

Elements:

(1) Knowingly

(2) (a) Create substantial risk of serious physical harm to any person other than the offender
   (*or*)
   (b) Cause physical harm to an occupied structure
   (*or*)
   (c) Create, through the offer or acceptance of an agreement for hire or other consideration, a substantial risk of serious physical harm to any occupied structure

(3) By means of fire or explosion

Penalty:

Violation of Division (2)(a), a felony of the first degree. Violation of Division (2)(b), a felony of the second degree.

Note:

R.C. § 2929.11(A) and (E) require restitution to the property owner and governmental authorities.

2909.03 Arson

Elements:

(1) Knowingly

(2) (a) Cause or create substantial risk of physical harm to any property of another without the other person's consent
(*or*)
   (b) Cause or create substantial risk of physical harm to any property of the offender or another, with purpose to defraud
(*or*)
   (c) Cause or create substantial risk of physical harm to statehouse, courthouse, school building, or other building or structure owned or controlled by state or any political subdivision, or any department, agency, instrumentality of either the state or a political subdivision, and used for public purpose
(*or*)
   (d) Cause, or create a substantial risk of, physical harm, through the offer or the acceptance of an agreement for hire or other consideration, to any property of another without the other person's consent or to any property of the offender or another with purpose to defraud
   (e) Cause, or create a substantial risk of, physical harm to any park, preserve, wildlands, brush-covered land, cut-over land, forest, timberland, greenlands, woods, or similar real property that is owned or controlled by another person, the state, or a political subdivision without the consent of the other person, the state, or the political subdivision;
(*or*)
   (f) With purpose to defraud, cause, or create a substantial risk of, physical harm to any park, preserve, wildlands, brush-covered land, cut-over land, forest, timberland, greenlands, woods, or similar real property that is owned or controlled by the offender, another person, the state, or a political subdivision
(3) By means of fire or explosion

Penalty:

Violation of (2)(a) above, value of property or amount of physicial harm less than $500, a misdemeanor of the first degree.

Violation of (2)(a) above, value of property or amount of physical harm $500 or more, a felony of the fourth degree.

ARSON AND RELATED OFFENSES 2909.05

Violation of (2)(b), (c), (e), or (f), a felony of the fourth degree.
Violation of (2)(d), a felony of the third degree.

Note:

R.C. § 2929.21(A) requires restitution to the property owner and governmental authorities.

2909.04 Disrupting Public Services

Elements:

(1) (a) Purposely by any means
     (or)
  (b) Knowingly, by damaging or tampering with property
(2) Interrupt or impair
  (a) TV, radio, telephone, telegraph, or other mass communications service
     (or)
  (b) Police, fire, other public service communications
     (or)
  (c) Radar, loran, radio, other electronic aids to air or marine navigation or communications
     (or)
  (d) Amateur or citizens band radio communications being used for public service or emergency communications
     (or)
  (e) Public transportation, including school bus transportation, water supply, gas, power, other utility service to public
     (or)
(3) Substantially impair
  (a) Ability of law enforcement officers, firemen, rescue personnel to respond to emergency or to protect and preserve any person or property from serious physical harm

Penalty:

Felony of the fourth degree.

2909.05 Vandalism

Elements:

Division (A):

(1) Knowingly cause serious physical harm to
(2) Occupied structure or any of its contents

Division (B)(1):
(1) Knowingly cause serious physical harm to
(2) Property owned or possessed by another and which is
   (a) Used by its owner or possessor in the owner or possessor's profession, business, trade, occupation, and value of property or physical harm is $500 or more
   (or)
   (b) Such property or equivalent necessary for its owner or possessor to engage in profession, business, trade, occupation

Division (B)(2):
(1) Knowingly cause serious physical harm to
(2) Property owned, leased, or controlled by a government entity

Division (C):
(1) Knowingly, and without privilege to do so, cause serious physical harm (involving $300 or more in value) to
(2) (a) Any tomb, monument, gravestone, or other similar structure used as a memorial for the dead
   (or)
   (b) Any fence, railing, curb, or other property used to protect, enclose, or ornament any place of burial
   (or)
   (c) A place of burial

Division (D):
(1) Knowingly, and without privilege to do so, cause physical harm to
(2) A place of burial
(3) By breaking and entering into a tomb, crypt, casket, or other structure that is used as a memorial for the dead or as an enclosure for the dead

Penalty:
Value of property or amount of physical harm less than $5,000, a felony of the fifth degree.
Value of property or amount of physical harm more than $5,000 but less than $100,000, a felony of the fourth degree.

Value of property or amount of physical harm more than $100,000, a felony of the third degree.

2909.06 Criminal Damaging or Endangering

Elements:

(1) Cause or create substantial risk of physical harm to property of another without consent
(2) (a) Knowingly, by any means
    (*or*)
    (b) Recklessly, by fire, explosion, flood, poison gas, poison, radioactive material, caustic or corrosive material, other inherently dangerous agency or substance

Penalty:

A misdmeanor of the second degree unless a risk of physical harm to any person, then a misdemeanor of the first degree. If the property involved in a violation of this section is an aircraft, an aircraft engine, propeller, appliance, spare part, or any other equipment or implement used or intended to be used in the operation of an aircraft and if the violation creates a risk of physical harm to any person, then a felony of the fifth degree. If the property involved in a violation is an aircraft, an aircraft engine, propeller, appliance, spare part, or any other equipment or implement used or intended to be used in the operation of an aircraft and if the violation causes substantial risk of physical harm to any person or if the property involved is an occupied aircraft, a felony of the fourth degree.

2909.07 Criminal Mischief

Elements:

(1) Without privilege knowingly move, deface, damage, destroy, or otherwise improperly tamper with property of another
    (*or*)
(2) With purpose to interfere with use or enjoyment of property of another, employ tear gas device, stink bomb, smoke generator, or other device, releasing a substance harmful or offensive to persons exposed, or that tends to cause public alarm

2909.07

(*or*)

(3) Without privilege to do so, knowingly move, deface, damage, destroy, or otherwise improperly tamper with bench mark, triangulation station, boundary marker, other survey station, monument, or marker

(*or*)

(4) Without privilege to do so, knowingly move, deface, damage, destroy, or otherwise improperly tamper with any safety device, property of another or the offender, when required or placed for safety of others, so as to destroy or diminish its effectiveness or availability for intended purpose

(5) With purpose to interfere with the use or enjoyment of the property of another, set a fire on the land of another or place personal property that has been set on fire on the land of another, which fire or personal property is outside and apart from any building, other structure, or personal property that is on that land

Penalty:

A misdemeanor of the third degree unless a risk of physical harm to any person, then a misdemeanor of the first degree. If the property involved in violation of this section is an aircraft, an aircraft engine, propeller, appliance, spare part, fuel, lubricant, hydraulic fluid, any other equipment, implement, or material used or intended to be used in the operation of an aircraft, or any cargo carried or intended to be carried in an aircraft and if the violation creates a risk of physical harm to any person, then a felony of the fifth degree. If the property involved in a violation is an aircraft, an aircraft engine, propeller, appliance, spare part, or any other equipment or implement used or intended to be used in the operation of an aircraft and if the violation causes substantial risk of physical harm to any person or if the property involved is an occupied aircraft, a felony of the fourth degree.

Note:

As used in this section, "safety device" means any fire extinguisher, fire hose, or fire axe, or any fire escape, emergency exit, or emergency escape equipment, or any life line, life-saving ring, life preserver, or life boat or raft, or any alarm, light, flare,

ARSON AND RELATED OFFENSES **2909.08** 49

signal, sign, or notice intended to warn of danger or emergency, or intended for other safety purposes, or any guard railing or safety barricade, or any traffic sign or signal, or any railroad grade crossing sign, signal, or gate, or any first aid or survival equipment, or any other device, apparatus, or equipment intended for protecting or preserving the safety of persons or property.

2909.08 Endangering Aircraft or Airport Operations

Elements:

[A](1) Knowingly
    (2) (a) (i) Throw an object at or drop an object upon
          (ii) Any moving aircraft
          (*or*)
      (b) (i) Shoot with a bow and arrow or discharge a firearm, air gun, or spring-operated gun
          (ii) At or toward any aircraft

[B](1) Knowingly or recklessly
    (2) Shoot with a bow and arrow or discharge a firearm, air gun, or spring-operated gun
    (3) Upon or over any airport operational surface

Penalty:

A violation of Division (A), a misdemeanor of the first degree unless a risk of physical harm to any person, then a felony of the fifth degree. A violation of Division (B), a misdemeanor of the second degree unless a risk of physical harm to any person, then a felony of the fifth degree (a violation while hunting results additionally in revocation or suspension of hunting license pursuant to R.C. § 1533.68). If violation creates a substantial risk of physical harm to any person or if the aircraft is occupied, a felony of the fourth degree.

Note:

Division (B) above does not apply to any federal or Ohio or other state officer, agent, or employee, or any law enforcement officer, who is authorized to discharge firearms and is acting within the scope of his duties; or to any person who, with the consent of the owner or operator of the airport operational surface or the authorized agent of either, is lawfully engaging in any hunting or sporting activity or is otherwise lawfully discharging a firearm. See R.C. § 2909.08(C). R.C § 2909.08(F) provides that any bow and arrow, air gun, spring-operated gun, or firearm used in a felony violation of this section shall be seized and forfeited, and disposed of pursuant to R.C. § 2933.41.

Definitions:

See R.C. § 2909.08(A) for definitions of "air gun," "firearm," "spring-operated gun," and "airport operational surface."

CHAPTER 2911

ROBBERY, BURGLARY, TRESPASS AND SAFECRACKING

ROBBERY

2911.01	Aggravated Robbery
2911.02	Robbery

BURGLARY

2911.11	Aggravated Burglary
2911.12	Burglary
2911.13	Breaking and Entering

TRESPASS

2911.21	Criminal Trespass
2911.21.1	Aggravated Trespass

SAFECRACKING

2911.31	Safecracking
2911.32	Tampering with Coin Machines

ROBBERY

2911.01 Aggravated Robbery

Elements:

(1) (a) Attempt or commit theft offense

  (*or*)

  (b) Flee immediately after the theft or attempt

(2) While

  (a) Having a deadly weapon on or about the offender's person or under the offender's control and either display the weapon, brandish it, indicate that the offender possesses it, or use it

  (*or*)

  (b) Having a dangerous ordnance on or about the offender's person or under the offender's control

  (*or*)

(c) Inflicting or attempting to inflict serious physical harm on another

Penalty:

Felony of the first degree.

2911.02 Robbery

Elements:

(1) (a) Attempt or commit theft offense
   (*or*)
   (b) Flee immediately after the attempt or offense
(2) While
   (a) Having a deadly weapon on or about the offender's person or under the offender's control
   (*or*)
   (b) Inflicting, or attempting to inflict, or threatening to inflict physical harm on another
   (*or*)
   (c) Use or threaten the immediate use of force against another

Penalty:

Violation of Divisions (2)(a) or (b), a felony of the second degree. Violation of Division (2)(c), a felony of the third degree.

BURGLARY

2911.11 Aggravated Burglary

Elements:

(1) Trespass in:
   (a) Occupied structure
   (*or*)
   (b) A separately secured or separately occupied portion thereof
(2) By force, stealth, or deception
(3) When another person other than an accomplice of the offender is present
(4) With purpose to commit in the structure or in the separately secured or separately occupied portion or the structure any

ROBBERY, BURGLARY, ETC.

criminal offense
(5) If any of the following apply:
   (a) The offender inflicts, attempts or threatens to inflict physical harm on another
      (*or*)
   (b) The offender has a deadly weapon or dangerous ordnance on or about the offender's person or under the offender's control

Penalty:
Felony of the first degree.

2911.12 Burglary

Elements:

(1) By means of force, stealth, or deception
(2) Trespass
(3) (a) In an occupied structure or in a separately secured or separately occupied portion of an occupied structure when another person other than an accomplice of the offender is present, with purpose to commit in the structure or in the separately secured or separately occupied portion of the structure any criminal offense
   (*or*)
   (b) In an occupied structure or in a separately secured or separately occupied portion of an occupied structure that is a permanent or temporary habitation of any person when any person other than an accomplice of the offender is present or likely to be present, with purpose to commit in the habitation any criminal offense
   (*or*)
   (c) In an occupied structure or in a separately secured or separately occupied portion of an occupied structure, with purpose to commit in the structure or separately occupied portion of the structure any criminal offense
   (*or*)
   (d) In a permanent or temporary habitation of any person when any person other than an accomplice of the offender is present or likely to be present

Penalty:
   Offense under (3)(a) or (3)(b), a felony of the second degree. Offense under (3)(c), a felony of the third degree. Offense under (3)(d), a felony of the fourth degree.

2911.13 Breaking and Entering

Elements:

Division (A):
(1) With purpose to commit a theft offense or any felony therein
(2) Trespass in unoccupied structure
(3) By force, stealth, or deception

Division (B):
(1) With purpose to commit a felony
(2) Trespass on land or premises of another

Penalty:
   A felony of the fifth degree.

TRESPASS

2911.21 Criminal Trespass

Elements:

(1) Without privilege to do so
(2) (a) Knowingly enter or remain on land or premises of another
       (or)
   (b) (i) Knowingly enter or remain on land or premises of another, use of which is lawfully restricted to certain persons, purposes, modes, or hours
       (ii) When the offender knows he is violating such restrictions or is reckless in that regard
           (or)
   (c) Recklessly enter or remain on the land or premises of another, as to which notice against unauthorized access or presence is given
       (i) By actual communication to the offender
           (or)
       (ii) In a manner prescribed by law

    (or)
  - (iii) By posting in a manner reasonably calculated to come to the attention of potential intruders
    (or)
  - (iv) By fencing or other enclosure manifestly designed to restrict access
    (or)
- (d) (i) Being on the land or premises of another
  - (ii) Negligently failing or refusing to leave
  - (iii) Upon being notified to do so by the owner or occupant, or the agent or servant of either

Penalty:

A misdemeanor of the fourth degree.

Note:

It is no defense to this charge that the premises were owned or controlled by a public agency, or that there was authority to enter when such authorization was obtained by deception.

"Land or premises," as used in this section, includes any land, building, structure, or place belonging to, controlled by, or in custody of another, and any separate enclosure or room, or portion thereof.

2911.21.1 Aggravated Trespass

Elements:
(1) (a) Enter
     (or)
   (b) Remain
(2) On the land or premises of another
(3) With purpose to commit
(4) On that land or those premises
(5) A misdemeanor the elements of which involve
(6) (a) Causing physical harm to another person
     (or)
   (b) Causing another person to believe that the offender will cause physical harm to him

Penalty:

A misdemeanor of the first degree.

Note:

See R.C. § 2919.25.1 for special provisions concerning repeat offenders and offenders violating prior protection orders or consent orders.

SAFECRACKING

2911.31 Safecracking

Elements:

(1) With purpose to commit an offense
(2) Knowingly enter, force entry into or tamper with a vault, safe or strongbox

Penalty:

A felony of the fourth degree.

2911.32 Tampering with Coin Machines

Elements:

(1) With purpose to commit a theft or to defraud
(2) Knowingly
(3) Enter, force entrance into, tamper with or insert any part of an instrument into
(4) A coin machine

Penalty:

A misdemeanor of the first degree. If the offender has previously been convicted under this section or for any theft offense, then a felony of the fifth degree.

CHAPTER 2913
THEFT AND FRAUD

IN GENERAL

2913.01	Definitions

THEFT

2913.02	Theft
2913.03	Unauthorized Use of a Vehicle
2913.04	Unauthorized Use of Property; Computer Property
2913.04.1	Possession or Sale of Unauthorized Cable Television Device

PASSING BAD CHECKS

2913.11	Passing Bad Checks

MISUSE OF CREDIT CARD

2913.21	Misuse of Credit Card

FORGERY

2913.31(A)	Forgery
2913.31(B)	Forging Identification Cards
	Selling Forged Identification Cards
	Distributing Forged Identification Cards
2913.32	Criminal Simulation
2913.33	Making or Using Slugs
2913.34	Trademark Counterfeiting

FRAUDS

2913.40	Medicaid Fraud
2913.42	Tampering with Records
2913.43	Securing Writings by Deception
2913.44	Personating an Officer
2913.44.1	Illegal Display of Law Enforcement Emblem
2913.45	Defrauding Creditors
2913.46	Illegal Use of Food Stamps or WIC Program Benefits
2913.47	Insurance Fraud

RECEIVING

2913.51	Receiving Stolen Property

VALUE

2913.61   Value of Stolen Property

AGGRAVATING CIRCUMSTANCES

2913.71   Degree of Offense When Certain Property Involved

THEFT

2913.02 Theft

Elements:

(1) Knowingly
(2) Obtain or exert control over property or services
(3) With purpose to deprive the owner thereof
(4) (a) Without consent of owner or person authorized to consent
    (*or*)
  (b) Beyond the scope of the express or implied consent of owner or person authorized to consent
    (*or*)
  (c) By deception
    (*or*)
  (d) By threat

Penalty:

A misdemeanor of the first degree if the value is less than $500. If value is $500 or more and is less than $5,000, or if object is one of the following listed in R.C. § 2913.71: credit card/printed form for check or other negotiable instrument which identifies the drawer, maker, or account, etc./motor vehicle license plate/temporary license placard or sticker/blank certificate of title, or manufacturer's or importer's certificate to a motor vehicle/blank form for any license listed in R.C. § 4507.01, then a felony of the fifth degree. If value is $5,000 or more and less than $100,000, or if the property stolen is a firearm or dangerous ordnance or if property is a motor vehicle as defined in R.C. § 4501.01, then a felony of the fourth degree. If the value is $100,000 or more, then a felony of the third degree.

If property stolen is any dangerous drug as defined in R.C.

THEFT AND FRAUD **2913.04** 59

§ 4729.02, a felony of the fourth degree. If property stolen is any dangerous drug as defined in R.C. § 4749.02, and offender has prior felony drug abuse conviction as defined in R.C. § 2925.01, a felony of the third degree.

2913.03 Unauthorized Use of a Vehicle

Elements:

Division (A):
(1) Knowingly
(2) Use or operate
(3) Aircraft, motor vehicle, motorboat, other motor propelled vehicle
(4) Without consent of owner or person authorized to give consent

Division (B):
(1) Knowingly
(2) Use or operate
(3) Aircraft, motor vehicle, motorcycle, motorboat, other motor propelled vehicle
(4) Without consent of owner or person authorized to give consent
(5) Remove from Ohio, or keep possession more than 48 hours

Penalty:
   (A) A misdemeanor of the first degree.
   (B) A felony of the fifth degree.

2913.04 Unauthorized Use of Property; Computer Property

Elements:

Division (A):
(1) Knowingly
(2) Use or operate
(3) Property of another
(4) Without owner's consent or consent of authorized person

Division (B):
(1) Knowingly
(2) Gain access to or cause access to be gained to
(3) Any computer, computer system, or computer network

(4) Without the consent of, or beyond the scope of the express or implied consent of,

(5) The owner of the computer, computer system, or computer network or other person authorized to give consent by the owner

Penalty:

(A) A misdemeanor of the fourth degree.

If committed for the purpose of devising or executing a scheme to defraud or to obtain property or services and the value of the property or services or the loss to the victim is less than $500, a misdemeanor of the first degree.

If the value of the property or services or the loss to the victim is $500 or more and is less than $5,000, a felony of the fifth degree.

If the value of the property or services or the loss to the victim is $5,000 or more and less than $100,000, a felony of the fourth degree.

If the value of the property or services or the loss to the victim is $100,000 or more, a felony of the third degree.

(B) A felony of the fifth degree.

2913.04.1 Possession or Sale of Unauthorized Cable Television Device

Elements:

Division (A):

(1) Knowingly

(2) Possess any device, including any instrument, apparatus, computer chip, equipment, decoder, descrambler, converter, software, or other device specially adapted, modified, or remanufactured for gaining access to cable television service

(3) Without securing authorization from or paying the required compensation to the owner or operator of the system that provides the cable television service

Division (B):

(1) Knowingly

(2) Sell, distribute, or manufacture any device, including any instrument, apparatus, computer chip, equipment, decoder,

THEFT AND FRAUD 2913.21

descrambler, converter, software, or other device specially adapted, modified, or remanufactured for gaining access to cable television service
(3) Without securing authorization from or paying the required compensation to the owner or operator of the system that provides the cable television service

Penalty:
    (A) A felony of the fifth degree.
    (B) A felony of the fourth degree.

PASSING BAD CHECKS

2913.11 Passing Bad Checks

Elements:

(1) Issue, transfer or cause to be issued or transferred
(2) Check or other negotiable instrument
(3) Knowing it will be dishonored
(4) With purpose to defraud

Penalty:
    A misdemeanor of the first degree. If value is $500 or more and less than $5,000, a felony of the fifth degree. If value is $5,000 or more and less than $100,000, a felony of the fourth degree. If value is $100,000 or more, a felony of the third degree.

MISUSE OF CREDIT CARD

2913.21 Misuse of Credit Card

Elements:

Division (A):
(1) Procure the issuance of a credit card by deception which is relied upon
    (*or*)
(2) Knowingly buy or sell a credit card from or to a person other than the issuer

Division (B): With a purpose to defraud

(1) Obtain control of a credit card to secure a debt
(*or*)
(2) Obtain property or services by use of a credit card, in one or more transactions, knowing or having reasonable cause to believe the card was expired, revoked, or was obtained, retained, or being used illegally
(*or*)
(3) Furnish property or services on the presentation of a credit card, knowing the card is being used illegally
(*or*)
(4) Representing or causing it to be represented to the issuer of a credit card that property/services were furnished, knowing the representation to be false

Division (C):
(1) With a purpose to violate this section
(2) Receive, possess, control or dispose of a credit card

Penalty:

If violation of (A), (B)(1), or (C), a misdemeanor of the first degree. If violation of (B)(2), (3), or (4) and cumulative retail value of property and services involved in one or more violations is $500 or less and the violations involve one or more credit card accounts and occur within a period of 90 consecutive days commencing on the date of the first violation, a misdemeanor of the first degree.

If violation of (B)(2), (3), or (4) and cumulative retail value of property and services involved in one or more violations is $500 or more and less than $5,000 and the violations involve one or more credit card accounts and occur within a period of 90 consecutive days commencing on the date of the first violation or if offender has previous conviction of a theft offense, a felony of the fifth degree.

If violation of (B)(2), (3), or (4) and cumulative retail value of property and services involved in one or more violations is $5,000 or more and less than $100,000 and the violations involve one or more credit card accounts and occur within a period of 90 consecutive days commencing on the date of the first violation or if offender has previous conviction of two or more theft offenses, a felony of the fourth degree.

If violation of (B)(2), (3), or (4) and cumulative retail value of property and services in one or more violations is $100,000 or more and violations involve one or more accounts and occur within a period of 90 consecutive days commencing on date of first violation, felony of the third degree.

FORGERY

2913.31(A) Forgery

Elements:

Division (A):

(1) With a purpose to defraud or knowing the person is facilitating a fraud
(2) (a) Forge another's writing without the other person's authority
    (or)
  (b) Forge a writing so that it
      (i) Appears to be genuine when it actually is spurious
          (or)
      (ii) Purports to be the act of another though actually unauthorized
          (or)
      (iii) Purports to have been executed at a time or place or with different terms from what in fact was the case
          (or)
      (iv) Purports to be a copy of an original when no such original existed
          (or)
  (c) Utter, or possess with purpose to utter, any writing known to have been forged

Penalty:

A felony of the fifth degree.

If property or services are involved and the victim suffers a loss and if the value of the property or services or the loss to the victim is $5,000 or more and less than $100,000, a felony of the fourth degree.

If property or services are involved and the victim suffers a loss and if the value of the property or services or the loss to the victim is $100,000 or more, a felony of the third degree.

2913.31(B) Forging Identification Cards
Selling Forged Identification Cards
Distributing Forged Identification Cards

Elements:

(1) Knowingly
(2) (a) Forge an identification card
   (*or*)
   (b) Sell or otherwise distribute a card that purports to be an identification card, knowing it to have been forged

Penalty:

A misdemeanor of the first degree. If previously convicted under this subsection, mandatory minimum fine of $250.

Note:

See also R.C. § 4301.63.6 for offenses involving false official identification cards.

"Identification card" is defined in the statute. See Glossary.

2913.32 Criminal Simulation

Elements:

(1) With a purpose to defraud or knowing the person is facilitating a fraud
(2) (a) Make or alter any object so that it appears to have value due to antiquity, rarity, curiosity, source, authorship but which it does not in fact possess
   (*or*)
   (b) Practice deception in making, retouching, editing or reproducing a photograph, movie film, video tape, phonograph record, recording tape
   (*or*)
   (c) Falsely or fraudulently make, simulate, forge, alter, or counterfeit any wrapper, label, stamp, cork, or cap prescribed by the Liquor Control Commission under Chapters 4301. and 4303., falsely or fraudulently cause to be made, simulated, forged, altered, or counterfeited any wrapper,

label, stamp, cork, or cap prescribed by the Liquor Control Commission under Chapters 4301. and 4303., or use more than once any wrapper, label, stamp, cork, or cap prescribed by the Liquor Control Commission under Chapters 4301. and 4303.

(or)

(d) Utter, or possess with a purpose to utter, any object known to have been simulated as above

Penalty:

A misdemeanor of the first degree.

If the loss to the victim is $500 or more and less than $5,000, a felony of the fifth degree.

If the loss to the victim is $5,000 or more and less than $100,000, a felony of the fourth degree.

If the loss to the victim is more than $100,000, a felony of the third degree.

2913.33 Making or Using Slugs

Elements:

(1) (a) With purpose to defraud, insert or deposit a slug in a coin machine

   (or)

(b) With purpose of enabling another to defraud by inserting or depositing in coin machine, make, possess or dispose of a slug

Penalty:

A misdemeanor of the second degree.

2913.34 Trademark Counterfeiting

Elements:

Division (A)(1):

(1) Attach, affix, or otherwise use
(2) A counterfeit mark
(3) In connection with the manufacture of goods or services
(4) Whether or not the goods or services are intended for sale or resale

Division (A)(2):
(1) Possess, sell, or offer for sale
(2) Tools, machines, instruments, materials, articles, or other items of personal property
(3) Knowing that they are designed for the production or reproduction of counterfeit marks

Division (A)(3):
(1) Purchase or otherwise acquire goods
(2) Keep or otherwise have the goods in the person's possession
(3) Knowing that a counterfeit mark is attached to, affixed to, or otherwise used in connection with the goods
(4) With the intent to sell or otherwise dispose of the goods

Division (A)(4):
(1) Sell, offer for sale, or otherwise dispose of goods in the person's possession
(2) Knowing that a counterfeit mark is attached to, affixed to, or otherwise used in connection with the goods

Division (A)(5):
(1) Sell, offer for sale, or otherwise provide services
(2) Knowing that a counterfeit mark is used in connection with that sale, offer for sale, or other provision of services

Penalty:

A violation of Division (A)(1) is a felony of the fifth degree. If the cumulative sales price of the goods or services to which or in connection with which the counterfeit mark is attached, affixed, or otherwise used in the offense is $5,000 or more but less than $100,000 or if the number of units of goods to which or in connection with which the counterfeit mark is attached, affixed, or otherwise used in the offense is more than 100 units but less than 1,000 units, a felony of the fourth degree. If the cumulative sales price of the goods or services to which or in connection with which the counterfeit mark is attached, affixed, or otherwise used in the offense is $100,000 or more or if the number of units of goods to which or in connection with which the counterfeit mark is attached, affixed, or otherwise used in the offense is 1,000 units or more, a felony of the third degree.

A violation of Division (A)(2) is a misdemeanor of the first

THEFT AND FRAUD 2913.40

degree. If the circumstances of the violation indicate that the tools, machines, instruments, materials, articles, or other items of personal property involved were intended for use in the commission of a felony, a felony of the fifth degree.

A violation of Divisions (A)(3), (4), or (5) is a misdemeanor of the first degree. If the cumulative sales price of the goods or services to which or in connection with which the counterfeit mark is attached, affixed, or otherwise used is $500 or more but less than $5,000, a felony of the fifth degree. If the cumulative sales price of the goods or services to which or in connection with which the counterfeit mark is attached, affixed, or otherwise used is $5000 or more but less than $100,000 or if the number of units of goods to which the counterfeit mark is attached, affixed, or otherwise used is more than 100 units but less than 1,000 units, a felony of the fourth degree. If the cumulative sales price of the goods or services to which or in connection with which the counterfeit mark is attached, affixed, or otherwise used is $100,000 or more or if the number of units of goods to which or in connection with which the counterfeit mark is attached, affixed, or otherwise used is 1,000 units or more, a felony of the third degree.

FRAUDS

2913.40 Medicaid Fraud

Elements:

Division (B):
(1) Knowingly
(2) Make or cause to be made
(3) False or misleading statement or representation
(4) For use in obtaining reimbursement from the Medical Assistance Program

Division (C)(1):
(1) (a) With purpose to commit fraud
   (*or*)
   (b) Knowing the person is facilitating a fraud
(2) Contrary to terms of provider agreement

(3) Charge, solicit, accept, or receive
(4) For goods or services the person provides under the Medical Assistance Program
(5) Any property, money or other consideration in addition to amount under Medical Assistance Program and provider agreement and authorized deductibles and co-payments

Division (C)(2):
(1) (a) With purpose to commit fraud
    (*or*)
 (b) Knowing the person is facilitating a fraud
(2) Solicit, offer, or receive
(3) Any remuneration other than authorized deductibles or co-payments, in cash or in kind, including but not limited to kickback or rebate
(4) In connection with furnishing goods and services for which whole or partial reimbursement is or may be made under the Medical Assistance Program

Division (D):
(1) Having submitted a claim for or provided goods or services under the Medical Assistance Program
(2) Knowingly
(3) Alter, falsify, destroy, conceal, or remove
(4) Any records that are necessary to fully disclose
(5) (a) Nature of all goods or services for which the claim was submitted, or for which reimbursement was received, by the person
    (*or*)
 (b) All income and expenditures upon which rates of reimbursements were based for the person
(6) For a period of six years after a reimbursement pursuant to that claim or a reimbursement for those goods or services is received under the Medical Assistance Program

Penalty:
    A misdemeanor of the first degree.
    If value of property, services, or funds is more than $500 and less than $5,000, a felony of the fifth degree.
    If value of property, services, or funds is more than $5,000

THEFT AND FRAUD   **2913.42**   69

and less than $100,000, a felony of the fourth degree.

If value of the property, services, or funds is $100,000 or more, a felony of the third degree.

Note:

Provisions of this section not intended to be exclusive remedies. See 2913.40 for definitions.

2913.42 Tampering with Records

Elements:

Division (A):

(1) (a) Falsify, destroy, remove conceal, alter, deface, or mutilate any writing, data, or record
   (*or*)
   (b) Utter any writing or record knowing it has been tampered with as above
(2) Knowing the person has no privilege to do so and with a purpose to defraud or knowingly to facilitate a fraud

Penalty:

For offense not involving data, and writing or record is not unrevoked will or record kept by or belonging to governmental agency, a misdemeanor of the first degree.

For offense not involving data, and writing or record is unrevoked will or record kept by or belonging to governmental agency, a felony of the fifth degree.

For offense involving data and the value of the data involved or the loss to the victim is less than $500, a misdemeanor of the first degree.

For offense involving data and the value of the data involved or the loss to the victim is $500 or more and is less than $5,000, a felony of the fifth degree.

For offense involving data and the value of the data involved or the loss to the victim is $5,000 or more and is less than $100,000, a felony of the fourth degree.

For offense involving data and the value of the data involved or the loss to the victim is $100,000 or more or if the offense is committed for the purpose of devising or executing a scheme to defraud or to obtain property or services and the value of the property or services or the loss to the victim is $5,000 or more, a felony of the third degree.

2913.43 Securing Writings by Deception

Elements:

(1) By deception
(2) Cause another to execute a writing disposing of or encumbering property or creating pecuniary obligation

Penalty:

A misdemeanor of the first degree. If property or obligation value is $500 or more but less than $5,000, a felony of the fifth degree. If property or obligation value is $5,000 or more but less than $100,000, a felony of the fourth degree. If property or obligation value is $100,000 or more, a felony of the third degree.

2913.44 Personating an Officer

Elements:

(1) (a) With purpose to defraud or knowingly to facilitate a fraud
     (*or*)
    (b) With purpose to induce another to buy property or services
(2) Personate a law enforcement officer, inspector, investigator or agent of any governmental agency

Penalty:

A misdemeanor of the first degree.

2913.44.1 Illegal Display of Law Enforcement Emblem

Elements:

(1) Knowingly display on a motor vehicle
(2) Emblem of a law enforcement agency or an organization of law enforcement officers
(3) By a person who is not entitled to do so

Penalty:

A minor misdemeanor.

2913.45 Defrauding Creditors

Elements:

(1) (a) Remove, conceal, destroy, encumber, convey, or otherwise deal with any of the person's property
(or)
(b) Misrepresent or refuse to disclose to fiduciary appointed to administer or manage the person's affairs or estate, the existence, amount, location of any of the person's property, or any other information regarding such property which the person is legally required to furnish fiduciary

(2) With purpose to defraud a creditor

Penalty:

A misdemeanor of the first degree.

If the value of the property involved is $500 or more and is less than $5,000, a felony of the fifth degree.

If the value of the property involved is $5,000 or more and is less than $100,000, a felony of the fourth degree.

If the value of the property involved is $100,000 or more, a felony of the third degree.

2913.46 Illegal Use of Food Stamps or WIC Program Benefits

Elements:
Division (B):

(1) Individual
(2) Knowingly
(3) Possess, buy, sell, use, alter, accept, or transfer
(4) Food stamp coupons, WIC program benefits, or any electronically transferred benefit
(5) In manner not authorized by Food Stamp Act of 1977 or the Child Nutrition Act of 1966

Division (C)(1):

(1) Organization
(2) Knowingly
(3) Allow an employee
(4) To sell, transfer, or trade items or services the purchase of

which is prohibited by the Food Stamp Act of 1977 or the Child Nutrition Act of 1966

(5) In exchange for food stamp coupons, WIC program benefits, or any electronically transferred benefit

Division (C)(2):
(1) Organization
(2) Negligently
(3) Allow an employee
(4) To sell, transfer, or exchange food stamp coupons, WIC program benefits, or any electronically transferred benefit
(5) For anything of value

Penalty:

When face value of food stamp coupons is less than $500, a felony of the fifth degree. When face value of food stamp coupons is $500 or more and less than $5,000, a felony of the fourth degree. If the value of the food stamp coupons is $5,000 or more and is less than $100,000, a felony of the third degree. If the value of the food stamp coupons is $100,000 or more, a felony of the second degree.

2913.47 Insurance Fraud

Elements:

(1) (a) With purpose to defraud
   (*or*)
   (b) Knowing that the person is facilitating a fraud
(2) (a) Present to or cause to be presented to an insurer any written or oral statement
   (*or*)
   (b) Assist, aid, abet, solicit, procure, or conspire with another to prepare or make any written or oral statement that is intended to be presented to an insurer
(3) If the statement is part of, or in support of
(4) (a) An application for insurance
   (*or*)
   (b) A claim for payment pursuant to a policy
   (*or*)
   (c) A claim for any other benefit pursuant to a policy

THEFT AND FRAUD 2913.48

(5) Knowing that the statement or any part of the statement is false or deceptive

Penalty:

A misdemeanor of the first degree. If the amount of the application or claim is $500 or more, but less than $5,000, a felony of the fifth degree. If the amount of the application or claim is $5,000 or more, but less than $100,000, a felony of the fourth degree. If the amount of the application or claim is $100,000 or more, a felony of the third degree.

Notes:

See statute for definitions of data, deceptive, insurer, policy, and statement specific to this offense.

This statute does not abrogate, waive, or modify 2317.02(A), concerning the attorney-client privilege.

2913.48 Workers' Compensation Fraud

Elements:

(1) (a) With purpose to defraud
   (*or*)
   (b) Knowing that the person is facilitating a fraud
(2) (a) Receive workers' compensation benefits to which the person is not entitled
   (*or*)
   (b) Make or present or cause to be made or presented a false or misleading statement with the purpose to secure payment for goods or services rendered under R.C. Chapters 4121., 4123., 4127., or 4131. or to secure workers' compensation benefits
   (*or*)
   (c) Alter, falsify, destroy, conceal, or remove any record or document that
     (i) is necessary to fully establish the validity of any claim filed with the bureau of workers' compensation or a self-insuring employer
       (*or*)
     (ii) is necessary to establish the nature of goods and services for which reimbursement or payment was

received or is requested from the bureau of workers' compensation or a self-insuring employer

(*or*)

(d) Enter into an agreement or conspiracy to defraud the bureau or a self-insuring employer by making or presenting or causing to be made or presented a false claim for workers' compensation benefits.

Penalty:

A misdemeanor of the first degree. If the value of the goods, services, property, or money stolen is $500 or more, but less than $5,000, a felony of the fifth degree. If the value of the goods, services, property, or money stolen is $5,000 or more, but less than $100,000, a felony of the fourth degree. If the value of the goods, services, property, or money stolen is $100,000 or more, a felony of the third degree.

RECEIVING

2913.51 Receiving Stolen Property

Elements:

(1) Receive, retain or dispose of property of another
(2) (a) Knowing

    (*or*)

  (b) Having reasonable cause to believe
(3) Such property has been obtained through commission of theft offense

Penalty:

A misdemeanor of the first degree. If the value of the property involved is $500 or more but less than $5,000, or if property involved is listed in 2913.71, a felony of the fifth degree. If the property is a motor vehicle as defined in 4501.01, if the property involved is a dangerous drug as defined in R.C. § 4729.02, or if the value of the property is $5,000 or more but less than $100,000, a felony of the fourth degree. If the value of the property is $100,000 or more, a felony of the third degree.

CHAPTER 2915

GAMBLING

2915.01	Definitions
2915.02	Gambling
2915.03	Operating a Gambling House
2915.04	Public Gaming
2915.05	Cheating; Corrupting Sports

BINGO

2915.07	Conducting Bingo Game
2915.09	Illegally Conducting Bingo Game
2915.10(A)	Failure to Maintain Bingo Records for Three Years
2915.10(C)	Illegal Acts Re Inspection of Bingo Game or Scheme or Game of Chance
2915.11(A)	Operation of Bingo Game by a Minor
2915.11(B)	Operation of Bingo Game by Former Offender

2915.02 Gambling

Elements:

(1) (a) Engage in bookmaking

     (*or*)

  (b) (i) Knowingly

     (ii) Engage in conduct that facilitates bookmaking (i.e. aid an illegal bookmaking operation, including without limitation placing a bet with a person engaged in or facilitating illegal bookmaking)

     (*or*)

  (c) (i) Establish, promote, or operate

     (ii) Any scheme or game of chance conducted for profit

     (*or*)

  (d) (i) Knowingly

     (ii) Engage in conduct that facilitates any scheme or game of chance conducted for profit (i.e., in any way knowingly and in the conduct or operation of any such scheme or game, including without limitation playing the scheme or game)

     (*or*)

  (e) (i) Knowingly

- (ii) Procure, transmit, exchange or engage in conduct that facilitates the procurement, transmission, or exchange of
- (iii) Information for use in establishing odds or determining winners in connection with
- (iv) Bookmaking or any scheme or game of chance conducted for profit

  (*or*)

(f) (i) Engage in betting or in playing any scheme or game of chance, except a charitable bingo game
- (ii) As a substantial source of income or livelihood

  (*or*)

(g) (i) With purpose to violate this section as set forth above
- (ii) Acquire, possess, control, or operate
- (iii) Any gambling device

  (*or*)

(h) (i) Receive
- (ii) Any commission, wage, salary, tip, reward, donation, gratuity, or other form of compensation
- (iii) Directly or indirectly
- (iv) For operating or assisting in the operation of
- (v) Any scheme or game of chance

Penalty:

A misdemeanor of the first degree. If prior gambling conviction, then a felony of the fifth degree.

Note:

This section does not prohibit conduct in connection with gambling expressly permitted by law (see R.C. § 2915.02(C)). This section does not apply to schemes or games of chance conducted by charitable organizations operating within the limits of R.C. § 2915.02(D).

2915.03 Operating a Gambling House

Elements:

(1) Being an owner, lessee, or person having control/supervision of premises

GAMBLING **2915.05** 77

(2) (a) Use or occupy premises for gambling in violation of R.C. § 2915.02
   (*or*)
   (b) Recklessly permit premises to be used or occupied for gambling as above

Penalty:

A misdemeanor of the first degree. If a prior gambling conviction, then a felony of the fifth degree.

2915.04 Public Gaming

Elements:

Division (A):

(1) While at a hotel, restaurant, tavern, store, arena, hall, or other place of public accommodation, business, amusement or resort
(2) Make a bet or play a game of chance

Division (B):

(1) Being an owner, lessee, or person having control/supervision of:
   (a) Premises as listed in Division (A)(1) above
(2) Recklessly permit such premises to be used or occupied for purpose of making a bet or playing a game of chance

Penalty:

A minor misdemeanor. If a prior gambling conviction, then a misdemeanor of the fourth degree.

2915.05 Cheating; Corrupting Sports

Elements:

Division (A):

(1) With purpose to defraud or to facilitate a fraud
(2) Engage in conduct designed to corrupt the outcome of
(3) (a) A bet
   (*or*)
   (b) A contest of knowledge, skill, or endurance that is not an athletic or sporting event
   (*or*)

(c) A scheme or game of chance

Division (B):

(1) Knowingly
(2) (a) Offer, give, solicit, or accept anything of value to corrupt the outcome of an athletic or sporting event
 (*or*)
 (b) Engage in conduct designed to corrupt the outcome of an athletic or sporting event

Penalty:

(A) A misdemeanor of the first degree. If potential gain is five hundred dollars ($500) or more or a prior gambling conviction or theft offense, then a felony of the fifth degree.

(B) A felony of the fifth degree. If a prior gambling or theft offense, then a felony of the fourth degree.

BINGO

2915.07 Conducting Bingo Game

Elements:

(1) Conduct or advertise
(2) Bingo game
(3) Without having obtained a bingo license pursuant to R.C. § 2915.08

Penalty:

A felony of the fourth degree.

2915.09 Illegally Conducting Bingo Game

Elements:

Division (A)(2):

(1) Being a charitable organization
(2) Conduct bingo game
(3) (a) Without using all gross receipts for paying prizes or the purposes listed in its license application
 (*or*)
 (b) Using an amount of the receipts above the amount reason-

ably and customarily spent for similar purchases, leases, hiring or advertising for
- (i) purchasing, or leasing bingo cards and other equipment used in conducting the bingo game
  (*or*)
- (ii) hiring security personnel for the bingo game
  (*or*)
- (iii) advertising the bingo game
  (*or*)
- (iv) renting premises in which to conduct the bingo game
  (*or*)
- (c) For each bingo session, deducting from the gross receipts a sum in excess of the lesser of $600 or 45% of the gross receipts as consideration for the use of the premises owned by the charitable organization conducting the game

Division (A)(1):
(1) Being a charitable organization
(2) Conduct bingo game without
- (a) Owning all equipment used to conduct the bingo game
  (*or*)
- (b) Leasing such equipment from a licensed charitable organization at a customary and reasonable rental rate

Divisions (A)(3), (4), (5):
(1) Being a charitable organization
(2) Conduct bingo game
(3) On premises not
- (a) Owned by charitable organization
  (*or*)
- (b) Leased from another charitable organization at a rate not exceeding $450 per session (Note: A charitable organization shall not lease premises that it owns to more than one other charitable organization per calendar week for the purpose of conducting bingo on the premises.)
  (*or*)
- (c) Leased from a person other than a charitable organization at a rental rate that is more than is customary and reasonable for premises similar in location, size, and quality, but

not exceeding $450 per session. (Note: Lessor other than charitable organization shall lease premises only and shall not provide special personnel, services or equipment.)
  (*or*)
  (d) Subleased from another charitable organization that leases from a person other than a charitable organization at a rate not exceeding $450 per session
  (*or*)
(4) Conduct more than two bingo sessions on any premises in any calendar week except that a volunteer firefighter's organization or a volunteer rescue service organization that conducts not more than five bingo sessions in a calendar year may conduct more than two bingo sessions in a seven-day period after notifying the attorney general when it will conduct the sessions.

(*or*)

(5) Fail to display its bingo license conspicuously at the location where the bingo game is conducted

(*or*)

(6) Fail to conduct the bingo in accordance with definition in R.C. § 2915.01(S)(1)

Division (B):

(1) Being a charitable organization
(2) Conduct a bingo game and
(3) (a) (i) Pay compensation to a bingo game operator for operating a bingo game or for preparing, selling or serving food or beverages at the site of the bingo game
    (*or*)
   (ii) Permit any auxiliary unit or society of the charitable organization to pay compensation to any bingo game operator who prepares, sells or serves food or beverages at a bingo session
    (*or*)
   (iii) Permit any auxiliary unit or society of the charitable organization to prepare, sell or serve beverages at a bingo session if the auxiliary unit or society pays compensation to the bingo game operators who prepare, sell or serve the food or beverages

GAMBLING **2915.09** 81

      (*or*)
- (b) Pay consulting fees to any person for any services performed in relation to the bingo game
  (*or*)
- (c) Pay concession fees to any person who provides refreshments to participants in the bingo game
  (*or*)
- (d) Conduct more than two bingo sessions in any seven-day period
  (*or*)
- (e) Pay out more than $3,500 in prizes during any bingo session
  (*or*)
- (f) (i) Do so at any time during the 10 hour period between midnight and 10 a.m.
  (*or*)
  - (ii) Do so at any time during, or within 10 hours of, a bingo game conducted for amusement only pursuant to R.C. § 2915.12
    (*or*)
  - (iii) Do so at any location, on any day of the week, or during any time period not specified on its bingo license
  (*or*)
- (g) Permit any person whom the charitable organization knows, or should have known, is under the age of 18 to work as a bingo game operator
- (h) Permit any person whom the charitable organization knows, or should have known, has been convicted of a felony or gambling offense to be a bingo game operator
- (i) Permit the lessor of the premises on which bingo is conducted, if the lessor is not a charitable organization, to provide the charitable organization with bingo game operators, security personnel, concessions, bingo equipment, or any other type of service or equipment

Division (C):
(1) Being a bingo game operation
(2) Receive or accept
(3) Directly or indirectly, regardless of the source

(4) Any commission, wage, salary, reward, tip, donation, gratuity or other form of compensation
(5) (a) For operating a bingo game
   (*or*)
   (b) For providing other work or labor at the site of the bingo game

Penalty:

Violation of (A)(2) is a felony of the fourth degree. Violation of (A)(1), (3), (4), (5), (B) or (C) is a minor misdemeanor. If prior conviction for violation of (A)(1), (3), (4), (5), (B), or (C) violation of (A)(1), (3), (4), (5), (B), or (C) is a misdemeanor of the first degree.

2915.10(A) Failure to Maintain Bingo Records for Three Years

Elements:

(1) Being a charitable organization
(2) Conduct bingo session or scheme or game of chance
(3) Fail to maintain the following records for at least three years from the date on which the bingo session or scheme or game of chance is conducted
   (a) An itemized list of the gross receipts of each session or scheme or game of chance
   (b) An itemized list of all expenses other than prizes that are incurred in conducting the bingo session, the name of each person to whom the expenses are paid, and a receipt for all of the expenses
   (c) A list of all prizes awarded during the bingo session or scheme or game of chance conducted by said organization and the name and address of all persons who are winners of prizes of $100 or more in value
   (d) An itemized list of the charitable recipients of the proceeds of the bingo session or scheme or game of chance, including the name and address of each recipient to whom the money is distributed, and if the organization uses the proceeds of a bingo session or the money or assets received from a scheme or game of chance for any purpose

set forth in R.C. § 2915.01(Z) or R.C. § 2915.02(D), a list of each purpose and an itemized list of each expenditure for each purpose
- (e) The number of persons who participate in any bingo session or scheme or game of chance that is conducted by the charitable organization
- (f) A list of receipts from the sale of food and beverages by the charitable organization or one of its auxiliary units or societies, if the receipts are excluded from the definition of "gross receipts" under R.C. § 2915.01(X)
- (g) An itemized list of all expenses incurred at each bingo session conducted by the charitable organization in the sale of food or beverages by the charitable organization or by an auxiliary unit or society of the charitable organization, the name of each person to whom the expenses are paid, and a receipt for all of the expenses

Penalty:
A misdemeanor of the first degree.

2915.10(C) Illegal Acts Re Inspection of Bingo Game or Scheme or Game of Chance

Elements:

(1) (a) Destroy, alter, conceal, withhold, or deny access to any accounts or records of a charitable organization that have been requested for examination
(*or*)
(b) Obstruct, impede, or interfere with any inspection, audit, or observation of
  (i) a bingo game or scheme or game of chance
  (*or*)
  (ii) premises where a bingo game or scheme or game of chance is operated
  (*or*)
(c) Refuse to comply with any reasonable request of, or obstruct, impede, or interfere with any other reasonable action undertaken by the attorney general or a local law enforcement agency pursuant to R.C. § 2915.10(B)

Penalty:
A misdemeanor of the first degree.

2915.11(A) Operation of Bingo Game by a Minor

Elements:

(1) Being under the age of 18
(2) Operate a bingo game

Penalty:
A misdemeanor of the third degree.

2915.11(B) Operation of Bingo Game by Former Offender

Elements:

(1) Being a person who has been convicted in any jurisdiction of
   (a) felony
      (*or*)
   (b) gambling offense
(2) Operate a bingo game

Penalty:
A misdemeanor of the first degree.

CHAPTER 2917

OFFENSES AGAINST THE PUBLIC PEACE

INCITING, RIOT, AND RELATED OFFENSES

2917.01	Inciting to Violence
2917.02	Aggravated Riot
2917.03	Riot
2917.04	Failure to Disperse
2917.05	Justifiable Use of Force to Suppress Riot

DISORDERLY CONDUCT

2917.11	Disorderly Conduct
2917.12	Disturbing a Lawful Meeting
2917.13	Misconduct at an Emergency

HARASSMENT

2917.21	Telephone Harassment

FALSE ALARMS

2917.31	Inducing Panic
2917.32	Making False Alarms

CROWD SAFETY

2917.40	Illegal Acts Re Crowd Control and Seating at Live Entertainment Performances
2917.41	Misconduct Involving a Public Transportation System

BLOCK PARENT SYMBOL

2917.46	Unauthorized Use of Block Parent Symbol

INCITING, RIOT, AND RELATED OFFENSES

2917.01 Inciting to Violence

Elements:

(1) Knowingly
(2) Engage in conduct designed to urge or incite another to commit an offense of violence

(3) Under circumstances where
   (a) The conduct creates clear and present danger that an offense of violence will result
      (*or*)
   (b) The conduct proximately results in an offense of violence

Penalty:

If the offense of violence that the other person is being urged or incited to commit is a misdemeanor, a misdemeanor of the first degree.

If the offense of violence that the other person is being urged or incited to commit is a felony, a felony of the third degree.

2917.02 Aggravated Riot

Elements:

Division (A):

(1) Participate with 4 or more others
(2) In a course of disorderly conduct contrary to R.C. § 2917.11
(3) (a) With a purpose to commit or facilitate a felony
      (*or*)
   (b) With purpose to commit or facilitate an offense of violence
      (*or*)
   (c) While the offender, or any participant to the knowledge of the offender, has a deadly weapon or dangerous ordnance on or about the offender's or participant's person or under the offender's or participant's control, uses, or intends to use same

Division (B):

(1) Being an inmate of a detention facility
(2) Violate Division (A)(3)(a) or (c)
(3) Violate Division (A)(3)(b) or R.C. § 2917.03

Penalty:

A violation of Division (A)(3)(a) or (c), a felony of the fifth degree.

A violation of Division (A)(3)(b) or (B)(2), a felony of the fourth degree.

A violation of Division (B)(3), a felony of the third degree.

2917.03 Riot

Elements:

Division (A):
1. Participate with 4 or more others
2. In a course of disorderly conduct contrary to R.C. § 2917.11
3. (a) With purpose to commit or facilitate a misdemeanor other than disorderly conduct
   (or)
   (b) With purpose to intimidate a public official or employee into taking or refraining from taking official action
   (or)
   (c) With a purpose to hinder, impede, obstruct function of government
   (or)
   (d) With a purpose to hinder, impede or obstruct the orderly administration of or instruction at an educational institution, or interfere with or disrupt its activities

Division (B):
1. Participate with 4 or more others
2. With purpose to do an act with unlawful force or violence
3. Although such act would otherwise be lawful

Penalty:
   A misdemeanor of the first degree.

2917.04 Failure to Disperse

Elements:

1. When five or more persons are participating in disorderly conduct in violation of R.C. § 2917.11
2. With other persons in vicinity and whose presence creates:
   (a) A likelihood of physical harm to persons/property
      (or)
   (b) Serious public inconvenience, annoyance, or alarm
3. And a law enforcement officer or other public official orders all of above to disperse
4. Knowingly fail to obey such order

Penalty:
A minor misdemeanor.

Note:
The offender can be either one of the participants in the disorderly conduct or one of the persons in the vicinity, so long as he or she is not peaceably assembled for a lawful purpose.

DISORDERLY CONDUCT

2917.11 Disorderly Conduct

Elements:

Division (A):
(1) Recklessly
(2) Cause inconvenience, annoyance or alarm to another by means of
   (a) Fighting/threatening harm to persons or property/violent or turbulent behavior
   (or)
   (b) Making unreasonable noise/offensively coarse utterances/gestures, displays, or communicating unwarranted and grossly abusive language to others
   (or)
   (c) Insulting/taunting/challenging another under circumstances in which such conduct is likely to provoke a violent response
   (or)
   (d) Hindering or preventing movement of persons upon a public street/road/highway/right-of-way, or to or from public/private property, so as to interfere with rights of others by acts that serve no lawful/reasonable purpose
   (or)
   (e) Creating a physically offensive condition or one that presents a risk of physical harm to persons/property by acts serving no lawful reasonable purpose

Division (B):
(1) While voluntarily intoxicated

(2) (a) In a public place or in the presence of 2 or more persons
    (1) Engage in conduct likely to be offensive
        (or)
    (2) Cause inconvenience, annoyance, or alarm to persons of ordinary sensibilities, which conduct the offender, if the offender were not intoxicated, should know is likely to have that effect on others
        (or)
  (b) Engage in conduct or create a condition that presents a risk of physical harm to the offender or another, or the property of another

Penalty:
A minor misdemeanor. If offender persists in disorderly conduct after reasonable warning or request to desist, or if the offense is committed within the vicinity of a school, a misdemeanor of the fourth degree.

Note:
The violation of a statute or ordinance of which an element is operating a motor vehicle, etc., or other vehicle while under influence of alcohol or any other drug of abuse, is not a violation of Division (B) above.

2917.12 Disturbing a Lawful Meeting

Elements:

(1) With a purpose to prevent or disrupt
(2) (a) Do anything which obstructs or interferes with the conduct of a meeting, procession, or gathering
        (or)
    (b) Make utterances, gestures, or displays which outrage the sensibilities of group

Penalty:
A misdemeanor of the fourth degree.

2917.13 Misconduct at an Emergency

Elements:

(1) Knowingly

- (a) Hamper lawful operations of any law enforcement officer, fireman, rescuer, medical or other authorized person, engaged in duties at a fire, accident, disaster, riot, or emergency

   (*or*)
- (b) Fail to obey a lawful order of any law enforcement officer engaged in duties at the scene or in connection with a fire, accident, disaster, riot, or emergency

Penalty:

A minor misdemeanor. If misconduct creates a risk of physical harm to persons or property, a misdemeanor of the fourth degree.

Note:

Nothing in this section shall be construed to limit access or deny information to any news media representative in the lawful exercise of his duties.

HARASSMENT

2917.21 Telephone Harassment

Elements:

Division (A):

(1) Knowingly

(2) (a) Make a telephone call

   (*or*)

   (b) Cause a telephone call to be made

   (*or*)

   (c) Permit a telephone call to be made from a telephone under the offender's control

(3) To another

(4) If the caller does any of the following:

   (a) Fails to identify the caller to the recipient of the telephone call and makes the telephone call with purpose to harass, abuse, or annoy any person at the premises to which the telephone call is made, whether or not conversation takes place during the telephone call

   (*or*)

OFFENSES AGAINST THE PUBLIC PEACE   **2917.21**   91

- (b) Describes, suggests, requests, or proposes that the caller, recipient of the telephone call, or any other person engage in, any sexual activity as defined in Division (C) of section 2907.01 of the Revised Code, and the recipient of the telephone call, or another person at the premises to which the telephone call is made, has requested, in a previous telephone call or in the immediate telephone call, the caller not to make a telephone call to the recipient of the telephone call or to the premises to which the telephone call is made

    (or)

- (c) During the telephone call, violates section 2903.21 of the Revised Code

    (or)

- (d) Knowingly states to the recipient of the telephone call that the caller intends to cause damage to or destroy public or private property, and the recipient of the telephone call, any member of the family of the recipient of the telephone call, or any other person who resides at the premises to which the telephone call is made owns, leases, resides, or works in, will at the time of the destruction or damaging be near or in, has the responsibility of protecting, or insures the property that will be destroyed or damaged

    (or)

- (e) Knowingly makes the telephone call to the recipient of the telephone call, to another person at the premises to which the telephone call is made, or to the premises to which the telephone call is made, and the recipient of the telephone call, or another person at the premises to which the telephone call is made, has previously told the caller not to call the premises to which the telephone call is made or not to call any persons at the premises to which the telephone call is made.

Division (B):

(1) (a) Make a telephone call

    (or)

  (b) Cause a telephone call to be made

    (or)

(c) Permit a telephone call to be made from a telephone under the offender's control
(2) With purpose to
    (a) Abuse
        (or)
    (b) Threaten
        (or)
    (c) Annoy
        (or)
    (d) Harass
(3) Another person

Penalty:

A misdemeanor of the first degree. If a previous conviction for violation of this section involving the same person, recipient, or premises, then a felony of the fifth degree.

FALSE ALARMS

2917.31 Inducing Panic

Elements:

(1) Cause
(2) The evacuation of a public place or serious public inconvenience or alarm
(3) By means of
    (a) Initiating or circulating a report or warning of alleged or impending fire, explosion, crime or other catastrophe, knowing such to be false
        (or)
    (b) Threatening to commit any offense of violence
        (or)
    (c) Committing any offense with reckless disregard of the likelihood that it will cause serious public inconvenience or alarm

Penalty:

A misdemeanor of the first degree. If the conduct results in physical harm to any person, then a felony of the fourth degree.

2917.32 Making False Alarms

Elements:

(1) (a) Initiate or circulate a report/warning of alleged or impending fire, explosion, crime, or other catastrophe
   (b) Knowing it to be both false and likely to cause public inconvenience/alarm
   (*or*)
(2) (a) Knowingly cause
   (b) A false alarm of fire or other emergency
   (c) To be transmitted to or within
   (d) A public or private organization dealing with emergencies which involve a risk of physical harm to persons/property
   (*or*)
(3) (a) Report to any law enforcement agency
   (b) Alleged offense or other incident
   (c) Knowing such did not occur

Penalty:

A misdemeanor of the first degree.

Note:

This section does not apply to any person conducting an authorized fire or emergency drill.

CROWD SAFETY

2917.40 Illegal Acts Re Crowd Control and Seating at Live Entertainment Performances

Elements:

Division (B)(1):

(1) (a) Sell
      (*or*)
   (b) Offer to sell
      (*or*)
   (c) Offer in return for a donation
(2) Ticket that is not numbered and that does not correspond to a specific seat for admission to
(3) (a) A live entertainment performance that is not exempted

under R.C. § 2917.40(D), that is held in a restricted entertainment area, and for which more than eight thousand tickets are offered to the public
(*or*)
  (b) A concert that is not exempted under R.C. § 2917.40(D) and for which more than three thousand tickets are offered to the public

Division (B)(2):
(1) Advertise
(2) A live entertainment performance that is not exempted under R.C. § 2917.40(D) that is held in a restricted entertainment area, and for which more than eight thousand tickets are offered to the public
(3) Without including the words "reserved seats only"

Division (C):
(1) (a) Being the owner of a restricted entertainment area
       (*or*)
    (b) Being the operator of a restricted entertainment area
(2) Fail to open, maintain and properly staff
(3) Number of entrances designated by R.C. § 2917.40(E)
(4) For a minimum of 90 minutes prior to the start of a live entertainment performance
(5) Held in a restricted entertainment area
(6) For which more than 3,000 tickets are
    (a) Sold
        (*or*)
    (b) Offered for sale
        (*or*)
    (c) Offered in return for a donation

Division (F):
(1) Enter into contract
(2) For a live entertainment performance
(3) That does not
    (a) Require
        (*or*)
    (b) Permit
(4) Compliance with R.C. § 2917.40

Penalty:

Misdemeanor of the first degree. If physical harm to person caused by violation, sentencing court must consider that factor in favor of imposing a term of imprisonment upon offender.

2917.41 Misconduct Involving a Public Transportation System

Elements:

Division (A):
(1) Evade payment
(2) Of known fares
(3) Of a public transportation system

Division (B):
(1) Alter any transfer, pass, ticket, or token
(2) Of a public transportation system
(3) With purpose of evading the payment of fares or of defrauding the system

Division (C):
(1) (a) Play sound equipment without proper use of a private earphone
(*or*)
(b) (i) Smoke, eat, or drink
(ii) In any area where such activity is clearly marked as being prohibited
(*or*)
(c) Expectorate upon a facility or vehicle
(2) While in any facility or vehicle
(3) Of a public transportation system

Division (D):
(1) Write, deface, draw, or otherwise mark
(2) On any facility or vehicle
(3) Of a public transportation system

Division (E):
(1) Fail to comply with lawful order
(*and*)
(2) Resist, obstruct, or abuse

(3) A public transportation system police officer in the performance of the officer's duties

Penalty:
Offense under Division (A), (B), (C), or (E) a misdemeanor of the fourth degree. Offense under Division (D), a misdemeanor of the third degree.

Definition:
See R.C. § 2917.41(G) for definition of "public transportation system."

BLOCK PARENT SYMBOL

2917.46 Unauthorized Use of Block Parent Symbol

Elements:
(1) With intent to identify a building as a block parent home or building
(2) (a) Display the block parent symbol, unless authorized
    (*or*)
   (b) Display a symbol that falsely gives the appearance of being the block parent symbol

Penalty:
A minor misdemeanor.

Note:
See R.C. §§ 3301.07.6, 3313.20.4 regarding adoption and use of block parent symbols.

CHAPTER 2919

OFFENSES AGAINST THE FAMILY

BIGAMY

2919.01	Bigamy

ABORTION

2919.11	Definition of Abortion
2919.12	Unlawful Abortion
2919.13	Abortion Manslaughter
2919.14	Abortion Trafficking
2919.15	Performing Unlawful Abortion Procedure
2919.17	Terminating or Attempting to Terminate Human Pregnancy After Viability
2919.18	Failure to Perform Viability Testing

NONSUPPORT AND RELATED OFFENSES

2919.21	Nonsupport or Contributing to Nonsupport of Dependents
2919.22	Endangering Children
2919.22.2	Parental Education Neglect
2919.23	Interference with Custody
2919.23.1	Interfering with Action to Issue or Modify Support Order
2919.24	Contributing to Unruliness or Delinquency of a Child

DOMESTIC VIOLENCE

2919.25	Domestic Violence
2919.27	Violating Protection Order, Consent Agreement, or Anti-Stalking Protection Order

BIGAMY

2919.01 Bigamy

Elements:

(1) Being married

(2) (a) Marry another

(*or*)

(b) Continue to cohabit with another in this state

Penalty:

A misdemeanor of the first degree.

Note:

It is an affirmative defense to a charge under this section that the actor's spouse was continuously absent for five years immediately preceding the purported subsequent marriage, and was not known by the actor to be alive within that time.

ABORTION

2919.12 Unlawful Abortion

Elements:

(1) Perform or induce abortion without informed consent of pregnant woman
   (or)
(2) Knowingly perform or induce abortion upon woman who is pregnant, unmarried, under eighteen, and unemancipated unless:
   (a) Person performing has given 24 hours actual notice to one parent, guardian, or custodian
      (or)
   (b) Woman has requested to notify one of certain specified relatives in lieu of parents, guardian, or custodian, affidavits containing specified information have been filed in juvenile court, the court has notified the person performing of the filing of the affidavits, the juvenile court has been given name and address of person performing, and the person performing has given 24 hours actual notice to the specified relative
      (or)
   (c) One parent, guardian, or custodian has given written consent
      (or)
   (d) Juvenile court has authorized woman to consent without notification pursuant to § 2151.85
      (or)
   (e) Juvenile court or court of appeals by inaction has construc-

tively authorized woman to consent without notification pursuant to § 2151.85 or 2505.07.3
(*or*)
(f) Parent, guardian, custodian, or specified relative notified in accordance with statute clearly and unequivocally expresses he or she does not wish to consult with the woman
(*or*)
(g) Reasonable efforts to give actual notice to appropriate person have failed, and 48 hours constructive notice has been given in manner specified in statute

Penalty:

A misdemeanor of the first degree. For subsequent offenses, under Division (1), a felony of the fourth degree. For subsequent offenses, under Division (2), a felony of the fifth degree.

Note:

Affirmative defense that woman provided false, misleading, or incorrect information on specified matters and person had no reasonable cause to disbelieve such information.

Affirmative defense that compliance not possible because immediate threat of serious risk to life or health of woman created emergency necessitating immediate performance or inducement of abortion.

Offender also liable for civil compensatory and exemplary damages.

Definition:
"Unemancipated" § 2919.12(F).

2919.13 Abortion Manslaughter

Elements:

Division (A):
(1) Purposely
(2) Take the life of a child
   (a) Born by attempted abortion
   (b) Alive when removed from the uterus of the pregnant woman

Division (B):
(1) Being a person performing an abortion
(2) Fail to take measures required by the exercise of medical judgment in light of the attending circumstances to preserve the life of a child who is alive when removed from the uterus of a pregnant woman

Penalty:
    A felony of the first degree.

2919.14 Abortion Trafficking

Elements:

(1) (a) Experiment upon
       (*or*)
   (b) Sell
(2) The aborted product of human conception

Penalty:
    Misdemeanor of first degree.

Note:
    This offense does not include autopsies pursuant to R.C. §§ 313.13, 2108.50.

2919.15 Performing Unlawful Abortion Procedure

Elements:
(1) Knowingly
(2) Perform or attempt to perform
(3) A dilation and extraction procedure
(4) On a pregnant woman

Penalty:
    A felony of the fourth degree.

Note:
    It is an affirmative defense that all other available abortion procedures would pose a greater risk to the health of the pregnant woman than the risk posed by the dilation and extraction procedure.

2919.17 Terminating or Attempting to Terminate Human Pregnancy After Viability

Elements:

Division (A):
(1) Purposely
(2) (a) Perform or induce
　　　(*or*)
　　(b) Attempt to perform or induce
(3) An abortion
(4) Upon a pregnant woman
(5) If the unborn human is viable unless the abortion is performed or induced or attempted to be performed or induced by a physician and that physician determines, in good faith and in the exercise of reasonable medical judgment,
　　(a) That the abortion is necessary to prevent the death of the pregnant woman or a serious risk of the substantial and irreversible impairment of a major bodily function of the pregnant woman
　　　(*or*)
　　(b) After making a determination relative to the viability of the unborn human in conformity with Division (A) of R.C. § 2919.18 that the unborn human is not viable

Division (B)(1):
(1) Physician
(2) Purposely
(3) (a) Perform or induce
　　　(*or*)
　　(b) Attempt to perform or induce
(4) An abortion
(5) Upon a pregnant woman when the unborn human is viable and when the physician has determined, in good faith and reasonable medical judgment, that the abortion is necessary to prevent the death of the pregnant woman or a serious risk of the substantial and irreversible impairment of a major bodily function of the pregnant woman, unless each of the following is satisfied:
　　(a) The physician certifies in writing that he has determined, in good faith and the exercise of reasonable medical judg-

ment, that the abortion is necessary to prevent the death of the pregnant woman or a serious risk of the substantial and irreversible impairment of a major bodily function of the pregnant woman
(*and*)

(b) The determination referred to in (5)(a) is concurred in by at least one other physician who certifies in writing that the concurring physician has determined, in good faith and the exercise of reasonable medical judgment, and following a review of the available medical records of and any available tests results pertaining to the pregnant woman, that the abortion is necessary to prevent the death of the pregnant woman or a serious risk of the substantial and irreversible impairment of a major bodily function of the pregnant woman
(*and*)

(c) The abortion is performed or induced or attempted to be performed or induced in a health care facility that has or has access to appropriate neonatal services for premature infants
(*and*)

(d) The physician who performs or induces or attempts to perform or induce the abortion terminates or attempts to terminate the pregnancy in the manner that provides the best opportunity for the unborn human to survive, unless that physician determines, in good faith and in the exercise of reasonable medical judgment, that the termination of the pregnancy in that manner poses a significantly greater risk of the death of the pregnant woman or a serious risk of the substantial and irreversible impairment of a major bodily function of the pregnant woman than would other available methods of abortion
(*and*)

(e) The physician who performs or induces or attempts to perform or induce the abortion has arranged for the attendance in the same room in which the abortion is to be performed or induced or attempted to be performed or induced of at least one other physician who is to take control of, provide immediate medical care for, and take

OFFENSES AGAINST THE FAMILY 2919.18

all reasonable steps necessary to preserve the life and health of the unborn human immediately upon the unborn human's complete expulsion or extraction from the pregnant woman

Penalty:
A felony of the fourth degree.

Note:
Division (B)(1) does not prohibit the performance or inducement or attempted performance or inducement of an abortion without prior satisfaction of each of the conditions described in Division (B)(1)(a)-(e) if the physician in good faith and reasonable medical judgment believes that a medical emergency exists that prevents compliance with one or more of those conditions.

2919.18 Failure to Perform Viability Testing

Elements:

Division (A)(1):
(1) Physician
(2) (a) Perform or induce
    (*or*)
    (b) Attempt to perform or induce
(3) An abortion
(4) Upon a pregnant woman after the beginning of her twenty-second week of pregnancy unless the physician determines in good faith and in the exercise of reasonable medical judgment, that the unborn human is not viable, and the physician makes that determination after performing a medical examination and after performance of gestational age, weight, lung maturity, or other tests of the unborn human that a reasonable physician making a determination as to whether an unborn human is or is not viable would perform or cause to be performed

Division (A)(2):
(1) Physician
(2) (a) Perform or induce
    (*or*)

(b) Attempt to perform or induce
(3) An abortion
(4) Upon a pregnant woman after the beginning of her twenty-second week of pregnancy without first entering the determination described in Division (A)(1) and the associated findings of the medical examination and tests in the medical record of the woman.

Penalty:

A misdemeanor of the fourth degree.

Note:

Divisions (A)(1) and (2) do not prohibit a physician from performing or inducing or attempting to perform or induce an abortion on a pregnant woman after the beginning of her twenty-second week of pregnancy if a medical emergency exists.

NONSUPPORT AND RELATED OFFENSES

2919.21 Nonsupport or Contributing to Nonsupport of Dependents

Elements:

Division (A):

(1) Abandon or fail to support adequately according to law
(2) (a) A spouse
   (*or*)
   (b) A child under 18, or a mentally or physically handicapped child under 21
   (*or*)
   (c) An aged/infirm parent or adoptive parent who is unable to provide adequately his own support through lack of ability/means
   (*or*)
   (d) Any other person whom, by law, court order or decree one is legally obligated to support

Division (B):

(1) Abandon or fail to provide support as established by a court order to

(2) Another person
(3) Whom by court order or decree,
(4) The person is legally obligated to support

Division (C):
(1) Aid, abet, induce, cause, encourage, or contribute to
(2) (a) Child
   (*or*)
   (b) Ward of juvenile court
(3) (a) Becoming a dependent child as defined in R.C. § 2151.04
   (*or*)
   (b) Becoming a neglected child as defined in R.C. § 2151.03

Penalty:

A misdemeanor of the first degree. If previously convicted under (A)(2)(b) or (B) of this section, or the court finds a failure to support under (A)(2)(b) or (B) of this section for a total accumulated period of 26 weeks out of 104 consecutive weeks, a felony of the fifth degree. If previously convicted of a felony violation of (A)(2)(b) or (B) of this section, a felony of the fourth degree.

Note:

It is an affirmative defense to a charge under this section that the actor was unable to provide adequate support, and provided such support as was within his ability and means. In addition, it is an affirmative defense to a charge under Division (A)(3) of this section that the parent abandoned, or failed to support the actor as required by law, while the actor was under age eighteen, or was mentally or physically handicapped and under age twenty-one.

Court costs and the attorney fees of adverse parties are to be assessed for a violation of a support order issued on or after 4-15-85.

It is not a defense to a charge under division (B) that the person whom a court has ordered the accused to support is being adequately supported by someone other than the accused.

2919.22 Endangering Children

Elements:

Division (A):
(1) Being a parent, guardian, custodian, person with custody or

control, or a person in loco parentis
(2) Create a substantial risk to the health or safety of
(3) A child under 18 or a mentally or physically handicapped person under 21
(4) By violating a duty of care, protection, or support

Division (B):
(1) (a) Abuse a child
    (*or*)
   (b) Torture/cruelly abuse a child
    (*or*)
   (c) Administer corporal punishment or use other physical disciplinary measures, or physically restrain a child in a cruel manner or for prolonged periods in a manner excessive under the circumstances and which creates substantial risk of serious physical harm
    (*or*)
   (d) Repeatedly administer unwarranted disciplinary measures to a child involving substantial risk that such conduct, if continued, will seriously impair or retard mental health/development if continued
    (*or*)
   (e) Entice, coerce, permit, encourage, compel, employ, hire, use, or allow the child to act, model, or in any other way participate in, or be photographed for, the production, presentation, dissemination, or advertisement of any material or performance that he knows or reasonably should know is obscene, as defined in R.C. § 2907.01, or any material or performance that is a sexually- or nudity-oriented matter
(2) When such child is under 18 or is a mentally or physically handicapped child under 21

Division (C):
(1) Operate a vehicle, streetcar, or trackless trolley
(2) Within this state
(3) In violation of Division (A) of R.C. § 4511.19
(4) When one or more children under 18 are in the vehicle, streetcar, or trackless trolley

OFFENSES AGAINST THE FAMILY — 2919.22

Penalty:

A violation of Division (A) or (B)(1)(a), a misdemeanor of the first degree unless serious physical harm to the child is involved, then a felony of the third degree. Where offender has previously been convicted under this section or of any offense involving neglect, abandonment, contributing to the delinquency of, or physical abuse of a child, a felony of the fourth degree. A violation of Division (B)(1)(b), (c) or (d), a felony of the third degree unless serious physical harm to the child, or there has been a previous conviction under R.C. § 2919.22, or an offense involving neglect, abandonment, contributing to the delinquency of, or physical abuse of a child, then a felony of the second degree. A violation of Division (B)(1)(e), a felony of the second degree. A violation of Division (C) with no violation of (E)(5)(b) or (c), a misdemeanor of the first degree. A violation of Division (C) with no violation of (E)(5)(c) and serious harm results to the child or the offender has been previously convicted of an offense under this section or any offense involving neglect, abandonment, contributing to the delinquency of, or physical abuse of a child, a felony of the fifth degree. A violation of Division (C) resulting in serious physical harm to the child involved and the offender has been previously convicted of a violation of Division (C) of this section, R.C. §§ 2903.06, 2903.07, or 2903.08, or R.C. § 2903.04 in a case in which the offender was subject to the sanctions described in Division (D) of that section, a felony of the fourth degree.

Note:

It is not a violation of a duty of care, protection or support under Division (A) when the parent, guardian, custodian, or person having custody or control of a child treats the physical or mental illness or defect of such child by spiritual means—through prayer alone, in accordance with the tenets of a recognized religious body.

Division (B) of this section does not apply to any material or performance that is produced, presented, or disseminated for a bona fide medical, scientific, educational, religious, governmental, judicial, or other proper purpose, by or to a physician, psychologist, sociologist, scientist, teacher, person pursuing bona fide studies or research, librarian, clergyman, prosecutor, judge, or other person having a proper interest in the material or performance.

Mistake of age is not a defense under (B)(1)(e) above.

As used in Division (B)(1)(e) of this section:

(a) "Material," "performance," and "sexual activity" have the same meanings as in section 2907.01 of the Revised Code.

(b) "Nudity-oriented matter" means any material or performance that shows a minor in a state of nudity and that, taken as a whole by the average person applying contemporary community standards, appeals to prurient interest.

(c) "Sexually oriented matter" means any material or performance that shows a minor participating or engaging in sexual activity, masturbation, or bestiality.

Any sentence of imprisonment imposed under (B)(1)(e) above is to be served consecutively to any other sentence of imprisonment.

Revised Code § 2933.16 provides that if an offender is convicted of or pleads guilty to a violation of R.C. § 2919.22(B), the court may suspend execution of sentence and place the offender on probation conditioned upon the participation of the offender, to the satisfaction of the court, in a program of clinically appropriate psychiatric or psychological treatment.

2919.22.2 Parental Education Neglect

Elements:
(1) Fail to attend a parental education or training program
(2) The person is required to attend pursuant to a policy adopted under § 3313.66.3

Penalty:
A misdemeanor of the the fourth degree.

2919.23 Interference with Custody

Elements:

Division (A):
(1) (a) Knowing the person is without privilege to do so
(*or*)

OFFENSES AGAINST THE FAMILY 2919.23

    (b) Being reckless in that regard
(2) Entice, take, keep or harbor from parent, guardian or custodian
(3) (a) A child under 18 or mentally/physically handicapped child under 21
      (*or*)
   (b) A person committed by laws to an institution for delinquent, unruly, neglected, abused, or dependent children
      (*or*)
   (c) A person committed by laws to an institution for the mentally ill/mentally retarded

Division (B):
(1) Aid, abet, induce, cause, or encourage
(2) (a) Child
      (*or*)
   (b) Ward of the juvenile court
(3) Who has been committed to the custody of any person, department, or public or private institution
(4) To leave the custody of that person, department, or institution
(5) Without legal consent

Penalty:

For a violation of Division (A)(3)(a), a misdemeanor of the first degree. If the child is removed from the state or if the offender previously has been convicted of an offense under this section, a felony of the fifth degree. If the child suffers physical harm as a result of the violation, a felony of the fourth degree.

For violation of Division (A)(3)(b) or (c), a misdemeanor of the third degree. For violation of Division (B), a misdemeanor of the first degree.

Note:

It is an affirmative defense to a charge of enticing or taking, under Division (A)(3)(a), above, that the actor reasonably believed that his conduct was necessary to preserve the child's health or safety. It is an affirmative defense to a charge of keeping or harboring under this section, that the actor in good faith gave notice to law enforcement or judicial authorities within a reasonable time after the child or committed person came under his shelter, protection or influence. Each day of violation of Division (B) is a separate offense.

2919.23.1 Interfering with Action to Issue or Modify Support Order

(1) By using physical harassment or threats of violence against another person
(2) (a) Interfere with the other person's initiation or continuance of
    (*or*)
    (b) Attempt to prevent the other person from initiating or continuing an action to issue or modify
(3) A support order under Chapter 3115., or under R.C. §§ 2151.23, 2151.23.1, 2151.33, 2151.36, 2151.49, 3105.18, 3105.21, 3109.05, 3111.13, 3113.04, 3113.07, or 3113.31

Penalty:

A misdemeanor of the first degree. If the offender has a prior conviction under this section or R.C. § 3111.29, a felony of the fourth degree.

2919.24 Contributing to the Unruliness or Delinquency of a Child

Elements:

(1) (a) Aid, abet, induce, cause, encourage, or contribute to
    (*or*)
    (b) Act in a way tending to cause
(2) (a) Child
    (*or*)
    (b) Ward of the juvenile court
(3) (a) Becoming (to become) an unruly child, as defined in R.C. § 2151.02.2
    (*or*)
    (b) Becoming (to become) a delinquent child, as defined in R.C. § 2151.02

Penalty:

A misdemeanor of the first degree.

Note:
Each day of violation is a separate offense.

DOMESTIC VIOLENCE

2919.25 Domestic Violence

Elements:

Division (A):
(1) Knowingly
(2) Cause or attempt to cause
(3) Physical harm
(4) To a family or household member

Division (B):
(1) Recklessly
(2) Cause
(3) Serious physical harm
(4) To a family or household member

Division (C):
(1) Knowingly
(2) By force or threat of force
(3) Cause
(4) A family or household member to believe
(5) The offender will cause imminent physical harm
(6) To the family or household member

Penalty:

Division (A) or (B), no previous conviction under this section or conviction under 2903.11, 2903.12, or 2903.13 involving person who was family or household member at time of violation, a misdemeanor of the first degree.

Division (A) or (B), previous conviction under this section or conviction under 2903.11, 2903.12, or 2903.13 involving person who was family or household member at time of violation, a felony of the fifth degree.

Division (C), no previous conviction under this section or conviction under 2903.11, 2903.12, or 2903.13 involving person who was family or household member at time of violation, a misdemeanor of the fourth degree.

Division (C), previous conviction under this section or conviction under 2903.11, 2903.12, or 2903.13 involving person who was family or household member at time of violation, a misdemeanor of the third degree.

Note:

Temporary protection order see R.C. § 2919.26. For duty of law enforcement agency to provide information regarding relief see R.C. § 3113.31.

2919.27 Violating Protection Order, Consent Agreement, or Anti-Stalking Protection Order

Elements:

(1) Recklessly
(2) Violate any terms
(3) Of protection order issued or consent agreement approved pursuant to R.C. § 2919.26 or § 3113.31
(4) Of an anti-stalking protection order issued pursuant to R.C. § 2903.21.3

Penalty:

A misdemeanor of the first degree. If the offender has one or more prior convictions/guilty pleas under this section, or two or more violations under 2903.21.1 or 2911.21.1, involving the same person who is subject of protection order or consent agreement, a felony of the fifth degree.

If a violation of Division (4) and there is a previous conviction or guilty plea to two or more violations of this section involving an anti-stalking protection order, two or more violations of R.C. §§ 2903.21, 2903.21.1, 2903.22, or 2911.21.1 that involve the same person who is the subject of the anti-stalking protection order, or two or more violations of R.C. § 2903.21.4 as it existed prior to the effective date of this amendment, a felony of the fifth degree.

CHAPTER 2921
OFFENSES AGAINST JUSTICE AND PUBLIC ADMINISTRATION

IN GENERAL

2921.01 Definitions

BRIBERY AND INTIMIDATION

2921.02 Bribery
2921.03 Intimidation
2921.04 Intimidation of Attorney, Victim or Witness in Criminal Case
2921.05 Retaliation

PERJURY

2921.11 Perjury
2921.12 Tampering with Evidence
2921.13 Falsification; in Theft Offense; to Purchase Firearm
2921.14 False Report of Child Abuse or Neglect

COMPOUNDING

2921.21 Compounding a Crime
2921.22 Failure to Report a Crime or Knowledge of a Death, or Burn Injury
2921.23 Failure to Aid a Law Enforcement Officer
2921.24 Disclosure of Confidential Information

OBSTRUCTING AND ESCAPE

2921.31 Obstructing Official Business
2921.32 Obstructing Justice
2921.32.1 Assaulting Police Dog or Horse or Handicapped Assistance Dog
2921.33 Resisting Arrest
2921.33.1 Failure to Comply with Order or Signal of Police Officer
2921.34 Escape
2921.35 Aiding Escape or Resistance to Authority
2921.36 Illegal Conveyance of Weapons or Prohibited Items Onto Detention Facility or Institution

PECULATION AND DERELICTION

2921.41	Theft in Office
2921.42	Having an Unlawful Interest in a Public Contract
2921.43	Soliciting or Receiving Improper Compensation
2921.44	Dereliction of Duty
2921.45	Interfering with Civil Rights

IMPERSONATING PEACE OFFICER

2921.51	Impersonating Peace Officer or Private Policeman

SHAM LEGAL PROCESS

2921.52	Using Sham Legal Process

BRIBERY AND INTIMIDATION

2921.02 Bribery

Elements:

Division (A):
(1) With purpose to corrupt or improperly influence
(2) A public servant or party official whether before or after attaining office
(3) With respect to the discharge of his duty
(4) Promise, offer or give any valuable thing or benefit

Division (B):
(1) Knowingly solicit or accept any valuable thing or benefit for himself or another person
(2) As a public servant or party official
(3) To corrupt or improperly influence him or another public servant or party official
(4) With respect to the discharge of his or the other servant's or official's duty
(5) Before or after attaining office

Division (C):
(1) With purpose to corrupt a witness or improperly influence his testimony in an official proceeding
(2) Promise, offer or give any valuable thing or benefit to said

witness or another person

(3) Either before or after he is subpoenaed or sworn

Division (D):
(1) Knowingly solicit or accept a valuable thing or benefit for himself or another person
(2) To corrupt or improperly influence acceptor's testimony in an official proceeding
(3) Either before or after he is subpoenaed or sworn as a witness

Penalty:
A felony of the third degree. If public servant or party official convicted, forever disqualified from holding public office, employment, or position of trust in state.

2921.03 Intimidation

Elements:

(1) Knowingly
(2) By force, unlawful threat of harm, or by filing, recording, or otherwise using a materially false or fraudulent writing with malicious purpose, in bad faith, or in a wanton and reckless manner
(3) Attempt to influence, intimidate or hinder a public servant, party official, an attorney or witness involved in a civil action or proceeding
(4) In the discharge of the duties of the public servant, party official, attorney or witness

Penalty:
A felony of the third degree.

2921.04 Intimidation of Attorney, Victim or Witness in Criminal Case

Elements:

Division (A):
(1) Knowingly
(2) Attempt to
(3) (a) Intimidate
(*or*)

(b) Hinder
(4) (a) A victim of crime
- (i) In filing of criminal charges
  (*or*)
- (ii) In prosecution of criminal charges
  (*or*)

(b) A witness in a criminal action or proceeding in the discharge of the duties of the witness

Division (B):
(1) Knowingly
(2) (a) By force
  (*or*)
  (b) By unlawful threat of harm to any person or property
(3) Attempt to
(4) (a) Influence
  (*or*)
  (b) Intimidate
  (*or*)
  (c) Hinder
(5) (a) A victim of crime
- (i) In filing of criminal charges
  (*or*)
- (ii) In prosecution of criminal charges
  (*or*)

(b) An attorney or witness involved in a criminal action or proceeding in the discharge of the duties of the attorney or witness

Penalty:

A violation of Division (A), a misdemeanor of the first degree. A violation of Division (B), a felony of the third degree.

Note:

Division (A) above does not apply to any person who, either prior or subsequent to the filing of the complaint, indictment, information, is either attempting to resolve a dispute pertaining to the alleged commission of a criminal offense, or is attempting to arbitrate, mediate, compromise, settle, or assist in the conciliation of that dispute pursuant to an authorization for arbitration, mediation, compromise, settlement, or conciliation of a dispute of that nature.

2921.05 Retaliation

Elements:

Division (A):
(1) Purposely
(2) (a) By force

   (or)

   (b) By unlawful threat of harm to any person or property
(3) Retaliate against a public servant, a party official, or an attorney or witness who was involved in a civil or criminal action or proceeding
(4) Because the public servant, party official, or attorney or witness discharged the duties of the public servant, party official, attorney, or witness

Division (B):
(1) Purposely
(2) (a) By force

   (or)

   (b) By unlawful threat of harm to any person or property
(3) Retaliate against the victim of a crime
(4) Because the victim filed or prosecuted criminal charges

Penalty:
   A felony of the third degree.

PERJURY

2921.11 Perjury

Elements:

(1) Knowingly
(2) (a) Make a false statement under oath or affirmation

   (or)

   (b) Swear or affirm the truth of a false statement previously made
(3) In an official proceeding

(4) When either statement is material to such proceeding

Penalty:

A felony of the third degree.

Note:

No conviction hereunder where proof of falsity rests solely upon contradictory testimony of one person other than defendant. However, where contradictory statements relating to the same material fact are made by the offender under oath or affirmation and within the period of the statute of limitations for perjury, it is not necessary for the prosecution to prove which statement was false, but only that one or the other was false.

A falsification is material, regardless of its admissibility in evidence, if it can affect the course or outcome of the proceeding. It is no defense to a charge under this section that the offender mistakenly believed a falsification to be immaterial.

2921.12 Tampering with Evidence

Elements:

(1) Knowing an official proceeding or investigation is in progress, or is about to be or is likely to be instituted
(2) (a) (i) Alter, destroy, conceal, or remove any record, document, or thing
   (ii) With purpose to impair its value or availability as evidence in such proceeding or investigation
   (*or*)
  (b) (i) Make, present, or use any record, document or thing
   (ii) Knowing it to be false
   (iii) With purpose to mislead a public official who is or may be engaged in a proceeding or investigation or with a purpose to corrupt the outcome of any proceeding or investigation

Penalty:

A felony of the third degree.

2921.13 Falsification; in Theft Offense; to Purchase Firearm

Elements:

(1) Knowingly

(a) Make a false statement
   (*or*)
(b) Swear or affirm the truth of a previous false statement

(2) When such is:
   (a) Made in official proceeding
      (*or*)
   (b) Made with purpose to incriminate another
      (*or*)
   (c) Made with purpose to mislead public official in performing his official function
      (*or*)
   (d) Made with a purpose to secure payment of unemployment compensation; aid to dependent children; disability assistance administered by the Department of Human Services; retirement benefits; economic development assistance as defined in § 9.66 of the revised code; or other benefits administered by governmental agency or paid out of public treasury
      (*or*)
   (e) Made with a purpose to secure issuance by governmental agency of license, permit, authorization, certificate, registration, release, or provider agreement
      (*or*)
   (f) Sworn or affirmed before notary public or other person empowered to administer oath
      (*or*)
   (g) In writing on or in connection with a report or return that is required or authorized by law
      (*or*)
   (h) In writing, and made with purpose to induce another to extend credit, employ offender; confer any degree, diploma, certificate of attainment, award of excellence, honor on offender; extend or bestow on offender any other valuable benefit or distinction when person to whom statement directed relies upon it to that person's detriment
      (*or*)
   (i) Made with purpose to commit or facilitate commission of theft offense

(or)
(j) Made to a probate court in connection with any action, proceeding, or other matter within its jurisdiction, either orally or in a written document, including but not limited to, an application, petition, complaint, or other pleading, or an inventory, account, or report
(or)
(k) Made on account, record, stamp, or other writing that is required by law
(or)
(l) Made in connection with the purchase of a firearm, as defined in RC § 2923.11, and in conjunction with the furnishing to the seller of the firearm of a fictitious or altered driver's or commercial driver's license or permit, a fictitious or altered identification card, or any other document that contains false information about the purchaser's identity
(or)
(t) Made in a document or instrument of writing that purports to be a judgment, lien, or claim of indebtedness and is filed or recorded with the secretary of state, a county recorder, or the clerk of a court of record*
*The lettering is the result of combining the amendments made by SB 269 and HB 644.

Division (B):
(1) In connection with the purchase of a firearm
(2) Knowingly furnish to the seller of the firearm a fictitious or altered driver's or commercial driver's license or permit, a fictitious or altered identification card, or any other document that contains false information about the purchaser's identity
(3) Venue

Penalty:
A violation of Divisions (2)(a), (b), (c), (d), (e), (f), (g), (h), (j), or (k), a misdemeanor of the first degree.

A violation of Division (2)(i) (falsification in a theft offense), a misdemeanor of the first degree. If the value of the property or services stolen is $500 or more and is less than $5,000, a felony of the fifth degree. If the value of the property or services stolen is $5,000 or more and less than $100,000, a felony of the fourth degree. If the value of the property or services stolen is $100,000 or more, a felony of the third degree.

A violation of Division (2)(I) or (B), a felony of the fifth degree.

2921.14 False Report of Child Abuse or Neglect

Elements:

(1) Knowingly
(2) (a) Make
   (*or*)
   (b) Cause another person to make
(3) A false report under 2151.42.1(B) that any person has committed an act or omission that resulted in a child being
   (a) An abused child as defined in 2151.03.1
   (*or*)
   (b) A neglected child as defined in 2151.03

Penalty:
   A misdemeanor of the first degree.

COMPOUNDING

2921.21 Compounding a Crime

Elements:

(1) Knowingly
(2) Demand, accept, or agree to accept
(3) Anything of value
(4) In consideration for abandoning or agreeing to abandon a pending prosecution

Penalty:
   A misdemeanor of the first degree.

Note:
   No crime if pending prosecution is for a violation of R.C. §§ 2913.02 (theft), 2913.11 (bad checks), 2913.21(B)(2) (credit cards), or 2913.47 (insurance fraud) and actor under this section

is the victim and the thing of value received did not exceed amount which actor reasonably believed due him as restitution for loss caused by offense.

2921.22 Failure to Report a Crime or Knowledge of a Death, or Burn Injury

Elements:

Division (A): Failure to report a crime (Felony)
(1) While having knowledge that a felony has been or is being committed
(2) Knowingly
(3) Fail to report
(4) To law enforcement authorities
(5) That a felony has been or is being committed

Division (B): Failure to report a crime (Injury from offense of violence)
(1) While a physician, limited practitioner, nurse, or person giving aid to a sick or injured person
(2) Negligently
(3) Fail to report
(4) To law enforcement authorities
(5) (a) Any gunshot wound treated or observed by the physician, limited practitioner, nurse, or person
   (or)
   (b) Any stab wound treated or observed by the physician, limited practitioner, nurse, or person
   (or)
   (c) Any serious physical harm to persons that the physician, limited practitioner, nurse, or person knows or has reasonable cause to believe resulted from an offense of violence

Division (C): Failure to report knowledge of a death
(1) (a) Having discovered the body of a person
   (or)
   (b) Having acquired the first knowledge of the death of any person
(2) Fail to report the death immediately to
(3) (a) Any physician known to be treating the deceased for a

condition from which death at such time would not be unexpected
(*or*)
- (b) A law enforcement officer
(*or*)
- (c) An ambulance service
(*or*)
- (d) An emergency squad
(*or*)
- (e) The coroner in a political subdivision in which the body is discovered, the death is believed to have occurred, or knowledge concerning the death is obtained

Division (D): Failure to report knowledge of a death (Facts bearing on investigation of death)
(1) Fail to provide
(2) (a) Upon request of the person to whom a report under (C) above was made
   (*or*)
   (b) To any law enforcement officer who has reasonable cause to assert the authority to investigate the circumstances surrounding the death
(3) Any facts within the person's knowledge that may have a bearing on the facts of the death

Division (E): Failure to report a burn injury
(1) (a) While a physician, nurse, or limited practitioner outside a hospital, sanitarium, or other medical facility who attends or treats a person who has sustained a
   (*or*)
   (b) While a manager, superintendent, or other person in charge of a hospital, sanitarium, or other medical facility in which a person is attended or treated for any
(2) Burn injury
(3) (a) Inflicted by an explosion or other incendiary device
   (*or*)
   (b) That shows evidence of having been inflicted in a violent, malicious, or criminal manner
(4) (a) Fail to report the burn injury immediately to the local arson

bureau if there is one in the jurisdiction in which the person is attended or treated or otherwise to local law enforcement authorities

(or)

(b) Fail to file within three working days after attending or treating the victim, a written report, on a form to be provided by the state fire marshal, with the state fire marshal

Penalty:

Violation of (A), (C), or (D), a misdemeanor of the fourth degree.

Violation of (B), or knowing violation of (E), a misdemeanor of the second degree.

Negligent violation of (E), a minor misdemeanor.

2921.23 Failure to Aid a Law Enforcement Officer

Elements:

(1) When called upon to assist law enforcement officer in preventing/halting commission of offense, or in apprehension or detention of an offender
(2) Negligently fail or refuse to render aid
(3) When such aid can be given without substantial risk of physical harm to person called upon

Penalty:

A minor misdemeanor.

2921.24 Disclosure of Confidential Information

Elements:

(1) Being an officer or employee
(2) (a) Of a law enforcement agency or court
    (or)
    (b) Of the office of the clerk of any court
(3) Disclose
(4) During the pendency of any criminal case
(5) The home address of any peace officer as defined in R.C. § 2935.01
(6) Who is a witness or arresting officer in the case

OFFENSES AGAINST JUSTICE **2921.32** 125

Penalty:
A misdemeanor of the fourth degree.

Note:
The court in which any criminal case is pending may order the disclosure of the home address of any peace officer in the case pursuant to a written request and for good cause shown. This section does not prohibit a peace officer from disclosing his own address, and does not apply to any person who discloses such address pursuant to a court order.

OBSTRUCTING AND ESCAPE

2921.31 Obstructing Official Business

Elements:

(1) Perform any act which hampers/impedes a public official in the performance of his lawful duties
(2) With a purpose to prevent, obstruct, or delay performance by a public official of his authorized acts
(3) Without having a privilege to do so

Penalty:
A misdemeanor of the second degree.

2921.32 Obstructing Justice

Elements:

(1) With a purpose
   (a) To hinder the discovery, apprehension, prosecution, conviction, or punishment of another for crime
      (or)
   (b) To assist another to benefit from the commission of a crime
(2) (a) Harbor or conceal another
      (or)
   (b) Provide another with money, transportation, a weapon, disguise or other means of avoiding discovery or apprehension
      (or)

(c) Warn another of impending discovery or apprehension
(*or*)
(d) Destroy or conceal physical evidence of a crime
(*or*)
(e) Induce anyone to withhold testimony or information, or elude legal process summoning the other person to testify or supply evidence
(*or*)
(f) Communicate false information to anyone

Penalty:

If the crime committed by the person aided is a misdemeanor, a misdemeanor of the same degree as the crime committed. If the crime committed by the person aided is a felony, then a felony of the fifth degree. If the person aided committed aggravated murder, murder, or a felony of the first or second degree and if the offender knows or has reason to believe that the crime committed is one of those offenses, a felony of the third degree.

2921.32.1 Assaulting Police Dog or Horse or Handicapped Assistance Dog

Elements:

Division (A):

(1) Knowingly
(2) Cause or attempt to cause
(3) Physical harm
(4) To a police dog or horse
(5) In either of the following circumstances:
   (i) the police dog or horse is assisting a law enforcement officer in the performance of the officer's official duties at the time the physical harm is caused or attempted
   (*or*)
   (ii) the police dog or horse is not assisting a law enforcement officer in the performance of the officer's official duties at the time the physical harm is caused or attempted, but the offender has actual knowledge that the dog or horse is a police dog or horse

OFFENSES AGAINST JUSTICE **2921.33** 127

Division (B):

(1) Knowingly
(2) Cause or attempt to cause
(3) Physical harm
(4) To a handicapped assistance dog
(5) In either of the following circumstances:
> (i) the handicapped assistance dog is assisting a blind, deaf, or mobility impaired person at the time the physical harm is attempted or caused
> (*or*)
> (ii) the handicapped assistance dog is not assisting a blind, deaf, or mobility impaired person at the time the physical harm is caused or attempted, but the offender has actual knowledge that the dog is a handicapped assistance dog

Penalty:

Where violation results in the death of the police dog or horse or handicapped assistance dog, a felony of the fourth degree. Where violation results in serious physical harm to the police dog or horse or handicapped assistance dog other than its death, a felony of the fifth degree. Where violation results in physical harm to the police dog or horse or handicapped assistance dog other than death or serious physical harm, a misdemeanor of the first degree. Where violation does not result in death, serious physical harm, or physical harm to the police dog or horse or handicapped assistance dog, a misdemeanor of the second degree.

2921.33 Resisting Arrest

Elements:

(1) Recklessly or by means of force
(2) Resist/interfere with lawful arrest
(3) Of himself or another

Penalty:

A misdemeanor of the second degree. If the offense is committed by an offender who brandishes a deadly weapon or who attempts to gain control of a deadly weapon that is in the possession of a law enforcement officer, a felony of the fifth degree.

2921.33.1 Failure to Comply With Order or Signal of Police Officer

Elements:

Division (A):
(1) Fail to comply
(2) With any lawful order or direction
(3) Of any police officer invested with authority to direct, control, or regulate traffic

Division (B):
(1) Operate a motor vehicle
(2) So as willfully to elude or flee
(3) A police officer
(4) After receiving a visible or audible signal
(5) From a police officer
(6) To bring his motor vehicle to a stop

Penalty:
   Division (A), a misdemeanor of the first degree.
   Division (B), a misdemeanor of the first degree, but a felony of the fourth degree if the trier of fact finds beyond a reasonable doubt that: (1) the offense was committed while the offender was fleeing immediately after committing a felony, (2) the operation of the motor vehicle was a proximate cause of serious physical harm to persons or property, or (3) the operation of the motor vehicle caused a substantial risk of serious physical harm to persons or property.

2921.34 Escape

Elements:

Division (A)(1):

(1) Knowing oneself to be under detention or being reckless in that regard
(2) (a) Purposely break or attempt to break that detention
      (*or*)

> (b) Purposely fail to return to detention, either following a temporary leave granted for a specific purpose or limited period, or at the time required when serving a sentence in intermittent confinement

Division (A)(2):
(1) No person who is sentenced as a sexually violent predator whose sentence has been modified and is restricted to a geographic area
(2) Knowing that the person is under a geographic restriction or being reckless in that regard
(3) (a) Purposely leave the geographic area to which the restriction applies
   (*or*)
   (b) Purposely fail to return to that geographic area following a temporary leave granted for a specific purpose or for a specific period of time

Penalty:

If the offender, at the time of the commission of the offense, was under detention as an alleged or adjudicated delinquent or unruly child, if the act for which the offender was under detention would not be a felony if committed by an adult, a misdemeanor of the first degree.

If the offender, at the time of the commission of the offense, was under detention in any other manner or was a sexually violent predator for whom the requirement that the entire prison term imposed pursuant to R.C. § 2971.03(A)(3) be served in a state correctional institution has been modified pursuant to R.C. § 2971.05, when the most serious offense for which the offender was under detention is aggravated murder, murder, or a felony of the first or second degree or, if the person was under detention as an alleged or adjudicated delinquent child, when the most serious act for which the person was under detention would be aggravated murder, murder, or a felony of the first or second degree if committed by an adult, a felony of the second degree.

If the offender, at the time of the commission of the offense, was under detention in any other manner or was a sexually violent predator for whom the requirement that the entire prison term imposed pursuant to R.C. § 2971.03(A)(3) be served in a state correctional institution has been modified pursuant to R.C. § 2971.05, when the most serious offense for which the offender was under detention is a felony of the third, fourth, or fifth degree or an unclassified felony or, if the person was under detention as an alleged or adjudicated delinquent child, when the most serious act for which the person was under detention would be a felony of the third, fourth, or fifth degree or an unclassified felony if committed by an adult, a felony of the third degree.

If the offender, at the time of the commission of the offense, was under detention in any other manner or was a sexually violent predator for whom the requirement that the entire prison term imposed pursuant to R.C. § 2971.03(A)(3) be served in a state correctional institution has been modified pursuant to R.C. § 2971.05, when the most serious offense for which the offender was under detention is a misdemeanor, a felony of the fifth degree.

If the offender, at the time of the commission of the offense, was under detention in any other manner or was a sexually violent predator for whom the requirement that the entire prison term imposed pursuant to R.C. § 2971.03(A)(3) be served in a state correctional institution has been modified pursuant to R.C. § 2971.05, when the person was found not guilty by reason of insanity and the person's detention consisted of hospitalization, institutionalization, or confinement in a facility under an order made pursuant to R.C. § 2945.40, 2945.401, or 2945.402, a felony of the fifth degree.

If the offender, at the time of the commission of the offense, was under detention in any other manner or was a sexually violent predator for whom the requirement that the entire prison term imposed pursuant to R.C. § 2971.03(A)(3) be served in a state correctional institution has been modified pursuant to R.C. § 2971.05, when the most serious offense for which the offender was under detention is a misdemeanor and when the person fails to return to the detention at a specified time following temporary leave granted for a specific purpose or limited period or at the time required when serving a sentence in intermittent confinement, a misdemeanor of the first degree.

OFFENSES AGAINST JUSTICE

2921.35 Aiding Escape or Resistance to Authority

Elements:

Division (A):
(1) With a purpose to promote or facilitate an escape or resistance to lawful authority
(2) (a) Convey into a detention facility
    (or)
    (b) Provide to anyone confined therein instruments or things which may be used to escape or resist authority

Division (B):
(1) Being confined in a detention facility
(2) Make, procure, conceal, unlawfully possess or give to another inmate
(3) Any instrument or thing which may be used for such purposes
(4) With a purpose to promote or facilitate escape or resistance to lawful authority

Penalty:
 A felony of the fourth degree and sentence of confinement imposed for (B) shall be consecutive to any other sentence.

2921.36 Illegal Conveyance of Weapons or Prohibited Items Onto Detention Facility or Institution

Elements:

(1) Knowingly
    (a) Convey or attempt to convey onto the grounds of
        (or)
    (b) Deliver or attempt to deliver to any person who is confined in
(2) (a) A detention facility
        (or)
    (b) An institution under the control of the department of mental health or the department of mental retardation and developmental disabilities
(3) (a) Any deadly weapon or dangerous ordnance as defined in R.C. § 2923.11
        (or)

(b) Any part of or ammunition for use in such deadly weapon or dangerous ordnance

(*or*)

(4) Any drug of abuse as defined in R.C. § 3719.01.1

(*or*)

(5) Any intoxicating liquor as defined in R.C. § 4301.01

or

(6) Cash

Penalty:

If involving (5) above, a misdemeanor of the second degree. If involving (4) above, a felony of the fifth degree. If involving (4) above, and offender is an officer or employee of the facility or institution, a felony of the fourth degree. If involving (3) above, a felony of the fourth degree. If involving (6) above and the offender has not been previously convicted under Division (D) of this section, a misdemeanor of the first degree. If involving (6) above and offender has been previously convicted under Division (D) of this section, a felony of the fifth degree.

PECULATION AND DERELICTION

2921.41 Theft in Office

Elements:

(1) Being a public official/party official
(2) Commit a theft offense:
   (a) Using the offender's office or permitting its use or assenting to its use in aid of such offense
   (*or*)
   (b) Involving property or service owned by this or any state, the United States, a county, municipal corporation, or township, or any political subdivision, department, or agency thereof, or by a political party, or which is part of a political campaign fund

Penalty:

A felony of the fifth degree. If the value of the property or services stolen is $500 or more and is less than $5,000, a felony

OFFENSES AGAINST JUSTICE 2921.42 133

of the fourth degree. If the value of the property or services stolen is $5,000 or more, a felony of the third degree.

Note:

A person convicted or pleading guilty hereunder is forever barred from office of public trust. In addition to any imprisonment or fine, the court shall require restitution. State retirement and deferred compensation benefits may be withheld to effect restitution and the prosecutor must notify the retirement and deferred compensation systems of the filing of charges.

2921.42 Having Unlawful Interest in a Public Contract

Elements:

Division (A):

(1) Being a public official
(2) Knowingly authorize or employ the authority or influence of his office:
   (a) To secure authorization of a public contract in which he, his family, or business associate has an interest
   (*or*)
   (b) To secure the investment of public funds in any share, bond, mortgage or other security which such public official, his family member or business associate has an interest, or is an underwriter, or receives any brokerage, origination or servicing fees

Division (B):

(1) (a) Being or having been a public official, during his term or within one year thereafter occupy a position of profit in the prosecution of a public contract authorized by him or by a legislative body, commission or board of which he was a member at the time of authorization, and which was not let by competitive bidding, or if let by competitive bidding, in which his is not the lowest and best bid
   (*or*)
   (b) Have an interest in profits or benefits of a public contract:
      (i)   Entered into by, or for the use of a political subdivision/governmental agency/instrumentality with which he is connected

      (*or*)
  (ii) Involving more than $150, not let by competitive bidding when so required by law

Penalty:
    Division (A), a felony of the fourth degree.
    Division (B), a misdemeanor of the first degree.

Note:
    A number of exceptions are set forth in section 2921.42(B) and (C).

2921.43 Soliciting or Receiving Improper Compensation

Elements:

Division (A):
(1) (a) Knowingly promise or give to a public servant
      (*or*)
  (b) Being a public servant, knowingly solicit or accept
(2) (a) Any compensation other than as allowed by law
    (i) To perform his official duties
        (*or*)
    (ii) To perform any other act in his public capacity
        (*or*)
    (iii) For the general performance of the duties of his public office or public employment
        (*or*)
    (iv) As a supplement to his public compensation
        (*or*)
  (b) Additional or greater fees or costs than allowed by law to perform his official duties

Division (B):
(1) (a) For one's own personal or business use (whether a public servant or not)
      (*or*)
  (b) For the personal or business use of a public servant or party official
(2) Solicit or accept anything of value in consideration of:
  (a) Appointing/securing/maintaining/renewing the appoint-

OFFENSES AGAINST JUSTICE

ment of anyone to public office, employment or agency
(*or*)
(b) Preferring/maintaining the status of any public employee with respect to his compensation, duties, placement, location, promotion or other material aspects of his employment

Division (C):
(1) Coerce a contribution
(2) For the benefit of a political party, campaign committee, legislative campaign fund, or political action committee
(3) In consideration of:
   (a) Appointing/securing/maintaining/renewing the appointment of anyone to public office, employment, or agency
   (*or*)
   (b) Preferring/maintaining the status of any public employee with respect to his compensation, duties, placement, location, promotion or other material aspects of his employment

Penalty:
A misdemeanor of the first degree and disqualified from public office, employment, or position of trust for 7 years.

2921.44 Dereliction of Duty

Elements:

Division (A):
(1) Being a law enforcement officer
(2) Negligently fail
(3) (a) To serve a warrant without delay
    (*or*)
   (b) To prevent/halt the commission of an offense, or to apprehend an offender, when it is in his power to do so alone or with available assistance

Division (B):
(1) Being a law enforcement, ministerial or judicial officer
(2) Negligently fail
(3) To perform one's duty in a criminal proceeding

Division (C):
(1) Being an officer in charge of a detention facility
(2) Negligently

(3) (a) Allow the facility to become littered or unsanitary
(*or*)
(b) Fail to provide prisoners with adequate food, clothing, bedding, shelter or medical attention
(*or*)
(c) Fail to control an unruly prisoner or prevent intimidation of or physical harm to a prisoner
(*or*)
(d) Allow a prisoner to escape
(*or*)
(e) Fail to observe all lawful and reasonable regulations for the management of the facility

Division (D):
(1) Being a public official of the state
(2) Recklessly
(3) (a) Create a deficiency
(*or*)
(b) Incur a liability
(*or*)
(c) Expend a greater sum than appropriated by general assembly for one year's use by the department, agency or institution with which the public official is connected

Division (E):
(1) Being a public servant
(2) Recklessly
(3) (a) Fail to perform a duty imposed by law
(*or*)
(b) Do any act forbidden by law with respect to one's office

Penalty:
A misdemeanor of the second degree.

2921.45 Interfering with Civil Rights

Elements:

(1) Being a public servant
(2) Under color of one's office, employment or authority
(3) Knowingly

(4) Deprive, or conspire or attempt to deprive another
(5) Of a constitutional or statutory right

Penalty:
    A misdemeanor of the first degree.

IMPERSONATING PEACE OFFICER

2921.51 Impersonating Peace Officer or Private Policeman

Elements:

Division (B):
(1) Impersonate
(2) (a) Peace officer
    (*or*)
   (b) Private policeman

Division (C):
(1) By impersonation of
(2) (a) Peace officer
    (*or*)
   (b) Private policeman
(3) (a) Arrest or detain any person
    (*or*)
   (b) Search any person
    (*or*)
   (c) Search the property of any person

Division (D):
(1) Impersonate
(2) (a) Peace officer
    (*or*)
   (b) Private policeman
    (*or*)
   (c) An officer, agent or employee of the state
(3) With purpose to facilitate the commission of an offense

Division (E):
(1) While impersonating

(2) (a) Peace officer
   (*or*)
   (b) Private policeman
   (*or*)
   (c) An officer, agent or employee of the state
(3) Commit a felony

Penalty:

Violation of (B) is a misdemeanor of the fourth degree. Violation of (C) or (D) is a misdemeanor of the first degree, unless the purpose of a violation of (D) is to commit or facilitate the commission of a felony, then a violation of (D) is a felony of the fourth degree. Violation of (E) is a felony of the third degree.

Note:

It is an affirmative defense to a charge under (B) that the impersonation of the peace officer was for a lawful purpose.

SHAM LEGAL PROCESS

2921.52 Using Sham Legal Process [M4, M1, F4 F3]

(1) Knowingly
(2) (a) Issue, display, deliver, distribute, or otherwise use sham legal process
   (*or*)
   (b) Use sham legal process to arrest, detain, search, or seize any person or the property of another
   (*or*)
   (c) Commit or facilitate the commission of an offense, using sham legal process
   (*or*)
   (d) Commit a felony by using sham legal process

Penalty:

A violation of Division (2)(a) is a misdemeanor of the fourth degree. A violation of Division (2)(b) or (c) is a misdemeanor of the first degree. If the purpose of the violation of Division (2)(c) is to commit or facilitate the commission of a felony, a felony of the fourth degree. A violation of Division (2)(d) is a felony of the third degree.

CHAPTER 2923

CONSPIRACY, ATTEMPT, AND COMPLICITY; WEAPONS CONTROL; CORRUPT ACTIVITY

CONSPIRACY, ATTEMPT, AND COMPLICITY

2923.01	Conspiracy
2923.02	Attempt
2923.03	Complicity

WEAPONS CONTROL

2923.11	Definitions
2923.12	Carrying Concealed Weapons
2923.12.1	Illegal Possession of Firearm in Liquor Permit Premises
2923.12.2	Illegal Conveyance or Possession of a Deadly Weapon or Dangerous Ordnance or Illegal Possession of an Object Indistinguishable From a Firearm on School Premises
2923.12.3	Illegal Conveyance of Deadly Weapon or Dangerous Ordnance Into Courthouse; Illegal Possession or Control in Courthouse
2923.13	Having Weapons While Under Disability
2923.13.1	Possession of Deadly Weapon While Under Detention
2923.14	Relief from Disability
2923.15	Using Weapons While Intoxicated
2923.16	Improperly Handling Firearms in Motor Vehicle
2923.16.1	Improperly Discharging Firearm At or Into Habitation or School
2923.17	Unlawful Possesion of Dangerous Ordnance; Illegally Manufacturing or Processing Explosives
2923.18	License or Permit to Possess Dangerous Ordnance
2923.19	Failure to Secure Dangerous Ordnance
2923.20	Unlawful Transactions in Weapons
2923.21	Improperly Furnishing Firearms to a Minor
2923.21.1	Underage Purchase of Firearm or Handgun
2923.22	Permitted Interstate Transactions in Firearms
2923.23	Immunity from Prosecution
2923.24	Possessing Criminal Tools

CORRUPT ACTIVITY

2923.32	Engaging in Pattern of Corrupt Activity

CONSPIRACY, ATTEMPT, AND COMPLICITY

2923.01 Conspiracy

Elements:

(1) With purpose
(2) To commit, promote or facilitate the commission of (a) aggravated murder or murder, (b) kidnapping, (c) compelling or promoting prostitution, (d) aggravated arson, or arson, (e) aggravated robbery, or robbery, (f) aggravated burglary, or burglary, or (g) engaging in a pattern of corrupt activity, or (h) corrupting another with drugs, a felony drug trafficking, manufacturing, processing, or possession offense, theft of drugs, or illegal possessing of drug documents, or (i) felony offense of unauthorized use of vehicle or (j) violation of R.C. Chapter 3734. relating to hazardous wastes, other than R.C. § 3734.18
(3) (a) Plan or aid in planning with another person or persons the commission of any of the specified offenses
    (*or*)
   (b) Agree with another person or persons that one or more will engage in conduct which facilitates commission of any of the specified offenses
(4) The offender, or one of his co-conspirators
   (a) Subsequent to the offender's entrance into the conspiracy
   (b) Does an overt act
   (c) Which is in furtherance of the conspiracy, and is of a character that manifests a purpose on the part of the actor that the object of the conspiracy be completed

Penalty:

A conspiracy to commit aggravated murder, murder, or an offense for which the maximum penalty is imprisonment for life, a felony of the first degree. A conspiracy to commit a first, second, third, or fourth degree felony is a felony of the next lesser degree. A conspiracy relating to hazardous waste provisions is a felony punishable by a fine up to $25,000 or imprisonment up to 18 months or both. A conspiracy to commit a fifth degree felony is a first degree misdemeanor.

If element (2)(g) applies, penalties may include a fine of 3 times the gross value gained or loss caused, court costs, costs of investigation and prosecution, and forfeiture of real and personal property.

Note:

When the offender knows or has reasonable cause to believe that a person with whom he conspires has also conspired or is conspiring with another to commit the same offense, then the offender is guilty of conspiracy with such other person, even though his identity may be unknown to the offender.

It is no defense to a charge of conspiracy that, in retrospect, commission of the offense which was the object of the conspiracy was impossible under the circumstances.

A conspiracy terminates when the offense or offenses which are its objects are committed, or when it is abandoned by all conspirators. In the absence of abandonment, it is no defense to a charge of conspiracy that no offense which was the object of the conspiracy was committed.

A person who conspires to commit more than one offense is guilty of only one conspiracy, when such offenses are the object of the same agreement or continuous conspiratorial relationship.

When a person is convicted of committing or attempting to commit a specific offense or a complicity in the commission of or attempt to commit such offense, he shall not be convicted of conspiracy involving the same offense.

The testimony of a co-conspirator alone is not enough to convict of conspiracy, unless the conspiracy results in an attempt to commit an offense or in the commission of an offense.

Affirmative defenses, see R.C. § 2923.01(I).

2923.02 Attempt

Elements:

(1) Purposely or knowingly (when purpose or knowledge is sufficient culpability)
(2) Engage in conduct that, if successful, would result in an offense

Penalty:

An attempt to commit aggravated murder, murder, or an offense for which the maximum penalty is imprisonment for life, a felony of the first degree. An attempt to violate hazardous waste provisions, R.C. Chapter 3734., other than R.C. § 3734.18, is a felony punishable by a fine up to $25,000 or imprisonment up to 18 months, or both. Other attempts are offenses of the next lesser degree than the offenses attempted. An attempt to commit a felony offense not specifically classified, other than a violation of R.C. Chapter 3734., a misdemeanor of the first degree. An attempt to commit a misdemeanor offense not specifically classified, a misdemeanor of the fourth degree. Attempt to commit minor misdemeanor, or to engage in conspiracy, is no offense.

Note:

A person may not be convicted of attempt if he is convicted of committing the attempted offense, of complicity in the commission of an offense, or of conspiracy to commit an offense.

It is no defense to a charge of attempt that, in retrospect, commission of the offense which was the object of the attempt was either factually or legally impossible under the attendant circumstances, if that offense could have been committed had the attendant circumstances been as the actor believed them to be.

It is an affirmative defense that the actor abandoned his effort to commit the offense or otherwise prevented its commission, under circumstances manifesting a complete and voluntary renunciation of his criminal purpose.

2923.03 Complicity

Elements:

(1) Acting with the culpability required in the principal offense
(2) (a) Solicit or procure another to commit the offense
   (*or*)
   (b) Aid or abet another to commit the offense
   (*or*)
   (c) Conspire with another to commit the offense in violation of R.C. § 2923.01

(*or*)
(d) Cause an innocent or irresponsible person to commit the offense

Penalty:
Same as that for principal offense.

Note:
A charge of complicity may be stated in terms of this section, or in terms of the principal offense. It is no defense that no person with whom the accused was in complicity has been convicted as a principal offender. However, it is an affirmative defense to a charge under this section that, prior to the commission of or attempt to commit the offense, the actor terminated his complicity, under circumstances manifesting a complete and voluntary renunciation of his criminal purpose.

WEAPONS CONTROL

2923.12 Carrying Concealed Weapons

Elements:

(1) Knowingly
(2) Carry or have concealed
(3) On the person ready at hand
(4) A deadly weapon or dangerous ordnance

Penalty:
Misdemeanor of the first degree.

Where previous conviction under this section or offense of violence, or weapon is loaded firearm, or ammunition is ready at hand or weapon is dangerous ordnance, a felony of the fourth degree.

If weapon is a firearm and the violation is committed at a premises for which a D permit has been issued, or if offense committed aboard aircraft or with purpose to carry concealed weapon aboard, a felony of the third degree.

2923.12.1 Illegal Possession of Firearm in Liquor Permit Premises

Elements:

(1) Possess
(2) Firearm
(3) In any room in which liquor is being dispensed
(4) In premises for which a D permit issued under R.C. Chapter 4303.

Penalty:
A felony of the fifth degree.

2923.12.2 Illegal Conveyance or Possession of a Deadly Weapon or Dangerous Ordnance or Illegal Possession of an Object Indistinguishable from a Firearm on School Premises

Elements:

Division (A)—Conveyance:

(1) Knowingly
(2) (a) Convey
 (*or*)
 (b) Attempt to convey
(3) (a) Deadly weapon
 (*or*)
 (b) Dangerous ordnance
(4) Onto school premises, into a school or school building, to a school activity, or onto a school bus

Division (B)—Possession:

(1) Knowingly
(2) Possess
(3) (a) Deadly weapon
 (*or*)
 (b) Dangerous ordnance
(4) On school premises, into a school or school building, to a school activity, or onto a school bus

Division (C):
(1) Knowingly
(2) Possess
(3) An object
   (a) that is indistinguishable from a firearm, whether or not capable of being fired
      (*and*)
   (b) the person indicates that the person possesses the object and that it is a firearm, or the person knowingly displays or brandishes the object and indicates that it is a firearm
(4) In a school or school building, at a school activity, or on a school bus

Penalty:

(A) or (B) A felony of the fifth degree.

If the offender has a previous conviction under this section, a felony of the fourth degree.

(C) A misdemeanor of the first degree.

Note:

This section does not apply to officers, agents, or employees of Ohio or any other state or the United States or to law enforcement officers authorized to carry deadly weapons or dangerous ordnance and acting within the scope of their duties, to any on-duty security officer employed by the board or governing body, or to any other person acting pursuant to written authorization to convey or possess deadly weapons or dangerous ordnance.

In addition to the penalties listed, the driver's license, permit, or nonresident operating privilege of any person who is under 19 shall be suspended for a period of 12 to 36 months

2923.12.3 Illegal Conveyance of Deadly Weapon or Dangerous Ordnance Into Courthouse; Illegal Possession or Control in Courthouse

Elements:

Division (A):
(1) Knowingly
(2) Convey

(3) Deadly weapon or dangerous ordnance
(4) Into a
   (a) courthouse
      (*or*)
   (b) other building or structure in which a courtroom is located

Division (B):
(1) Knowingly
(2) (a) Possess
      (*or*)
   (b) Have under the person's control
(3) Deadly weapon or dangerous ordnance
(4) In a
   (a) courthouse
      (*or*)
   (b) other building or structure in which a courtroom is located

Penalty:

A felony of the fifth degree. If the offender previously has been convicted of a violation of Division (A) or (B) of this section, a felony of the fourth degree.

2923.13 Having Weapons While Under Disability

Elements:

Division (A):
(1) Knowingly
(2) Acquire, have, carry, or use
(3) Firearm/dangerous ordnance
(4) While
   (a) A fugitive from justice
      (*or*)
   (b) Under indictment, or convicted of any felony offense of violence, or adjudicated a delinquent child for the commission of a felony offense of violence
      (*or*)
   (c) Under indictment, or previously convicted of offenses involving illegal possession, use, sale, administration, distribution, trafficking in drugs of abuse, or adjudicated a delinquent child for commission of such offense

(or)
- (d) Drug dependent person/in danger of becoming drug dependent or a chronic alcoholic
  (or)
- (e) Adjudicated mentally incompetent

(5) Unless relieved of above disabilities under R.C. § 2923.14

Division (B):
(1) Person convicted of first or second degree felony
(2) Knowingly
(3) Violate Division (A)
(4) Within 5 years of the date of the person's release
   (a) From imprisonment
      (or)
   (b) From post-release control that is imposed for the commission of a first or second degree felony

Penalty:
   (A) Felony of the fifth degree.
   (B) Felony of the third degree.

2923.13.1 Possession of Deadly Weapon While Under Detention

Elements:
(1) Possess
(2) Deadly weapon
(3) While under detention at a detention facility

Penalty:

If the offender, at the time of the commission of the offense, was under detention as an alleged or adjudicated delinquent child or unruly child and if at the time the offender commits the act for which the offender was under detention it would not be a felony if committed by an adult, a misdemeanor of the first degree.

If the offender, at the time of the commission of the offense, was under detention in any other manner:

When the most serious offense for which the person was under detention is aggravated murder or murder and regardless of when the aggravated murder or murder occurred, or if the person was under detention as an alleged or adjudicated delinquent child, when the most serious act for which the person was under detention would be aggravated murder or murder if committed by an adult and regardless of when that occurred, a felony of the first degree.

When the most serious offense for which the person was under detention is a felony of the first degree committed on or after July 1, 1996, or an aggravated felony of the first degree committed prior to July 1, 1996, a felony of the second degree.

If the person was under detention as an alleged or adjudicated delinquent child, the most serious act for which the person was under detention was committed on or after July 1, 1996, and would be a felony of the first degree if committed by an adult, or was committed prior to July 1, 1996, and would have been an aggravated felony of the first degree if committed by an adult, a felony of the second degree.

When the most serious offense for which the person was under detention is a felony of the second degree committed on or after July 1, 1996, or an aggravated felony of the second degree or a felony of the first degree committed prior to July 1, 1996, a felony of the third degree.

If the person was under detention as an alleged or adjudicated delinquent child, the most serious act for which the person was under detention was committed on or after July 1, 1996, and would be a felony of the second degree if committed by an adult, or was committed prior to July 1, 1996, and would have been an aggravated felony of the second degree or a felony of the first degree if committed by an adult, a felony of the third degree.

When the most serious offense for which the person was under detention is a felony of the third degree committed on or after July 1, 1996, or an aggravated felony of the third degree or a felony of the second degree committed prior to July 1, 1996, or is a felony of the third degree committed prior to July 1, 1996, that, if it had been committed on or after July 1, 1996, also would be a felony of the third degree, a felony of the fourth degree.

If the person was under detention as an alleged or adjudicated delinquent child, the most serious act for which the person was under detention was committed on or after July 1, 1996, and would be a felony of the third degree if committed by an adult, or was committed prior to July 1, 1996, and would have been an aggravated felony of the third degree or a felony of the second degree if committed by an adult, or was committed prior to July 1, 1996, would have been a felony of the third degree if committed by an adult, and, if it had been committed on or after July 1, 1996, also would be a felony of the third degree if committed by an adult, a felony of the fourth degree.

When the most serious offense for which the person was under detention is a felony of the fourth or fifth degree committed on or after July 1, 1996, is a felony of the third degree committed prior to July 1, 1996, that, if committed on or after July 1, 1996, would be a felony of the fourth degree, is a felony of the fourth degree committed prior to July 1, 1996, or is an unclassified felony or misdemeanor regardless of when the unclassified felony or misdemeanor is committed, a felony of the fifth degree.

If the person was under detention as an alleged or adjudicated delinquent child, the most serious act for which the person was under detention was committed on or after July 1, 1996, and would be a felony of the fourth or fifth degree if committed by an adult, was committed prior to July 1, 1996, and would have been a felony of the third degree if committed by an adult, and, if it had been committed on or after July 1, 1996, would be a felony of the fourth degree if committed by an adult, was committed prior to July 1, 1996, and would have been a felony of the fourth degree if committed by an adult, and, or would be an unclassified felony if committed by an adult regardless of when the act is committed, a felony of the fifth degree.

2923.15 Using Weapons While Intoxicated

Elements:

(1) Use or carry
(2) Any firearm/dangerous ordnance
(3) While under influence of alcohol or drug of abuse

Penalty:
   Misdemeanor of the first degree.

2923.16 Improperly Handling Firearms in Motor Vehicle

Elements:

Division (A):
(1) While in or on a motor vehicle
(2) Knowingly discharge a firearm

Division (B):
(1) Knowingly
(2) Transport or have a loaded firearm
(3) In a motor vehicle
(4) So that firearm is accessible to operator or passenger without leaving the vehicle

Division (C):
(1) Knowingly
(2) Transport or have firearm
(3) In motor vehicle
(4) Unless unloaded and carried:
   (a) In closed package, box, or case
      (*or*)
   (b) In compartment accessible only by leaving vehicle
      (*or*)
   (c) In plain sight and secured in rack or holder made for that purpose
      (*or*)
   (d) In plain sight with action open or weapon stripped (if firearm will not permit this, in plain sight)

Penalty:

A violation of (A) or (B) is a misdemeanor of first degree. Violation of (C) is a misdemeanor of fourth degree.

Note:

As used here, "unloaded" means, with respect to a firearm employing a percussion cap, flintlock, or other obsolete ignition system, when the weapon is uncapped, or when the priming charge is removed from the pan.

2923.16.1 Improperly Discharging Firearm At or Into Habitation or School

Elements:

(1) Without privilege to do so
(2) Knowingly
(3) Discharge a firearm
(4) At or into
  (a) Occupied structure that is a permanent or temporary habitation of any individual
    (*or*)
  (b) School (See Note below.)

Penalty:

A felony of the third degree. If previously convicted under this section, a felony of the second degree.

Note:

This section does not apply to any officer, agent, or employee of Ohio, any other state, or the United States, or to any law enforcement officer who discharges the firearm while acting within the scope of the officer's, agent's, or employee's duties.

As enacted, the statute refers to "an occupied structure that is a permanent or temporary habitation of any individual or a school;" it is unclear whether the "occupied structure" limitation applies to schools.

2923.17 Unlawful Possession of Dangerous Ordnance; Illegally Manufacturing or Processing Explosives

Elements:

Division (A):

(1) Knowingly
(2) Acquire, have, carry or use
(3) Dangerous ordnance

Division (B):

(1) Manufacture or process an explosive
(2) At any location in this state
(3) Unless the person first has been issued a license, certificate or registration, or permit to do so from a fire official of a political

CONSPIRACY, ATTEMPT, AND COMPLICITY

subdivision of the state or from a fire marshal

Penalty:
- (A) A felony of the fifth degree.
- (B) A felony of the second degree.

Note:

This section does not apply to, among others listed in R.C. § 2923.17, the holders of a license or temporary permit issued and in effect pursuant to R.C. § 2923.18, with respect to dangerous ordnance lawfully acquired, possessed, carried, or used for the purposes and in the manner specified in such license or permit.

2923.19 Failure to Secure Dangerous Ordnance

Elements:

(1) Negligently
(2) Fail to take proper precautions to
(3) (a) Secure against theft, acquisition or use by unauthorized or incompetent person
 (*or*)
 (b) Insure safety of persons and property
(4) In acquiring, possessing, carrying or using
(5) Dangerous ordnance

Penalty:

A misdemeanor of the second degree.

2923.20 Unlawful Transactions in Weapons

Elements:

A. (1) Recklessly
 (2) Sell, lend, give or furnish
 (3) Firearm
 (4) To any person prohibited under R.C. §§ 2923.13 (Having weapons while under disability), 2923.15 (Using weapons while intoxicated)
 (*or*)
B. (1) Recklessly
 (2) Sell, lend, give or furnish
 (3) Dangerous ordnance

(4) To any person prohibited under R.C. §§ 2923.13 (Having weapons while under disability), 2923.15 (Using weapons while intoxicated), 2923.17 (Unlawful possession of dangerous ordnance)
   (*or*)
C. (1) Possess
   (2) Firearm/dangerous ordnance
   (3) With purpose to dispose of it in violation of A or B above
   (*or*)
D. (1) Manufacture, possess for sale, sell or furnish
   (2) To any person (other than law enforcement agency for use in police work)
   (3) Brass knuckles, cestus, billy, blackjack, sandbag, switchblade knife, springblade knife, gravity knife or similar weapon
   (*or*)
E. (1) When transferring dangerous ordnance to another
   (2) Negligently
   (3) Fail to require transferee to exhibit identification, license, permit, showing him authorized to acquire dangerous ordnance under R.C. § 2923.17 (unlawful possession of dangerous ordnance)
   (*or*)
F. (1) When transferring dangerous ordnance to another
   (2) Negligently
   (3) Fail to take a complete record of the transaction and forthwith forward the record of the transaction to the sheriff of the county of the safety director or police chief of the municipality where the transaction takes place
   (*or*)
G. (1) Knowingly
   (2) Fail to report to law enforcement authority
   (3) Forthwith
   (4) Loss or theft
   (5) Firearm or dangerous ordnance under person's control

Penalty:

Violation of (A), (B), or (C), a felony of the fourth degree.

Violation of (D), (E), or (F), a misdemeanor of the second degree.

Violation of (G), a misdemeanor of the fourth degree.

2923.21 Improperly Furnishing Firearms to a Minor

Elements:

(1) Sell a firearm to person under 18
 (*or*)
(2) Subject to Division (B) of this section sell a handgun to person under 21
 (*or*)
(3) Furnish firearm to a person under 18 or subject to Division (B) of this section, furnish any handgun to a person who is under 21, except for purpose of lawful hunting/instruction in firearms safety, care, handling or marksmanship under direct supervision or control of responsible adult
 (*or*)
(4) Sell or furnish a firearm to a person 18 or older if the seller or furnisher knows, or has reason to know, that the person is purchasing or receiving the firearm for the purpose of selling or furnishing the firearm to a person under 18
 (*or*)
(5) Sell or furnish a handgun to a person 21 or older if the seller or furnisher knows, or has reason to know, that the person is purchasing or receiving the firearm for the purpose of selling or furnishing the firearm to a person under 21
 (*or*)
(6) Purchase or attempt to purchase any firearm with the intent to sell or furnish the firearm to a person under 18
 (*or*)
(7) Purchase or attempt to purchase any handgun with the intent to sell or furnish the firearm to a person under 21

Penalty:
 A felony of the fifth degree.

Note:
 Divisions (A)(1) and (2) of this section do not apply to the sale or furnishing of a handgun to a person 18 or older and under

21 if the person is a law enforcement officer who is properly appointed or employed as a law enforcement officer and has received firearms training approved by the Ohio Peace Officer Training Council or equivalent firearms training

2923.21.1 Underage Purchase of Firearm or Handgun

Elements:

(A)(1) No person under 18
    (2) Shall purchase or attempt to purchase
    (3) A firearm

Penalty:

If found guilty the minor is considered a delinquent child and is subject to an order of disposition as provided in R.C. § 2151.35.5.

(B)(1) No person under 21
    (2) Shall purchase or attempt to purchase
    (3) A handgun

Penalty:

A misdemeanor of the second degree.

Note:

Division (B) of this section does not apply to the purchase or attempted purchase of a handgun by a person 18 or older and under 21 if the person is a law enforcement officer who is properly appointed or employed as a law enforcement officer and has received firearms training approved by the Ohio Peace Officer Training Council or equivalent firearms training.

2923.24 Possessing Criminal Tools

Elements:

(1) Have possession or control of
(2) Any substance, device, instrument, or article
(3) With purpose to use it criminally

Penalty:

A misdemeanor of the first degree. If the circumstances indicate that the substance, device, instrument, or article involved in the offense was intended for use in the commission of a felony, a felony of the fifth degree.

Note:

Prima facie evidence of criminal purpose is established by the following: Possession or control of any dangerous ordnance, or the materials or parts for making dangerous ordnance, in the absence of circumstances indicating such dangerous ordnance, materials, or parts are intended for legitimate use; possession or control of any substance, device, instrument, or article commonly used for criminal purposes, under circumstances indicating such item is intended for criminal use.

CORRUPT ACTIVITY

2923.32 Engaging in Pattern of Corrupt Activity

Elements:

(A)(1) Being employed by or associated with any enterprise
   (2) Conduct or participate in affairs of enterprise
   (3) Directly or indirectly
   (4) (a) Through pattern of corrupt activity
       (*or*)
     (b) Through collection of unlawful debt
       (*or*)

(B)(1) (a) Through pattern of corrupt activity
       (*or*)
     (b) Through collection of unlawful debt
   (2) Acquire or maintain
   (3) Directly or indirectly
   (4) Interest in or control of
   (5) Any enterprise or real property
       (*or*)

(C)(1) Knowingly having received
   (2) Any proceeds
   (3) Derived
   (4) Directly or indirectly
   (5) (a) From pattern of corrupt activity
       (*or*)

    (b) From collection of any unlawful debt
(6) Use or invest
(7) Directly or indirectly
(8) (a) Any part of those proceeds
      (*or*)
    (b) Any proceeds derived from use/investment of those proceeds
(9) (a) In acquisition of any title to, right, interest, or equity in real property
      (*or*)
    (b) In establishment or operation of any enterprise

Penalty:

A felony of the second degree.

If at least one of the incidents of corrupt activity is a felony of the first, second, or third degree, aggravated murder, or murder, if at least one of the incidents of corrupt activity was a felony under the laws of this state that was committed prior to the effective date of this amendment and that would constitute a felony of the first, second, or third degree, aggravated murder, or murder, if committed on or after the effective date of this amendment, or if at least one of the incidents of corrupt activity is a felony under the laws of the United States or of another state that, if committed in this state on or after the effective date of this amendment, would constitute a felony of the first, second, or third degree, aggravated murder, or murder under the laws of this state, a felony of the first degree.

Also, fine of 3 times gross value gained/loss caused, court costs, costs of investigation/prosecution, criminal forfeiture of real and personal property.

Note:

See R.C. § 2923.31 for definitions.
See R.C. § 2923.33 for preserving reachability of property.
See R.C. § 2923.34 for provisions regarding civil proceedings.
See R.C. § 2923.35 for provisions regarding disposition of property forfeited, fines, and civil penalties.

See R.C. § 2923.36 for provisions regarding corrupt activity liens.

See R.C. § 2923.32(A)(3) regarding purchase of securities on open market without intent to control issuer.

CHAPTER 2925

DRUG OFFENSES

2925.01 Definitions

CORRUPTING; TRAFFICKING

2925.02	Corrupting Another with Drugs
2925.03	Trafficking in Drugs
2925.04	Illegal Manufacture of Drugs or Cultivation of Marihuana
2925.05	Funding of Drug or Marihuana Trafficking
2925.06	Illegal Administration or Distribution of Anabolic Steroids
2925.09	Offenses Involving Unapproved Drugs; Dangerous Drug Offenses Involving Livestock

DRUG ABUSE

2925.11	Possession of Drugs
2925.12	Possessing Drug Abuse Instruments
2925.13	Permitting Drug Abuse
2925.14	Drug Paraphernalia

DRUG THEFT

2925.22	Deception to Obtain a Dangerous Drug
2925.23	Illegal Processing of Drug Documents

HARMFUL INTOXICANTS

2925.31	Abusing Harmful Intoxicants
2925.32	Trafficking in Harmful Intoxicants; Improperly Dispensing or Distributing Nitrous Oxide
2925.33	Possessing Nitrous Oxide in Motor Vehicle

DRUG SAMPLES

2925.36	Illegal Dispensing of Drug Samples
2925.37	Offenses Involving Counterfeit Controlled Substances

CORRUPTING; TRAFFICKING

2925.02 Corrupting Another with Drugs

Elements:

Division (A)(1):
(1) Knowingly
(2) By force, threat, or deception

DRUG OFFENSES **2925.02**

(3) Administer to another or induce or cause another to use
(4) A controlled substance

Division (A)(2):
(1) Knowingly
(2) By any means
(3) Administer or furnish to another or induce or cause another to use
(4) A controlled substance
(5) With purpose to cause serious physical harm to the other person, or with purpose to cause the other person to become drug dependent

Division (A)(3):
(1) Knowingly
(2) By any means
(3) Administer or furnish to another or induce or cause another to use
(4) A controlled substance
(5) And thereby cause serious physical harm to such person, or cause such person to become drug dependent

Division (A)(4) (a-c):
(1) Knowingly
(2) By any means
(3) (a) Administer or furnish a controlled substance to a juvenile who is at least two years the offender's junior
   (*or*)
   (b) Induce or cause a juvenile who is at least two years the offender's junior to use a controlled substance
   (*or*)
   (c) Induce or cause a juvenile who is at least two years the offender's junior to commit a felony drug abuse offense
(4) When the offender knows the age of the juvenile or is reckless in that regard

Division (A)(4)(d):
(1) Use a juvenile
(2) To perform any surveillance activity that is intended to prevent
(3) (a) The detection of the offender or any other person in the

commission of
(*or*)
(b) The arrest of the offender or any other person for the commission of

(4) A felony drug abuse offense

(5) Whether or not the offender knows the age of the juvenile

Penalty:

Schedule I or II substance, except marihuana: A felony of the second degree, with mandatory prison term, mandatory minimum fine of $7,500, if offense committed in the vicinity of a school, a felony of the first degree with mandatory prison term and mandatory minimum fine of $10,000. If the offender as a result of the violation is a major drug offender, a mandatory 10 year prison term and a possible additional prison term of 1-10 years.

Schedule III, IV, or V substance: A felony of the second degree, with presumption of prison term, mandatory minimum fine of $7,500. If offense committed in the vicinity of a school, a felony of the second degree with mandatory prison term and mandatory minimum fine of $7,500.

Marihuana: A felony of the fourth degree. If offense committed in the vicinity of a school, a felony of the third degree with mandatory minimum fine of $5,000.

Note:

"Drug dependent person" is defined in R.C. § 3719.01.1, and "felony drug abuse offense" is defined in R.C. § 2925.01.

See statute for special provisions concerning attorneys and professionally licensed persons convicted under this statute.

See statute for provisions exempting indigents from mandatory minimum fines.

See statute for provisions allowing revocation or suspension of driver's and commercial driver's licenses.

2925.03 Trafficking in Drugs

Elements:

(1) Knowingly

(2) Sell or offer to sell

(3) A controlled substance

DRUG OFFENSES **2925.03** 163

Penalty:

AGGRAVATED TRAFFICKING IN DRUGS:

If the drug involved is a Schedule I or II substance (except marihuana, cocaine, LSD, heroin, and hashish), a felony of the fourth degree. If the offense was committed in the vicinity of a school, a felony of the third degree with a mandatory minimum fine of $5,000. If the amount of the drug involved exceeds the bulk amount but does not exceed five times the bulk amount, a felony of the third degree with a mandatory prison term and mandatory minimum fine of $5,000 (if committed in the vicinity of a school or a juvenile, a felony of the second degree with a mandatory prison term and mandatory minimum fine of $7,500). If the amount of the drug involved exceeds five times the bulk amount but does not exceed fifty times the bulk amount, a felony of the second degree with a mandatory prison term and mandatory minimum fine of $7,500 (if committed in the vicinity of a school or a juvenile, a felony of the first degree with a mandatory prison term and mandatory minimum fine of $10,000). If the amount of the drug involved exceeds fifty times the bulk amount but does not exceed one hundred times the bulk amount, regardless of whether the offense was committed within the vicinity of a school or a juvenile, a felony of the first degree with a mandatory prison term and mandatory minimum fine of $10,000. If the amount of the drug involved exceeds one hundred times the bulk amount and regardless of whether the offense was committed within the vicinity of a school or a juvenile, a felony of the first degree with a mandatory prison term and mandatory minimum fine of $10,000.

TRAFFICKING IN DRUGS:

If the drug involved is a Schedule III, IV, or V substance, a felony of the fifth degree. If the offense was committed in the vicinity of a school, a felony of the fourth degree. If the amount of the drug involved exceeds the bulk amount but does not exceed five times the bulk amount, a felony of the fourth degree (if committed in the vicinity of a school or a juvenile, a felony of the third degree with a presumptive prison term and mandatory minimum fine of $5,000). If the amount of the drug involved exceeds five times the bulk amount but does not exceed fifty times the bulk amount, a felony of the third degree with a presumptive prison term and a mandatory minimum fine of $5,000 (if committed in the vicinity of a school or a juvenile, a felony of the second degree with a presumptive prison term and mandatory minimum fine of $7,500). If the amount of the drug involved exceeds fifty times the bulk amount, a felony of the second degree with a mandatory prison term and a mandatory minimum fine of $7,500 (if committed in the vicinity of a school or a juvenile, a felony of the first degree with a mandatory prison term and mandatory minimum fine of $10,000).

TRAFFICKING IN MARIHUANA:

If the drug involved in the violation is marihuana or a compound, mixture, preparation, or substance containing marihuana other than hashish, a felony of the fifth degree. If the offense was committed in the vicinity of a school, a felony of the fourth degree. If the amount of the drug involved exceeds 200 grams, but does not exceed 1,000 grams, a felony of the fourth degree (if committed in the vicinity of a school or a juvenile, a felony of the third degree with a mandatory minimum fine of $5,000). If the amount of the drug involved exceeds 1,000 grams, but does not exceed 5,000 grams, a felony of the third degree with a mandatory minimum fine of $5,000 (if committed in the vicinity of a school or a juvenile, a felony of the second degree with a presumptive prison term and a mandatory minimum fine of $7,500). If the amount of the drug involved exceeds 5,000 grams, but does not exceed 20,000 grams, a felony of the third degree with a presumptive prison term and a mandatory minimum fine of $5,000 (if committed in the vicinity of a school or a juvenile, a felony of the second degree with a presumptive prison term and a mandatory minimum fine of $7,500). If the amount of the drug involved exceeds 20,000 grams, a felony of the second degree with a mandatory prison term and a mandatory minimum fine of $7,500 (if committed in the vicinity of a school or a juvenile, a felony of the first degree with a mandatory prison term and a mandatory minimum fine of $10,000). If the offense involves a gift of 20 grams or less and is a first offense, a minor misdemeanor. If the offense involves a gift of 20 grams or less and there is a prior offense, a misdemeanor of the third degree. If the offense involves a gift of 20 grams or less and the offense was committed in the vicinity of a school or the vicinity of a juvenile, a misdemeanor of the third degree.

TRAFFICKING IN COCAINE:

If the drug involved in the violation is cocaine or a compound, mixture, preparation, or substance containing cocaine, a felony of the fifth degree. If the offense was committed in the vicinity of a school, a felony of the fourth degree. If the amount of the drug involved exceeds five grams, but does not exceed ten grams that is not in unit dose form or exceeds one gram but does not exceed five grams in unit dose form, a felony of the fourth degree (if committed in the vicinity of a school or a juvenile, a felony of the third degree with a presumptive prison term and a mandatory minimum fine of $5,000). If the amount of the drug involved exceeds ten grams, but does not exceed one hundred grams that is not in unit dose form or exceeds five grams but does not exceed ten grams in unit dose form, a felony of the third degree with a mandatory prison term and a mandatory minimum fine of $5,000 (if committed in the vicinity of a school or a juvenile, a felony of the second degree with a mandatory prison term and a mandatory minimum fine of $7,500). If the amount of the drug involved exceeds one hundred grams, but does not exceed five hundred grams that is not in unit dose form or exceeds ten grams but does not exceed twenty-five grams in unit dose form, a felony of the second degree with a mandatory prison term and a mandatory minimum fine of $7,500 (if committed in the vicinity of a school or a juvenile, a felony of the first degree with a mandatory prison term and a mandatory minimum fine of $10,000). If the amount of the drug involved exceeds five hundred grams, but does not exceed one thousand grams that is not in unit dose form or exceeds twenty-five grams but does not exceed one hundred grams in unit dose form, a felony of the first degree with a mandatory prison term and a mandatory minimum fine of $10,000. If the amount of the drug involved exceeds one thousand grams that is not in unit dose form or exceeds one hundred grams in unit dose form, a felony of the first degree with a mandatory prison term and a mandatory minimum fine of $10,000.

TRAFFICKING IN LSD:

If the drug involved in the violation is LSD, a felony of the fifth degree. If the offense was committed in the vicinity of a school, a felony of the fourth degree. If the amount of the drug involved exceeds ten unit doses but does not exceed fifty unit doses of LSD in a solid form or exceeds one gram but does not exceed five grams of LSD in a liquid concentrate, liquid extract, or liquid distillate form, a felony of the fourth degree with a presumptive prison term (if committed in the vicinity of a school or a juvenile, a felony of the third degree with a presumptive prison term and a mandatory minimum fine of $5,000). If the amount of the drug involved exceeds fifty unit doses but does not exceed two hundred fifty unit doses of LSD in a solid form or exceeds five grams but does not exceed twenty-five grams of LSD in a liquid concentrate, liquid extract, or liquid distillate form, a felony of the third degree with a mandatory prison term and a mandatory minimum fine of $5,000 (if committed in the vicinity of a school or a juvenile, a felony of the second degree with a mandatory prison term and a mandatory minimum fine of $7,500). If the amount of the drug involved exceeds two hundred fifty unit doses but does not exceed one thousand unit doses of LSD in a solid form or exceeds twenty-five grams but does not exceed one hundred grams of LSD in a liquid concentrate, liquid extract, or liquid distillate form, a felony of the second degree with a mandatory prison term and a mandatory minimum fine of $7,500 (if committed in the vicinity of a school or a juvenile, a felony of the first degree with a mandatory prison term and a mandatory minimum fine of $10,000). If the amount of the drug involved exceeds one thousand unit doses but does not exceed five thousand unit doses of LSD in a solid form or exceeds one hundred grams but does not exceed five hundred grams of LSD in a liquid concentrate, liquid extract, or liquid distillate form, a felony of the first degree with a mandatory prison term and a mandatory minimum fine of $10,000. If the amount of the drug involved exceeds five thousand unit doses of LSD in a solid form or exceeds five hundred grams of LSD in a liquid concentrate, liquid extract, or liquid distillate form, a felony of the first degree with a mandatory prison term and a mandatory minimum fine of $10,000.

TRAFFICKING IN HEROIN:

If the drug involved in the violation is heroin or a compound, mixture, preparation, or substance containing heroin, a felony of the fifth degree. If the offense was committed in the vicinity of a school, a felony of the fourth degree. If the amount of the drug involved exceeds one gram but does not exceed five grams, a felony of the fourth degree with a presumptive prison term (if committed in the vicinity of a school or a juvenile, a felony of the third degree with a presumptive prison term and a mandatory minimum fine of $5,000). If the amount of the drug involved exceeds five grams but does not exceed ten grams, a felony of the third degree with a presumptive prison term and a mandatory minimum fine of $5,000 (if committed in the vicinity of a school or a juvenile, a felony of the second degree with a presumptive prison term and a mandatory minimum fine of $7,500). If the amount of the drug involved exceeds ten grams but does not exceed fifty grams, a felony of the second degree with a mandatory prison term and a mandatory minimum fine of $7,500 (if committed in the vicinity of a school or a juvenile, a felony of the first degree with a mandatory prison term and a mandatory minimum fine of $10,000). If the amount of the drug involved exceeds fifty grams but does not exceed two hundred fifty grams, a felony of the first degree with a mandatory prison term and a mandatory minimum fine of $10,000.

TRAFFICKING IN HASHISH:

If the drug involved in the violation is hashish or a compound, mixture, preparation, or substance containing hashish, a felony of the fifth degree. If the offense was committed in the vicinity of a school, a felony of the fourth degree. If the amount of the drug involved exceeds ten grams but does not exceed fifty grams of hashish in a solid form or exceeds two grams but does not exceed ten grams of hashish in a liquid concentrate, liquid extract, or liquid distillate form, a felony of the fourth degree (if committed in the vicinity of a school or a juvenile, a felony of the third degree with a mandatory minimum fine of $5,000). If the amount of the drug involved exceeds fifty grams but does not exceed two hundred fifty grams of hashish in a solid form or exceeds ten grams but does not exceed fifty grams of hashish in a liquid concentrate, liquid extract, or liquid distillate form, a felony of the third degree with a mandatory minimum fine of $5,000 (if committed in the vicinity of a school or a juvenile, a felony of the second degree with a presumptive prison term and a mandatory minimum fine of $7,500). If the amount of the drug involved exceeds two hundred fifty grams but does not exceed one thousand grams of hashish in a solid form or exceeds fifty grams but does not exceed two hundred fifty grams of hashish in a liquid concentrate, liquid extract, or liquid distillate form, a felony of the third degree with a presumptive prison term and a mandatory minimum fine of $5,000 (if committed in the vicinity of a school or a juvenile, a felony of the second degree with a presumptive prison term and a mandatory minimum fine of $7,500). If the amount of the drug involved exceeds one thousand grams of hashish in a solid form or exceeds two hundred fifty grams of hashish in a liquid concentrate, liquid extract, or liquid distillate form, a felony of the second degree with a mandatory prison term and a mandatory minimum fine of $7,500 (if committed in the vicinity of a school or a juvenile, a felony of the first degree with a mandatory prison term and a mandatory minimum fine of $10,000).

Note:

See statute for provisions exempting indigents from mandatory minimum fines.

See statute for provisions allowing revocation or suspension of driver's and commercial driver's licenses.

2925.04 Illegal Manufacture of Drugs or Cultivation of Marihuana

Elements:
(1) Knowingly
(2) Cultivate
(3) Marihuana
(4) Venue

DRUG OFFENSES   **2925.05**

(*or*)
(1) Knowingly
(2) Manufacture or otherwise engage in
(3) Any part of the production of a controlled substance
(4) Venue

Penalty:

If the drug involved is any compound, mixture, preparation or substance included in Schedule I or II (except marihuana), a felony of the second degree. Mandatory minimum fine: $7,500. If the violation involves the sale, offer to sell, or possession of a Schedule I or II controlled substance (except marihuana) and if the offender, as a result of the violation, is a major drug offender, sentencing pursuant to R.C. § 2929.14(D). Mandatory minimum fine: $7,500. If the drug involved is any compound, mixture, preparation or substance included in Schedule III, IV, or V, a felony of the third degree. Mandatory minimum fine: $5,000. If the drug involved is marihuana, a minor misdemeanor. If the amount of marihuana involved equals or exceeds one hundred grams but does not exceed two hundred grams, a misdemeanor of the fourth degree. If the amount of marihuana involved exceeds two hundred grams but does not exceed one thousand grams, a felony of the fifth degree. If the amount of marihuana involved exceeds one thousand grams but does not exceed five thousand grams, a felony of the third degree. Mandatory minimum fine: $10,000. If the amount of marihuana involved exceeds five thousand grams but does not exceed twenty thousand grams, a felony of the third degree. Mandatory minimum fine: $10,000. If the amount of marihuana involved exceeds twenty thousand grams, a felony of the second degree. Mandatory minimum fine: $7,500.

2925.05 Funding of Drug or Marihuana Trafficking

Elements:
(1) Knowingly
(2) Provide
(3) Money
    (*or*)

Other items of value
(4) To another person
(5) With the purpose that the recipient of the money or items of value use them to obtain any controlled substance
(6) For the purpose of selling or offering to sell the controlled substance
   (*or*)
   For the purpose of violating R.C. § 2925.04
(7) Venue

Penalty:

AGGRAVATED FUNDING OF DRUG TRAFFICKING

If the drug involved is any compound, mixture, preparation or substance included in Schedule I or II (except marihuana), a felony of the first degree. Mandatory minimum fine: $10,000. If the violation involves the sale, offer to sell, or possession of a Schedule I or II controlled substance (except marihuana) and if the offender, as a result of the violation, is a major drug offender, sentencing under R.C. § 2929.14. Mandatory minimum fine: $10,000.

FUNDING OF DRUG TRAFFICKING

If the drug involved is any compound, mixture, preparation or substance included in Schedule III, IV, or V, a felony of the second degree. Mandatory minimum fine: $7,500.

FUNDING OF MARIHUANA TRAFFICKING

If the drug involved is marihuana, a felony of the third degree. Mandatory minimum fine: $5,000.

2925.06 Illegal Administration or Distribution of Anabolic Steroids

Elements:
(1) Knowingly
(2) Administer to
   (*or*)
   Prescribe to
   (*or*)
   Dispense for administration to
(3) A human being

(4) Any anabolic steroid not approved by the FDA for administration to human beings
(5) Venue

Penalty:

A felony of the fourth degree.

2925.09 Offenses Involving Unapproved Drugs; Dangerous Drug Offenses Involving Livestock

Elements:

Division (A):
(1) Administer, dispense, distribute, manufacture, possess, sell, or use
(2) Any drug, other than a controlled substance, that is not approved by the United States Food and Drug Administration, or the United States Department of Agriculture, unless one of the following applies:
   (a) The United States Food and Drug Administration has approved an application for investigational use in accordance with the "Federal Food, Drug, and Cosmetic Act," 52 Stat. 1040 (1938), 21 U.S.C.A. 301, as amended, and the drug is used only for the approved investigational use
   (or)
   (b) The United States Department of Agriculture has approved an application for investigational use in accordance with the federal "Virus Serum-Toxin Act," 37 Stat. 832 (1913), 21 U.S.C.A. as amended, 151, as amended, and the drug is used only for the approved investigational use
   (or)
   (c) A practitioner, other than a veterinarian, prescribes or combines two or more drugs as a single product for medical purposes
   (or)
   (d) A pharmacist, pursuant to a prescription, compounds and dispenses two or more drugs as a single product for medical purposes

Division (B)(2):
(1) Administer, dispense, distribute, manufacture, possess, sell, or use
(2) Any dangerous drug to or for livestock or any animal that is generally used for food or in the production of food, unless the drug is prescribed by a licensed veterinarian by prescription or other written order and the drug is used in accordance with the veterinarian's order or direction

Penalty:

A felony of the fourth degree and a felony of the third degree on subsequent offenses.

Note:

Division (B)(2) of this section does not apply to a registered wholesale distributor of dangerous drugs, a licensed terminal distributor of dangerous drugs, or a person who possesses, possesses for sale, or sells, at retail, a drug in accordance with Chapters 3719., 4729., or 4741. of the Revised Code.

DRUG ABUSE

2925.11 Possession of Drugs

Elements:

(1) Knowingly
(2) Obtain, possess or use
(3) A controlled substance

Penalty:

AGGRAVATED POSSESSION OF DRUGS:

If the drug involved is a Schedule I or II substance (except marihuana, cocaine, LSD, heroin, and hashish), a felony of the fifth degree. If the amount of the drug involved exceeds the bulk amount but does not exceed five times the bulk amount, a felony of the third degree with a presumptive prison term and mandatory minimum fine of $5,000. If the amount of the drug involved exceeds five times the bulk amount but does not exceed fifty times the bulk amount, a felony of the second degree with a mandatory prison term and mandatory minimum fine of $7,500. If the amount of the drug involved exceeds fifty times the bulk amount but does not exceed one hundred times the bulk amount, a felony of the first degree with a mandatory prison term and mandatory minimum fine of $10,000. If the amount of the drug involved exceeds one hundred times the bulk amount, a felony of the first degree with a mandatory prison term of ten years plus possible additional term and mandatory minimum fine of $10,000.

POSSESSION OF DRUGS:

If the drug involved is a Schedule III, IV, or V substance, a misdemeanor of the third degree. If the offender has previously been convicted of a drug abuse offense, a misdemeanor of the second degree. If the amount of the drug involved exceeds the bulk amount but does not exceed five times the bulk amount, a felony of the fourth degree. If the amount of the drug involved exceeds five times the bulk amount but does not exceed fifty times the bulk amount, a felony of the third degree with a presumptive prison term and a mandatory minimum fine of $5,000. If the amount of the drug involved exceeds fifty times the bulk amount, a felony of the second degree with a mandatory prison term and a mandatory minimum fine of $7,500.

POSSESSION OF MARIHUANA:

If the drug involved in the violation is marihuana or a compound, mixture, preparation, or substance containing marihuana other than hashish, a minor misdemeanor. If the amount of the drug involved equals or exceeds 100 grams but does not exceed 200 grams, a misdemeanor of the fourth degree. If the amount of the drug involved exceeds 200 grams but does not exceed 1,000 grams, a felony of the fifth degree. If the amount of the drug involved exceeds 1,000 grams but does not exceed 5,000 grams, a felony of the third degree with a mandatory minimum fine of $5,000. If the amount of the drug involved exceeds 5,000 grams but does not exceed 20,000 grams, a felony of the third degree with a presumptive prison term and a mandatory minimum fine of $5,000. If the amount of the drug involved exceeds 20,000 grams, a felony of the second degree with a mandatory prison term and a mandatory minimum fine of $7,500.

POSSESSION OF COCAINE:

If the drug involved in the violation is cocaine or a compound, mixture, preparation, or substance containing cocaine, a felony of the fifth degree. If the amount of the drug involved exceeds five grams but does not exceed twenty-five grams that is not in unit dose form or exceeds one gram but does not exceed five grams in unit dose form, a felony of the fourth degree with a presumptive prison term. If the amount of the drug involved exceeds twenty-five grams but does not exceed one hundred grams that is not in unit dose form or exceeds five grams but does not exceed ten grams in unit dose form, a felony of the third degree with a mandatory prison term and a mandatory minimum fine of $5,000. If the amount of the drug involved exceeds one hundred grams but does not exceed five hundred grams that is not in unit dose form or exceeds ten grams but does not exceed twenty-five grams in unit dose form, a felony of the second degree with a mandatory prison term and a mandatory minimum fine of $7,500. If the amount of the drug involved exceeds five hundred grams but does not exceed one thousand grams that is not in unit dose form or exceeds twenty-five grams but does not exceed one hundred grams in unit dose form, a felony of the first degree with a mandatory prison term and a mandatory minimum fine of $10,000. If the amount of the drug involved exceeds one thousand grams that is not in unit dose form or exceeds one hundred grams in unit dose form, a felony of the first degree with a mandatory prison term and a possible additional term and a mandatory minimum fine of $10,000.

POSSESSION OF LSD:

If the drug involved in the violation is LSD, a felony of the fifth degree. If the amount of the drug involved exceeds ten unit doses, but does not exceed fifty unit doses of LSD in a solid form or exceeds one gram but does not exceed five grams of LSD in a liquid concentrate, liquid extract, or liquid distillate form, a felony of the fourth degree. If the amount of the drug involved exceeds fifty unit doses, but does not exceed two hundred fifty unit doses of LSD in a solid form or exceeds five grams but does not exceed twenty-five grams of LSD in a liquid concentrate, liquid extract, or liquid distillate form, a felony of the third degree with a presumptive prison term and a mandatory minimum fine of $5,000. If the amount of the drug involved exceeds two hundred fifty unit doses, but does not exceed one thousand unit doses of LSD in a solid form or exceeds twenty-five grams but does not exceed one hundred grams of LSD in a liquid concentrate, liquid extract, or liquid distillate form, a felony of the second degree with a mandatory prison term and a mandatory minimum fine of $7,500. If the amount of the drug involved exceeds one thousand unit doses, but does not exceed five thousand unit doses of LSD in a solid form or exceeds one hundred grams but does not exceed five hundred grams of LSD in a liquid concentrate, liquid extract, or liquid distillate form, a felony of the first degree with a mandatory prison term and a mandatory minimum fine of $10,000. If the amount of the drug involved exceeds five thousand unit doses of LSD in a solid form or exceeds five hundred grams of LSD in a liquid concentrate, liquid extract, or liquid distillate form, a felony of the first degree with a mandatory prison term and a possible additional term and a mandatory minimum fine of $10,000.

POSSESSION OF HEROIN:

If the drug involved in the violation is heroin or a compound, mixture, preparation, or substance containing heroin, a felony of the fifth degree. If the amount of the drug involved exceeds one gram but does not exceed five grams, a felony of the fourth degree. If the amount of the drug involved exceeds five grams but does not exceed ten grams, a felony of the third degree with a presumptive prison term and a mandatory minimum fine of $5,000. If the amount of the drug involved exceeds ten grams but does not exceed fifty grams, a felony of the second degree with a mandatory prison term and a mandatory minimum fine of $7,500. If the amount of the drug involved exceeds fifty grams but does not exceed two hundred fifty grams, a felony of the first degree with a mandatory prison term and a mandatory minimum fine of $10,000. If the amount of the drug involved exceeds two hundred fifty grams, a felony of the first degree with a mandatory prison term plus a possible additional prison term and a mandatory minimum fine of $10,000.

POSSESSION OF HASHISH:

If the drug involved in the violation is hashish or a compound, mixture, preparation, or substance containing hashish, a minor misdemeanor. If the amount of the drug equals or exceeds five grams but does not exceed ten grams of hashish in a solid form or equals or exceeds one gram but does not exceed two grams of hashish in a liquid concentrate, liquid extract, or liquid distillate form, a misdemeanor of the fourth degree. If the amount of the drug involved exceeds ten grams but does not exceed fifty grams of hashish in a solid form or exceeds two grams but does not exceed ten grams of hashish in a liquid concentrate, liquid extract, or liquid distillate form, a felony of the fifth degree. If the amount of the drug involved exceeds fifty grams but does not exceed two hundred fifty grams of hashish in a solid form or exceeds ten grams but does not exceed fifty grams of hashish in a liquid concentrate, liquid extract, or liquid distillate form, a felony of the third degree with a mandatory minimum fine of $5,000. If the amount of the drug involved exceeds two hundred fifty grams but does not exceed one thousand grams of hashish in a solid form or exceeds fifty grams but does not exceed two hundred fifty grams of hashish in a liquid concentrate, liquid extract, or liquid distillate form, a felony of the third degree with a presumptive prison term and a mandatory minimum fine of $5,000. If the amount of the drug involved exceeds one thousand grams of hashish in a solid form or exceeds two hundred fifty grams of hashish in a liquid concentrate, liquid extract, or liquid distillate form, a felony of the second degree with a mandatory prison term and a mandatory minimum fine of $7,500.

Note:

Arrest or conviction for a minor misdemeanor violation of this section does not constitute a criminal record and need not be reported by the person so arrested or convicted in response to any inquiries about the person's criminal record, including any inquiries contained in any application for employment, license, or other right or privilege made in connection with the person's appearance as a witness.

This section does not apply to manufacturers, practitioners, pharmacists, owners of pharmacies, and other persons whose conduct was in accordance with Chapters 3719, 4715, 4729, 4731 and 4741 of the Revised Code.

This section does not apply to any person who obtained the controlled substance pursuant to a prescription issued by a practitioner, where the drug is in the original container in which it was dispensed to such person.

See statute for provisions exempting some parties from provisions concerning anabolic steroids.

See statute for special provisions concerning attorneys and professionally licensed persons convicted under this statute.

See statute for provisions exempting indigents from mandatory minimum fines.

See statute for provisions allowing revocation or suspension of driver's and commercial driver's licenses.

See statute for special provisions concerning pregnant offenders.

2925.12 Possessing Drug Abuse Instruments

Elements:

(1) Knowingly
(2) Make, obtain, possess, or use
(3) Any instrument, article, or thing the customary and primary purpose of which is for the administration or use of a dangerous drug, other than marihuana
(4) When the instrument involved is a hypodermic or syringe, whether or not of crude or extemporized manufacture or assembly

(*and*)

(5) The instrument, article or thing involved has been used by the offender
   (a) To unlawfully administer or use a dangerous drug, other than marihuana,
   (*or*)
   (b) To prepare a dangerous drug, other than marihuana, for unlawful administration or use

Penalty:

A misdemeanor of the second degree. If prior drug abuse conviction, a misdemeanor of the first degree.

Note:

This section does not apply to manufacturers, practitioners, pharmacists, owners of pharmacies, and other persons whose conduct was in accordance with Chapters 3719, 4715, 4729, 4731, and 4741 of the Revised Code.

See statute for special provisions concerning attorneys and professionally licensed persons convicted under this statute.

See statute for provisions allowing revocation or suspension of driver's and commercial driver's licenses.

2925.13 Permitting Drug Abuse

Elements:

Division (A):
(1) Being the owner, operator, or person in charge of a locomotive, watercraft, aircraft, or other vehicle as defined in R.C. § 4501.01(A)
(2) Knowingly
(3) Permit such vehicle to be used for commission of felony drug abuse offense

Division (B):
(1) Being the owner, lessee, or occupant, or having custody, control, or supervision of premises, or real estate, including vacant land
(2) Knowingly
(3) Permit premises, or real estate, including vacant land, to be used for commission of a felony drug abuse offense
(4) By another person

Penalty:

A misdemeanor of the first degree.

If the felony drug offense in question involves corrupting another with drugs (2925.02), or the sale of a controlled substance [violation of 2925.03], and was committed in the vicinity of a school or a juvenile, a felony of the fifth degree.

Note:

See statute for special provisions concerning attorneys and professionally licensed persons convicted under this statute.

See statute for provisions allowing revocation or suspension of driver's and commercial driver's licenses.

2925.14 Drug Paraphernalia

Elements:

Illegal Use or Possession of Drug Paraphernalia [Division (C)(1)]

(1) Knowingly
(2) (a) Use
   (or)
   (b) Possess with purpose to use
(3) Drug paraphernalia

Dealing in Drug Paraphernalia [Division (C)(2)]

(1) Knowingly
(2) (a) Sell
   (or)
   (b) Possess with purpose to sell
   (or)
   (c) Manufacture with purpose to sell
(3) Drug paraphernalia
(4) If the person knows or reasonably should know the equipment, product, or material will be used as drug paraphernalia

Selling Drug Paraphernalia to Juveniles [Divisions (C)(2), (F)(3)]

(1) Knowingly
(2) (a) Sell
   (or)
   (b) Possess with purpose to sell
   (or)
   (c) Manufacture with purpose to sell
(3) Drug paraphernalia
(4) To a juvenile

Illegal Advertising of Drug Paraphernalia [Division (C)(3)]

(1) Place an advertisement
(2) In any newspaper, magazine, handbill, or other publication that is published and printed, and circulates primarily within this state
(3) Knowing that the purpose of the advertisement is to promote

the illegal sale in this state of the equipment, product, or material that the offender intended or designed for use as drug paraphernalia

Penalty:

Illegal use or possession of drug paraphernalia [Division (C)(1)], a misdemeanor of the fourth degree.

Dealing in drug paraphernalia [Division (C)(2)], a misdemeanor of the second degree.

Selling drug paraphernalia to juveniles [Divisions (C)(2), (F)(3)], a misdemeanor of the first degree.

Illegal advertising of drug paraphernalia [Division (C)(3)], a misdemeanor of the second degree.

Notes:

See Glossary for definition of drug paraphernalia.

See R.C. § 2925.14 for special provisions regarding seizure and disposal.

See statute for special provisions concerning attorneys and professionally licensed persons convicted under this statute.

See statute for provisions allowing revocation or suspension of driver's and commercial driver's licenses.

This statute does not apply to manufacturers, practitioners, pharmacists, owners of pharmacies, and other persons whose conduct is in accordance with Chapter 3719, 4715, 4729, 4731, or 4741 of the Revised Code.

This statute is not to be construed to prohibit the possession or use of a hypodermic as authorized by Section 3119.17.2 of the Revised Code.

DRUG THEFT

2925.22 Deception to Obtain a Dangerous Drug

Elements:

(1) By deception as defined in R.C. § 2913.01
(2) (a) Procure the administration of, a prescription for, or the dispensing of, a dangerous drug
   (*or*)
   (b) Possess an uncompleted preprinted prescription blank used for writing a prescription for a dangerous drug

DRUG OFFENSES **2925.23**

Penalty:

If the drug involved is a schedule I or II substance, except marihuana, a felony of the fourth degree.

If the drug involved is a schedule III, IV, or V substance or marihuana, a felony of the fifth degree.

Note:

See statute for special provisions concerning attorneys and professionally licensed persons convicted under this statute.

See statute for provisions allowing revocation or suspension of driver's and commercial driver's licenses.

2925.23 Illegal Processing of Drug Documents

Elements:

Division (A):
(1) Knowingly
(2) Make a false statement in any prescription, order, report, or record required by R.C. Chapter 3719 or 4729.

Division (B):
(1) (a) Intentionally make, utter, or sell
   (or)
   (b) Knowingly possess
(2) A false or forged
   (a) Prescription
   (or)
   (b) Uncompleted preprinted prescription blank used for writing a prescription
   (or)
   (c) Official written order
   (or)
   (d) License for a terminal distributor of dangerous drugs as required in R.C. 4729.60
   (or)
   (e) Registration certificate for a wholesale distributor of dangerous drugs as required in R.C. § 4729.60

Division (C):
(1) By theft, as defined in R.C. § 2913.02
(2) Acquire

(3) (a) A prescription
   (*or*)
   (b) An uncompleted preprinted prescription blank used for writing a prescription
   (*or*)
   (c) An official written order
   (*or*)
   (d) A blank official written order
   (*or*)
   (e) A license or blank license for a terminal distributor of dangerous drugs as required in R.C. § 4729.60
   (*or*)
   (f) A registration certificate or blank registration certificate for a wholesale distributor of dangerous drugs as required in R.C. § 4729.60

Division (D):
(1) Knowingly
(2) Make or affix
(3) Any false or forged label
(4) To a package or receptacle containing any dangerous drug

Penalty:
   If a schedule I or II controlled substance (except marihuana) is involved, a felony of the fourth degree. If a schedule III, IV, or V substance or marihuana is involved, a felony of the fifth degree.

Note:
   See statute for special provisions concerning attorneys and professionally licensed persons convicted under this statute.
   See statute for provisions allowing revocation or suspension of driver's and commercial driver's licenses.

HARMFUL INTOXICANTS

2925.31 Abusing Harmful Intoxicants

Elements:

(1) Except for lawful research, clinical, medical, dental, or veterinary purposes
(2) Obtain, possess, or use

DRUG OFFENSES **2925.32** 183

(3) A harmful intoxicant
(4) With purpose to induce intoxication or similar physiological effects

Penalty:

A misdemeanor of the fourth degree. If prior drug abuse conviction, a misdemeanor of the first degree.

Note:

This section does not apply to lawful research, clinical, medical, dental, or veterinary purposes.

See statute for special provisions concerning attorneys and professionally licensed persons convicted under this statute.

See statute for provisions allowing revocation or suspension of driver's and commercial driver's licenses.

2925.32 Trafficking in Harmful Intoxicants; Improperly Dispensing or Distributing Nitrous Oxide

Elements:

Division (A)(1):
(1) Knowingly
(2) Dispense or distribute
(3) A harmful intoxicant (excluding nitrous oxide)
(4) To a person age 18 or older
(5) Believing or having reason to believe that the harmful intoxicant will be used in violation of R.C. § 2925.31

Division (A)(2):
(1) Knowingly
(2) Dispense or distribute
(3) A harmful intoxicant (excluding nitrous oxide)
(4) To a person under age 18
(5) Believing or having reason to believe that the harmful intoxicant will be used in violation of R.C. § 2925.31

Division (B)(1):
(1) Knowingly
(2) Dispense or distribute
(3) Nitrous oxide
(4) To a person age 21 or older

(5) Knowing or having reason to believe that the nitrous oxide will be used in violation of R.C. § 2925.31

Division (B)(2):
(1) Knowingly
(2) Dispense or distribute
(3) Nitrous oxide
(4) To a person under 21
(5) Except for lawful medical, dental or clinical purposes

Division (B)(3):
(1) Sell
(2) Device that allows the purchaser to inhale nitrous oxide from cartridges or to hold nitrous oxide released from cartridges for purposes of inhalation
(3) At the time a cartridge of nitrous oxide is sold to another person

Division (B)(4):
(1) Being a person who dispenses or distributes nitrous oxide in cartridges
(2) Fail to comply with
(3) (a) The record-keeping requirements established under Division (F) of this section
   (*or*)
   (b) The labeling and transaction identification requirements established under Division (F) of this section

Penalty:
  (A)(1) and (2), (B)(1), (2), and (3). A felony of the fifth degree. If the offender previously has been convicted of a drug abuse offense, a felony of the fourth degree.
  (B)(4). A misdemeanor of the fourth degree.

Note:
  Division (A)(2) of this section does not prohibit dispensing or distributing a harmful intoxicant to a person under 18 if a written order from the juvenile's parent or guardian is provided to the dispenser or distributor or dispensing or distributing gasoline or diesel fuel to a person under 18 if the dispenser or distributor does not know or have reason to believe the product will be used in violation of R.C.

§ 2925.31. A person is not required to obtain a written order from the parent or guardian of a person under age 18 in order to distribute or dispense gasoline or diesel fuel to the person.

The sale of such a device as described in Division (B)(3) constitutes a rebuttable presumption that the person knew or had reason to believe that the purchaser intended to abuse the nitrous oxide.

This section does not apply to products used in making, fabricating, assembling, transporting, or constructing a product or structure by manual labor or machinery for sale or lease to another person, or to the mining, refining, or processing of natural deposits.

In addition to any other sanction imposed for trafficking in harmful intoxicants, the court shall suspend for not less than six months or more than five years the driver's or commercial driver's license or permit of any person who is convicted of or has pleaded guilty to trafficking in harmful intoxicants. If the offender is a professionally licensed person or a person who has been admitted to the bar by order of the supreme court, in addition to any other sanction imposed, the court forthwith shall comply with R.C. § 2925.38.

2925.33 Possessing Nitrous Oxide in Motor Vehicle

(1) Possess
(2) An open cartridge of nitrous oxide
(3) (a) While operating or being a passenger in or on a motor vehicle on a street, highway, or other public or private property open to the public for purposes of vehicular traffic or parking
   (*or*)
   (b) While being in or on a stationary motor vehicle on a street, highway, or other public or private property open to the public for purposes of vehicular traffic or parking
(4) Unless authorized under Chapter 3719, 4715, 4729, 4731, 4741, or 4765

Penalty:
   A misdemeanor of the fourth degree.

DRUG SAMPLES

2925.36 Illegal Dispensing of Drug Samples

Elements:

(1) Knowingly
(2) Furnish
(3) Another
(4) A sample drug

Penalty:

If the drug involved is a compound, mixture, preparation, or substance included in schedule I or II with the exception of marihuana, a felony of the fifth degree

If the offense was committed in the vicinity of a school or juvenile and the drug involved is a compound, mixture, preparation, or substance included in schedule I or II with the exception of marihuana, a felony of the fourth degree.

If the drug involved is a compound, mixture, preparation, or substance included in schedule III, IV, or V or is marihuana, a misdemeanor of the second degree.

If the offense was committed in the vicinity of a school or juvenile and the drug involved is a compound, mixture, preparation, or substance included in schedule III, IV, or V or is marihuana, a misdemeanor of the first degree.

Note:

See statute for special provisions concerning attorneys and professionally licensed persons convicted under this statute.

See statute for provisions allowing revocation or suspension of driver's and commercial driver's licenses.

2925.37 Offenses Involving Counterfeit Controlled Substances

Elements:

Division (A):
(1) Knowingly
(2) Possess
(3) Any counterfeit controlled substance

DRUG OFFENSES **2925.37** 187

Division (B):
(1) Knowingly
(2) Make, sell, offer to sell, or deliver
(3) Any substance
(4) Knowing it is a counterfeit controlled substance

Division (C):
(1) Make, possess, sell, offer to sell, or deliver
(2) Any punch, die, plate, stone, or other device
(3) Knowing or having a reason to know
(4) That it will be used to print or reproduce a trademark, trade name or other identifying mark
(5) Upon a counterfeit controlled substance

Division (D):
(1) Sell, offer to sell, give, or deliver
(2) Any counterfeit controlled substance
(3) To a juvenile

Division (E):
(1) Directly or indirectly represent
(2) A counterfeit controlled substance
(3) As a controlled substance
(4) By describing its effects
(5) As the physical or psychological effects associated with the use of controlled substances

Division (F):
(1) Directly or indirectly falsely represent or advertise
(2) A counterfeit controlled substance
(3) As a controlled substance

Penalty:
(A) Misdemeanor of the first degree.
(B), (C), (D), (E), or (F) Felony of the fifth degree. If the offense was committed in the vicinity of a school or juvenile, a felony of the fourth degree.

Note:
See statute for special provisions concerning attorneys and professionally licensed persons convicted under this statute.
See statute for provisions allowing revocation or suspension of driver's and commercial driver's licenses.

CHAPTER 2927

MISCELLANEOUS CRIMINAL CODE OFFENSES

2927.01	Abuse of a Corpse
2927.02	Illegal Distribution of Cigarettes or Other Tobacco Products
2927.03	Interference With Fair Housing Rights
2927.11	Desecration
2927.12	Ethnic Intimidation
2927.13	Selling or Donating Contaminated Blood
2927.21	Duty to Report Escape of Animal
2927.24	Contaminating Substance for Human Consumption or Use; Spreading False Report

2927.01(A)   Abuse of a Corpse

Elements:

(1) Without authority of law
(2) Treat a human corpse
(3) In a manner which the offender knows would outrage reasonable family sensibilities

Penalty:

A misdemeanor of the second degree.

2927.01(B)   Gross Abuse of a Corpse

Elements:

(1) Without authority of law
(2) Treat a human corpse
(3) In a manner that would outrage reasonable community sensibilities

Penalty:

A felony of the fifth degree.

2927.02   Illegal Distribution of Cigarettes or Other Tobacco Products

Elements:

Division (A):

MISCELLANEOUS CRIMINAL CODE OFFENSES 2927.02

(1) (a) Being a manufacturer, producer, distributor, wholesaler, or retailer of cigarettes or other tobacco products
   (*or*)
   (b) Being an agent, employee, or representative of any of the above
(2) (a) (i) Give, sell, or otherwise distribute
      (ii) Cigarettes or other tobacco products
      (iii) To any person under 18 years of age
         (*or*)
   (b) (i) Give away, sell, or distribute
      (ii) Cigarettes or other tobacco products
      (iii) In any place that does not have posted in a conspicuous place
      (iv) A sign stating that giving, selling, or otherwise distributing cigarettes or other tobacco products to a person under 18 years of age is against the law

Division (B):
(1) (a) Sell
      (*or*)
   (b) Offer to sell
(2) Cigarettes or other tobacco products
(3) From a vending machine which is *not*
   (a) In an area within a factory, business, office, or other place not open to the general public
      (*or*)
   (b) In an area to which persons under the age of eighteen years are not generally permitted access
      (*or*)
   (c) In a place not identified in (3)(a) or (b) above, where the vending machine is
      (i) Located within the immediate vicinity, plain view, and control of the person who owns or operates the place, or an employee of such person, so that all cigarettes and other tobacco product purchases from the vending machine will be readily observed by the person who owns or operates the place or an employee of such person

(*and*)
   (ii) Inaccessible to the public when the place is closed

Penalty:

A misdemeanor of the fourth degree, unless there has been a previous conviction, then a misdemeanor of the third degree.

Notes:

For purposes of this section, a vending machine located in any unmonitored area, including an unmonitored coatroom, restroom, hallway, or outer waiting area, shall not be considered located within the immediate vicinity, plain view, and control of the person who owns or operates the place, or an employee of such person.

"Vending machine" has the same definition as "coin machine" as defined in R.C. § 2913.01. (See Glossary.)

2927.03 Interference With Fair Housing Rights

Elements:

(1) Whether or not acting under color of law

(2) (a) By force

    (*or*)

  (b) By threat of force

(3) Willfully

(4) (a) Injure, intimidate, or interfere with

    (*or*)

  (b) Attempt to injure, intimidate or interfere with

(5) Any person

(6) (a) (i) Because of race, color, religion, sex, familial status, national origin, handicap, or ancestry

      (*and*)

   (ii) Because that person is or has been

     (A) Selling, purchasing, renting, financing, occupying, or contracting for any housing accommodations

       (*or*)

     (B) Negotiating for the sale, purchase, rental, financing, or occupation of any housing accommodations

       (*or*)

     (C) Applying for or participating in any service, organization, or facility relating to the business of selling or renting housing accommodations

(*or*)

(b) (i) (A) Because that person is or has been

(*or*)

(B) In order to intimidate that person or any other person or class of persons from

(ii) (A) Participating, without discrimination on account of race, color, religion, sex, familial status, national origin, handicap, or ancestry, in any of the activities, services, organizations, or facilities described in 6(a)(ii), above

(*or*)

(B) Affording another person or class of persons opportunity to participate, without discrimination on account of race, color, religion, sex, familial status, national origin, handicap, or ancestry, in any of the activities, services, organizations, or facilities described in 6(a)(ii), above

(*or*)

(c) (i) (A) Because that person is or has been

(*or*)

(B) In order to discourage that person or any other person from

(ii) (A) Lawfully aiding or encouraging other persons to participate, without discrimination on account of race, color, religion, sex, familial status, national origin, handicap, or ancestry, in any of the activities, services, organizations, or facilities described in 6(a)(ii) above

(*or*)

(B) Participating lawfully in speech or peaceful assembly opposing any denial of the opportunity to participate, without discrimination on account of race, color, religion, sex, familial status, national origin, handicap, or ancestry, in any of the activities, services, organizations, or facilities described in 6(a)(ii), above

Penalty:
A misdemeanor of the first degree.

2927.11 Desecration

Elements:

(1) Purposely
(2) Deface, damage, pollute or physically mistreat
(3) (a) The United States flag or the flag of Ohio
   (*or*)
   (b) A public monument
   (*or*)
   (c) A historical or commemorative marker, or any structure, Indian mound or earthwork, thing or site of great historical or archaeological interest
   (*or*)
   (d) A place of worship or its furnishings, or religious artifacts or sacred texts within the place of worship
   (*or*)
   (e) A work of art or museum piece
   (f) Any object of reverence or devotion
(4) Without privilege to do so

Penalty:

A misdemeanor of the second degree. Offense under 3(d) above, a misdemeanor of the first degree, with additional fine of up to $4,000.

2927.12 Ethnic Intimidation

Elements:

(1) Violate R.C. § 2903.21, 2903.22, 2909.06, 2909.07, or 2917.21(A)(3), (4), or (5)
(2) By reason of the race, color, religion, or national origin
(3) Of another person or group of persons

Penalty:

Next higher degree than offense which is a necessary element.

2927.13 Selling or Donating Contaminated Blood

Elements:

(1) With knowledge that he is a carrier of a virus that causes Acquired Immune Deficiency Syndrome

(2) (a) Sell
　　　(*or*)
　　(b) Donate
(3) (a) The person's blood
　　　(*or*)
　　(b) The person's plasma
　　　(*or*)
　　(c) A product of the person's blood
(4) If the person knows or should know that it is being accepted for the purpose of transfusion to another individual

Penalty:
　Felony of the fourth degree.

2927.21　Duty to Report Escape of Animal

Elements:
(1) Being the owner or keeper of animal
　　(a) Not indigenous to Ohio
　　　(*or*)
　　(b) Presenting risk of serious physical harm to persons or property
(2) Fail to report the animal's escape to appropriate law enforcement officer and to clerk of council or township clerk within one hour after one discovers the escape or reasonably should have discovered it

Penalty:
　A misdemeanor of the first degree.

Note:
　If the office of the clerk of a legislative authority or township clerk is closed to the public at the time a report is required by this section, then it is sufficient compliance with this section if the owner or keeper makes the report within one hour after the office is next open to the public.

2927.24 Contaminating Substance for Human Consumption or Use; Spreading False Report

Elements:

Division (B) (Contaminating a substance for human consumption or use)
(1) (a) Knowingly
   (b) Mingle a poison or other harmful substance with
   (c) (i) food
      (or)
      (ii) drink
      (or)
      (iii) nonprescription drug
      (or)
      (iv) prescription drug
      (or)
      (v) pharmaceutical product
   (or)
(2) (a) Knowingly
   (b) Place a poison or other harmful substance in a
   (c) (i) spring
      (or)
      (ii) well
      (or)
      (iii) reservoir
      (or)
      (iv) public water supply
(3) If the person knows or has reason to know that
(4) (a) The food
      (or)
   (b) drink
      (or)
   (c) nonprescription drug
      (or)
   (d) prescription drug
      (or)
   (e) pharmaceutical product
      (or)

MISCELLANEOUS CRIMINAL CODE OFFENSES 2927.24

(f) water

(5) May be ingested or used by another person

Division (C) (Spreading a false report of contamination)

(1) Inform another person
(2) That a poison or other harmful substance
(3) Will be placed in
(4) (a) A food
   (or)
   (b) drink
   (or)
   (c) nonprescription drug
   (or)
   (d) prescription drug
   (or)
   (e) other pharmaceutical drug
   (or)
   (f) spring
   (or)
   (g) well
   (or)
   (h) reservoir
   (or)
   (i) public water supply
(5) If the placement of the poison or other harmful substance would be a violation of Division (B) of this section
(6) The person knows that the information is
   (a) false
      (and)
   (b) will likely be disseminated to the public

Penalty:

A violation of Division (B) is a felony of the first degree. If the offense involved an amount of poison or other harmful substance sufficient to cause death if ingested or used by a person or if the offense resulted in serious physical harm to another person, an aggravated felony of the first degree requiring life imprisonment. A violation of Division (C) is a felony of the fourth degree.

CHAPTER 2929

PENALTIES AND SENTENCING

IN GENERAL

2929.01	Definitions

PENALTIES FOR MURDER

2929.02	Penalties for Murder
2929.02.1	Notice to Supreme Court of Indictment Charging Aggravated Murder; Plea
2929.02.2	Determination of Aggravating Circumstances
2929.02.3	Defendant May Raise Matter of Age
2929.02.4	Investigation Services and Experts for Indigent
2929.03	Imposing Sentence for Aggravated Murder
2929.04	Criteria for Imposing Death or Imprisonment for a Capital Offense
2929.05	Appellate Review of Death Sentence
2929.06	Resentencing After Vacation of Death Sentence or Life Imprisonment Without Parole

PENALTIES FOR FELONY

2929.11	Purposes of Felony Sentencing; Discrimination Prohibited
2929.12	Considerations in Imposing Sentence for Felony
2929.13	Considerations in Imposing Sanctions for Felony
2929.14	Imposition of Definite Prison Term for Felony; Additional Terms
2929.15	Sanctions Where Prison Term Not Required
2929.16	Community Residential Sanctions; Participation in County Jail Industry Program
2929.17	Nonresidential Sanctions
2929.18	Financial Sanctions; Restitution
2929.18.1	Determination of Offender's Ability to Pay; Withholding or Deduction Orders
2929.19	Sentencing Hearing
2929.20	Reduction of Stated Prison Term Through Judicial Release

PENALTIES FOR MISDEMEANOR

2929.21	Penalties for Misdemeanor
2929.22	Imposing Sentence for Misdemeanor

IMPRISONMENT

2929.22.1	Type of Institution Where Term of Imprisonment to be Served
2929.22.3	Reimbursement for Costs of Confinement for Misdemeanor
2929.23	Electronically Monitored House Arrest; Certification of Devices; Device Fund
2929.24	Prosecutor to Notify Appropriate Licensing Board
2929.25	Additional Fine for Certain Offenders; Collection of Fines; Crime Victims Recovery Fund

REIMBURSEMENT BY ARSONIST

2929.28	Arsonist to Reimburse Agencies for Costs of Investigation and Prosecution

ORGANIZATIONAL PENALTIES

2929.31	Organizational Penalties

MULTIPLE SENTENCES

2929.41	Multiple Sentences

MODIFICATION OF SENTENCE

2929.51	Modification of Sentence

OFFENSES PRIOR TO JANUARY 1, 1974

2929.61	Prosecution for Offenses Committed Prior to January 1, 1974; Third or Fourth Degree Felony Committed Between That Date and July 1, 1983

PENALTY TABLE (post 7-1-96)

Offense	Minimum Term	Maximum Term	Maximum Fine	Maximum Organizational Fine
Aggravated Murder	Life	Death	$25,000	$100,000
Murder	15 yrs	Life	$15,000	$ 50,000
F-1	3 yrs	10 yrs	$20,000	$ 25,000
F-2	2 yrs	8 yrs	$15,000	$ 20,000
F-3	1 yrs	5 yrs	$10,000	$ 15,000
F-4	6 mos	18 mos	$ 5,000	$ 10,000
F-5	6 mos	12 mos	$ 2,500	$ 7,500
M-1	None	6 mos	$ 1,000	$ 5,000
M-2	None	90 days	$ 750	$ 4,000
M-3	None	60 days	$ 500	$ 3,000
M-4	None	30 days	$ 250	$ 2,000
M-M	None	None	$ 100	$ 1,000

CHAPTER 2933

SEARCH WARRANTS

2933.32　Conducting Unauthorized Body Cavity or Strip Search; Failure to Prepare Proper Report
2933.42　Contraband
2933.52　Interception of Wire or Oral Communication
2933.59　Presenting Altered Record of Intercepted Communication

2933.32　Conducting Unauthorized Body Cavity or Strip Search; Failure to Prepare Proper Report

Elements:

(A) Conducting unauthorized body cavity or strip search
(1) Law enforcement officer, other employee of a law enforcement agency, physician, registered nurse, or licensed practical nurse
(2) Conducts or causes to be conducted
(3) (a) A body cavity search
   (or)
   (b) A strip search
(4) Where any of the following requirements is not met
   (a) (i) 1. A law enforcement officer or employee of a law enforcement agency
      2. Has probable cause to believe, based upon the nature of the offense with which the person is charged, the circumstances of his arrest, and his prior conviction record (if known)
      3. That the person is concealing evidence of the commission of a criminal offense, including fruits or tools of a crime, contraband, or a deadly weapon as defined in R.C. § 2923.11
      4. That could not otherwise be discovered
         (or)
   (ii) The search is conducted for a legitimate medical or hygienic reason
      (and)

- (b) The search is conducted
    - (i) Following issuance of a search warrant authorizing the search (unless there is a legitimate medical reason or medical emergency justifying the warrantless search)
      (*and*)
    - (ii) Under sanitary conditions
      (*and*)
    - (iii) By a physician or registered nurse or licensed practical nurse registered or licensed to practice in this state
      (*and*)
    - (iv) After a law enforcement officer or employee of a law enforcement agency obtains written authorization therefor from the person in command of the agency or from his specific designee (unless there is a legitimate medical reason or medical emergency making obtaining such authorization impracticable)
      (*and*)
    - (v) By a person or persons of the same sex as the person being searched
      (*and*)
    - (vi) In a manner and in a location that permits only the person(s) conducting the search and the person searched to observe it

(B) Failure to prepare proper report
(1) Following completion of a body cavity search or strip search
(2) Person(s) conducting the search
(3) Fail(s) to prepare a written report containing all of the following
   - (a) The written authorization for the search by the person in command of the law enforcement agency (if required)
     (*and*)
   - (b) The name of the person searched
     (*and*)
   - (c) The name of the person(s) conducting the search, and the time and date of and place at which the search was conducted
     (*and*)

SEARCH WARRANTS

(d) A list of items recovered during the search (if any)
(*and*)
(e) The facts upon which the law enforcement agency officer or employee based his probable cause for the search, including his review of the nature of the offense with which the person is charged, the circumstances of his arrest, and his prior conviction record (if known)
(*and*)
(f) If the search was conducted without issuance of a search warrant or without the granting of a written authorization, the legitimate medical reason or emergency that justified the warrantless search or made obtaining written authorization impracticable

Penalty:

A violation of Division (A), a misdemeanor of the first degree.
A violation of Division (B), a misdemeanor of the fourth degree.

Note:

R.C. § 2933.32(C)(2) provides that a copy of the required body cavity or strip search report is to be kept on file in the law enforcement agency, and that another copy is to be given to the person searched. This section does not apply to searches of persons sentenced to and serving a term in a detention facility, as defined in R.C. § 2921.01, R.C. § 2933.32(D).

Definitions: See R.C. § 2933.32(A) for definitions of "body cavity search" and "strip search."

2933.42 Contraband

Elements:

(1) (A) Possess
    (*or*)
  (B) Conceal
    (*or*)
  (C) Transport
    (*or*)
  (D) Receive
    (*or*)
  (E) Purchase

(or)
- (F) Sell
  (or)
- (G) Lease
  (or)
- (H) Rent
  (or)
- (I) Otherwise transfer

(2) Any contraband

Penalty:

Seizure and forfeiture under certain conditions — see 2933.42 and 2933.43.

2933.52 Interception of Wire or Oral Communication

Elements:

(1) (A) Purposely
  - (B) (i) Intercept
      (or)
    - (ii) Attempt to intercept
      (or)
    - (iii) Procure any other person to intercept or attempt to intercept
  - (C) (i) Any wire communication
      (or)
    - (ii) Any oral communication

(or)

(2) (A) Purposely
  - (B) (i) Use
      (or)
    - (ii) Attempt to use
      (or)
    - (iii) Procure any other person to use or attempt to use
  - (C) Any interception device which
    - (i) Is affixed to, or otherwise transmits a signal through a wire, cable, satellite, microwave or other similar method of connection used in wire communications
      (or)

       (ii) Transmits communications by radio, or interferes with the transmission of communication by radio
   (D) To intercept any wire or oral communication
     (or)
(3) (A) Purposely
   (B) (i) Disclose
       (or)
      (ii) Attempt to disclose
   (C) To any person
   (D) (i) The contents of
       (or)
      (ii) Any evidence derived from the contents of
   (E) Any wire communication or any oral communication
   (F) Knowing or having reason to know
   (G) That the contents or evidence was obtained
   (H) Through the interception of wire or oral communication in violation of R.C. Section 2933.51 to 2933.66

Penalty:

A felony of the fourth degree.

Note:

See statute for exclusions. See R.C. § 2933.51 for definitions.
For other provisions concerning telephone offenses, see Ohio Revised Code Chapter 4931.

2933.59 Presenting Altered Record of Intercepted Communication

Elements:

(1) With intent to present the altered recording or resume
(2) (a) In any judicial proceeding
     (or)
   (b) In any proceeding under oath or affirmation
(3) Purposefully
   (a) Edit
     (or)
   (b) Alter
     (or)
   (c) Tamper with

(or)
   (d) Attempt to alter, edit, or tamper with
(4) Any recording or resume of any intercepted wire or oral communication
(5) Present or permit presentation of any altered recording or resume
(6) (a) In any judicial proceeding
      (or)
   (b) In any proceeding under oath or affirmation
(7) Without fully indicating the nature of the changes made

Penalty:
   A felony of the third degree.

SELECTED MISCELLANEOUS AND TRAFFIC OFFENSES

3716.11	Adulterated Food
3719.32	Regulating the Sale of Poisons
3773.21	Firearms, Discharging
3773.21.1	Firearms, Discharging Over Highway
4301.62	Opened Container
4511.19	Motor Vehicles, Operating While Under the Influence
4511.19.2	Operation of Motor Vehicle While License Suspended Under 4511.19.1 (Driving While Under Implied Consent Suspension)
4511.20, 4511.20.1	Motor Vehicles, Reckless Driving
4511.20.2	Motor Vehicles, Operating Without Reasonable Control
4511.21	Motor Vehicles, Speed Limits/Assured Clear Distance
4549.04.2	Motor Vehicles, Master Car Keys

3716.11 Adulterated Food

Elements:

(1) With knowledge, or having reasonable cause to believe, another may suffer physical harm or be seriously inconvenienced or annoyed
(2) (A) Place a pin, needle, razor blade, glass, laxative, drug of abuse, or other harmful/hazardous object/substance in food or confections
   (*or*)
   (B) Furnish to another food or confections adulterated in violation of (A) above

Penalty:
   A misdemeanor of the first degree.

3719.32 Regulating the Sale of Poisons

Elements:
(1) Knowingly
(2) Sell or deliver
(3) (a) To any person other than in the manner prescribed by law
   (*or*)

(b) To a minor under 16 in the manner prescribed by law but without written order of an adult
(4) (a) Any of the substances listed in this section [includes many scheduled drugs]
  (*or*)
  (b) Any poisonous compounds, combinations, or preparations thereof

Penalty:
A minor misdemeanor.

3773.21 Firearms, Discharging

Elements:

(1) Not being the owner of the enclosure involved
(2) Discharge a firearm
(3) On a lawn, park, pleasure ground, orchard, or grounds appurtenant to a schoolhouse, church or inhabited dwelling, such being the property of another or of a charitable institution

Penalty:
A misdemeanor of the fourth degree.

3773.21.1 Firearms, Discharging Over Highway

Elements:

(1) Discharge a firearm
(2) Upon or over a public road or highway

Penalty:
A misdemeanor of the fourth degree.

4301.62 Opened Container

Elements:

(1) Have in one's possession
(2) An opened container of beer or intoxicating liquor
(3) (A) In a state liquor store
  (*or*)
  (B) On the premises of the holder of any permit issued by the department of liquor control

SELECTED MISCELLANEOUS OFFENSES **4511.19** 207

      (*or*)
- (C) In any other public place
      (*or*)
- (D) While operating or being a passenger in or on a motor vehicle on any street, highway, or other public or private property open to the public for purposes of vehicular travel or parking
      (*or*)
- (E) While being in or on a stationary motor vehicle on any street, highway, or other public or private property open to the public for purposes of vehicular travel or parking

Penalty:
A minor misdemeanor.

Note:
The statute specifies exceptions for beer or intoxicating liquor which has been lawfully bought for consumption on certain permit premises or convention premises.

4511.19 Motor Vehicles, Operating While Under the Influence

Elements:

Division (A)(1):
1. Operate any vehicle, streetcar, or trackless trolley
2. Within this state
3. While under the influence of
4. Alcohol or drug of abuse or combination thereof

Division (A)(2), (3), (4):
1. Operate any vehicle, streetcar or trackless trolley
2. Within this state
3. While having a concentration of
   - (A) .10 of 1% or more by weight of alcohol in the blood
     (*or*)
   - (B) .10 of 1 gram or more by weight of alcohol per 210 liters of breath
     (*or*)

(C) .14 of 1 gram or more by weight of alcohol per 100 milliliters of urine

Penalty:

If no conviction, within five years of the offense, under this section or a similar municipal ordinance, or under 2903.04 (involuntary manslaughter) in a case in which the offender was subject to the sanctions described in Division (D), 2903.06 (aggravated vehicular homicide), 2903.07 (vehicular homicide), 2903.08 (aggravated vehicular assault), or a municipal ordinance similar to 2903.07, in a case in which the jury or judge found that the offender was under the influence, a misdemeanor of the first degree, with mandatory minimum imprisonment of three consecutive days (or a three day intervention program) and a mandatory fine of $200 to $1000.

If the offender has been convicted, within five years of the offense, of one offense under this or a similar municipal ordinance, or under 2903.04 (involuntary manslaughter) in a case in which the offender was subject to the sanctions described in Division (D), 2903.06 (aggravated vehicular homicide), 2903.07 (vehicular homicide), 2903.08 (aggravated vehicular assault), or a municipal ordinance similar to 2903.07, in a case in which the jury or judge found that the offender was under the influence, a misdemeanor of the first degree, with mandatory minimum imprisonment of ten consecutive days (or mandatory minimum imprisonment of five consecutive days followed immediately by electronically monitored house arrest of at least 18 days) and a mandatory fine of $300 to $1500.

If the offender has been convicted, within five years of the offense, of two offenses under this section or similar municipal ordinance, or under 2903.04 (involuntary manslaughter) in a case in which the offender was subject to the sanctions described in Division (D), 2903.06 (aggravated vehicular homicide), 2903.07 (vehicular homicide), 2903.08 (aggravated vehicular assault), or a municipal ordinance similar to 2903.07, in a case in which the jury or judge found that the offender was under the influence, mandatory minimum imprisonment of thirty consecutive days, or to a longer definite term of not more than one year (or mandatory minimum imprisonment of fifteen consecutive days followed im-

SELECTED MISCELLANEOUS OFFENSES 4511.19

mediately by electronically monitored house arrest of at least 55 days) and a mandatory fine of $500 to $2500.

If the offender has been convicted, within five years of the offense, of three or more offenses under this section or similar municipal ordinance, or under 2903.04 (involuntary manslaughter) in a case in which the offender was subject to the sanctions described in Division (D), 2903.06 (aggravated vehicular homicide), 2903.07 (vehicular homicide), 2903.08 (aggravated vehicular assault), or a municipal ordinance similar to 2903.07, in a case in which the jury or judge found that the offender was under the influence, mandatory minimum imprisonment of sixty consecutive days, or to a longer definite term of not more than one year, and a mandatory fine of $750 to $10,000.

Notes:

Vehicle immobilization and forfeiture orders are provided for in 4511.19.3.

Immediate seizure and suspension of license for refusal or positive test is provided for in 4511.19.1.

License suspension, revocation and disqualification are provided for in 4507.16.

Division (B)(1), (2), or (3):

(1) Being under 21 years of age
(2) Operate any vehicle, streetcar, or trackless trolley
(3) Within this state
(4) While having a concentration of at least
   (A) .02 of 1% but less than .10 of 1% by weight of alcohol in the blood
     (*or*)
   (B) .02 of 1 gram but less than .10 of 1 gram by weight of alcohol per 210 liters of breath
     (*or*)
   (C) .028 of 1 gram but less than .14 of 1 gram by weight of alcohol per 100 milliliters of the urine

Penalty:

If no conviction, within one year of the offense, under this section or similar municipal ordinance, or under 2903.04 (involuntary manslaughter) in a case in which the offender was subject to the sanctions described in Division (D), 2903.06 (aggravated vehicular homicide), 2903.07 (vehicular homicide), 2903.08 (aggravated vehicular assault), or a municipal ordinance similar to 2903.07, in a case in which the jury or judge found that the offender was under the influence, a misdemeanor of the fourth degree, with a mandatory suspension of the offender's driver's or commercial driver's license or permit or nonresident operating privilege for no less than 60 days and no more than two years.

If the offender has been convicted or plead guilty to, within one year of the offense, of one offense under this section or similar municipal ordinance, or under 2903.04 (involuntary manslaughter) in a case in which the offender was subject to the sanctions described in Division (D), 2903.06 (aggravated vehicular homicide), 2903.07 (vehicular homicide), 2903.08 (aggravated vehicular assault), or municipal ordinance similar to 2903.07, in a case in which the jury or judge found that the offender was under the influence, a misdemeanor of the third degree, with a mandatory suspension of the offender's driver's or commercial driver's license or permit or nonresident operating privilege for no less than 60 days and no more than two years.

4511.19.2 Operation of Motor Vehicle While License Suspended Under 4511.19.1 (Driving While Under Implied Consent Suspension)

Elements:

(1) Operate a vehicle
(2) Upon the highways or streets within this state
(3) When one's license or permit to drive has been suspended under R.C. § 4511.19.1 or R.C. § 4511.19.6

Penalty:
A misdemeanor of the first degree.

Note:
License suspension is provided for in 4511.99(B).

4511.20, 4511.20.1 Motor Vehicles, Reckless Driving

Elements:

4511.20

(a) Operate motor vehicle, trackless trolley, or streetcar
(b) On any street or highway
(c) In willful or wanton disregard of the safety of persons or property
(d) Venue

(*or*)

4511.20.1

(a) Operate motor vehicle, trackless trolley, or streetcar
(b) On public or private property other than streets or highways
(c) In willful or wanton disregard of the safety of persons or property
(d) Venue

Penalty:

A minor misdemeanor. Second offense within one year of the first, a misdemeanor of the fourth degree. Subsequent offenses within one year of the first, misdemeanors of the third degree.

Note:

Competition among vehicles with the consent of the property owner is excepted under 4511.20.1.

4511.20.2 Motor Vehicles, Operating Without Reasonable Control

Elements:

(1) Operate a motor vehicle, trackless trolley, or streetcar
(2) On any street, highway, or property open to the public for vehicular traffic
(3) Without being in reasonable control
(4) Of the vehicle, trackless trolley, or streetcar

Penalty:

A minor misdemeanor.

4511.21 Motor Vehicles, Speed Limits/Assured Clear Distance

Elements:

Speed Limits

(1) Operate a motor vehicle, trackless trolley, or streetcar
(2) At a speed greater or less than is reasonable or proper, having due regard to the traffic, surface, and width of the street or highway and any other conditions

(or)

(1) Operate a motor vehicle, trackless trolley, or streetcar upon a street or highway
(2) (A) At a speed exceeding 55 miles per hour, except upon a freeway as provided in 4511.21(B)(10)

(or)

(B) At a speed exceeding 65 miles per hour, except upon a freeway as provided in 4511.21(B)(10) (motor vehicles weighing in excess of 8,000 pounds empty or noncommercial buses are excepted from this provision and are governed by the following provision (2)(C)

(or)

(C) At a speed exceeding 55 miles per hour upon a freeway if the motor vehicle weighs in excess of 8,000 pounds empty or is a noncommercial bus

Assured Clear Distance

(1) Drive any motor vehicle, trackless trolley, or streetcar
(2) In and upon any street or highway
(3) At a greater speed than will permit him to bring it to a stop within the assured clear distance ahead

Penalty:

A minor misdemeanor. Second offense within one year of the first, a misdemeanor of the fourth degree. Subsequent offenses within one year of the first, misdemeanor of the third degree.

Note:

See statute for speeds considered prima-facie lawful in absence of lower limits declared by director of transportation or local authorities.

4549.04.2 Motor Vehicles, Master Car Keys

Elements:

(1) Sell or dispose of
(2) Master key for more than one motor vehicle
(3) Knowing or having reasonable cause to believe key will be used to commit offense

(*or*)

(1) Buy, receive or possess
(2) Master key for more than one motor vehicle
(3) With purpose to use it to commit a crime

Penalty:

A minor misdemeanor. Second offense within one year of the first, a misdemeanor of the fourth degree. Subsequent offenses within one year of the first, misdemeanors of the third degree.

PART II

LAW ENFORCEMENT PROCEDURES

This part of the handbook contains three sections. The first is a list of the section numbers and subjects of several statutes which are likely to be of importance to law enforcement officers in the performance of their daily duties. The second is an outline of basic search and seizure principles, and the third is a condensed time table for hearings and trials in criminal cases.

2933.21	Search Warrant
2933.22	Probable Cause
2933.23	Affidavit for Search Warrant
2933.23.1	Statutory Precondition for Nonconsensual Entry
2933.24	Contents of Search Warrant; Report of Inspection Findings
2933.24.1	Inventory of Property Taken
2933.32	Body Cavity and Strip Searches; Conducting Unauthorized Search; Failure to Prepare Proper Report (See preceding section of this handbook)
2933.41	Disposition of Property Held by Law Enforcement Agency
2933.58	Eavesdropping; Wiretapping
2935.02	Accused May Be Arrested in Any County
2935.03	Arrest Without Warrant; Pursuit Outside Jurisdiction
2935.05	Affidavit Filed in Case of Arrest Without Warrant
2935.07	Person Arrested Without Warrant Shall Be Informed of Cause of Arrest
2935.09	Accusation by Affidavit to Cause Arrest or Prosecution
2935.10	Procedure upon Filing Affidavit or Complaint; Withdrawal of Unexecuted Warrants
2935.12	Forcible Entry in Making Arrest
2935.13	Proceedings Upon Arrest
2935.14	Rights of Person Arrested
2935.20	Right to Counsel
2935.24	Warrants Transmitted by Teletype or Similar Means

2935.26	Issuance of Citation for Minor Misdemeanor
2935.27	Security for Certain Traffic Offenses; Notice of Penalties
2935.28	Names of Traffic Law Violators Damaging Real Property to be Provided to Owner
2935.29	Definition of Fresh Pursuit and State
2935.30	Authority of Foreign Police
2935.31	Hearing Before Magistrate in County of Arrest
2939.28	Exemption from Arrest (Persons entering state in obedience to summons)
2945.71	Time Within Which Hearing or Trial Must be Held
2945.72	Extension of Time for Hearing or Trial
2945.73	Discharge for Delay in Trial
2950.01	Habitual Sex Offenders; Definitions
2950.02	Habitual Sex Offenders; Duty to Register
2950.99	Habitual Sex Offenders; Penalties
2951.02	Criteria for Probation; Conditions of Probation
2961.01	Civil Rights of Convicted Felons
2961.03	Revocation of License in Certain Cases
2963.34	Escape and Aiding Escape

SEARCH AND SEIZURE

(For detailed coverage, see *Anderson's Ohio Criminal Practice and Procedure,* Second Edition.)

PURSUANT TO WARRANT

I. Issuance of Warrant
   A. By judge of court of record who is satisfied that probable cause exists
   B. To search and seize any:
      1. Evidence of the commission of a criminal offense
         or
      2. Contraband, the fruits of crime, or things otherwise criminally possessed.
         or
      3. Weapons or other things by means of which a crime has been committed or reasonably ap-

      if:
1. a. Notice of intention to search is given and
   b. Admittance is refused
   or
2. a. Notice would endanger officer or others
   or
   b. Notice would lead to destruction of evidence or escape
   or
   c. Would be futile under the circumstances

  E. Statutory precondition for nonconsensual entry may be waived in appropriate circumstances

  F. A copy of the warrant and receipt for property seized shall be:
1. Given to the person from whom or from whose premises the property was taken
   or
2. Left at the place from which the property was taken

III. Return of Warrant
A. To be made promptly
B. To be accompanied by written inventory of any property taken
   1. Inventory to be made in presence of two of the following:
      a. Applicant for the warrant
      b. Person from whose possession or premises the property was taken
      c. Credible person other than one of the above if one of the above is not present
   2. Inventory shall be verified by officer

WARRANTLESS SEARCH AND SEIZURE

I. Consent Search

LAW ENFORCEMENT PROCEDURES

        pears about to be committed
- C. Located within the court's territorial jurisdictio[n]
- D. Upon request of a prosecuting attorney or l[aw] forcement officer
- E. On the basis of an affidavit or affidavits
    1. Sworn to before a judge of a court of reco[rd]
    2. Establishing grounds for issuance
        - a.
            - i. Naming or describing the person t[o be] searched

                or
            - ii. Particularly describing the place to [be] searched
        - b. Describing the property to be searched f[or] and seized
        - c. Stating substantially the offense in relation thereto
        - d. Stating the factual basis for the affiant's belief that such property is there located
- F. Identifying the property
- G. Naming or describing the person or place to be searched
- H. Directed to a law enforcement officer
- I. Commanding the officer to search the person or place named for the property specified
- J. Within three days
- K. Designating a judge to whom it shall be returned
- L. May contain waiver of statutory precondition for nonconsensual entry

II. Service of Warrant
- A. Within three days of issuance
- B.
    1. During the hours from 7:00 a.m. to 8:00 p.m.

        or
    2. As otherwise specifically authorized in the warrant by the issuing court
- C. Officer may enter only house or building described in warrant
- D. Officer may break down outer or inner door or window

LAW ENFORCEMENT PROCEDURES

    A. Consent must be freely and voluntarily given
    B. Voluntariness determined by totality of circumstances
    C. Consent can be given only by one who has sufficient interest in the place searched or the property seized
    D. Simple failure to resist does not equal consent

II. Stop and Frisk
    A. Stop and search of outer clothing for weapons justified when there is reasonable belief that criminal activity may be occurring and that the suspect is armed and presently dangerous
    B. Frisk of lawfully detained suspect must be founded on reasonable belief based upon specific articulable facts that suspect is armed and presently dangerous
    C. Reasonable belief may be provided by a reliable informant
    D. Limited search may be made of part of stopped vehicle into which something has been furtively placed by occupant

III. Search Incident to Arrest
    A. Arrest must be lawful
    B. Limited to arrestee's person or area within arrestee's immediate control (purpose of search is to find weapons that could be used against officer or to effect escape, and to prevent loss or destruction of evidence)
    C. Search must be substantially contemporaneous in time and place with the arrest
    D. Fingerprints, photos, inventory of personal effects, other evidence obtained through routine processing is admissible
    E. Evidence of crime need not be related to offense which led to arrest

IV. Plain View
    A. Objects within plain view of officer with a right to

be in that position are subject to seizure (does not constitute a "search")
B. Incriminating nature of seized materials must be immediately apparent

V. Exigent Circumstances
A. Probable cause also required
B. Hot pursuit
C. Prevent destruction of evidence
D. Render aid
E. Fire and crime scenes

VI. Open Fields
A. No warrant required (4th Amendment refers to "houses" and "effects")
B. "No Trespassing" sign does not bring open fields under protection of the 4th Amendment
C. Area immediately surrounding home not an open field
D. Wooded area may qualify as an open field

VII. Abandoned Property — seizure does not constitute a search; thus no 4th Amendment protection

VIII. Automobile
A. The "Automobile Exception"
1. Justification
a. Mobility (similar to exigent circumstances exception)
b. Reduced expectation of privacy
2. Probable cause required
3. Generally applied to cars stopped while being driven
4. If there is probable cause to believe vehicle contains contraband and full warrantless search would be justified, the vehicle may be searched after impoundment
B. Impoundment
1. Justification

LAW ENFORCEMENT PROCEDURES 221

        a. Protect police from possible harm
        b. Safeguard property found in auto
        c. Prevent claims for lost property
    2. Vehicle must be impounded
    3. Must be routine inventory search; not pretext for warrantless evidentiary search (similar to processing of arrestee — III. D., above)
    4. Also, see VIII A. 4., above.
  C. Incident to Lawful Arrest
    1. Justification
        a. Find weapons that could be used against officer or to effect escape
        b. Prevent loss or destruction of evidence
    2. May search passenger compartment incident to lawful arrest of any occupant and examine contents of any containers, even after the suspect has been arrested and placed in the police car
  D. Pursuant to Traffic Violation
    1. Must be probable cause to believe driver or vehicle has been involved in some other criminal conduct
    2. Limited search may be made of part of vehicle into which something has been furtively placed by occupant
    3. Events occurring after vehicle stopped (for example, weapon or other contraband in plain view inside vehicle) may constitute probable cause for "stop and frisk" (II., above), or "lawful arrest" (VIII. C., above) type search

TIME TABLE

Type of Hearing of Trial	Generally Time Limit	Time Limit When Accused Confined*
Trials in mayors' or police courts (regardless of offense)	30 days	10 days
Trials for minor misdemeanors (regardless of court)	30 days	10 days
Trials for 3rd and 4th degree misdemeanors for which maximum penalty does not exceed 60 days (regardless of court)	45 days	15 days
Trials for 1st and 2nd degree misdemeanors for which maximum penalty exceeds 60 days (regardless of court)	90 days	30 days
Preliminary hearings in felony cases	15 days	10 days
Trials for felony	270 days	90 days

*As the chart indicates, each day of confinement counts as 3 days.

PART III

CRIMINAL RULES

Pursuant to its rulemaking powers, the Supreme Court has adopted the Rules of Criminal Procedure. Certain of these rules which pertain particularly to problems confronted by the peace officer and which are appropriate for a quick reference manual such as this have been selected and are reproduced in their entirety in this section. It should be emphasized that these are only a few of the criminal rules and that these rules are separate from and additional to the Criminal Code itself.

Crim. R. 3	Complaint
Crim. R. 4	Warrant or Summons
Crim. R. 4.1	Optional Procedure in Minor Misdemeanor Cases
Crim. R. 41	Search and Seizure
Crim. R. 46	Bail

RULE 3

COMPLAINT

The complaint is a written statement of the essential facts constituting the offense charged. It shall also state the numerical designation of the applicable statute or ordinance. It shall be made upon oath before any person authorized by law to administer oaths.

RULE 4

WARRANT OR SUMMONS: ARREST

(A) Issuance.

(1) Upon complaint.

If it appears from the complaint, or from an affidavit or affidavits filed with the complaint, that there is probable cause to believe that an offense has been committed, and that the defendant has committed it, a warrant for the arrest of the defendant, or a summons in lieu of a warrant, shall be issued by a judge, magistrate, clerk of court, or officer of the court designated by the judge, to any law enforcement officer authorized by law to execute or serve it.

The finding of probable cause may be based upon hearsay in whole or in part, provided there is a substantial basis for believing the source of the hearsay to be credible and for believing that there is a factual basis for the information furnished. Before ruling on a request for a warrant, the issuing authority may require the complainant to appear personally and may examine under oath the complainant and any witnesses. Such testimony shall be admissible at a hearing on a motion to suppress, if it was taken down by a court reporter or recording equipment.

The issuing authority shall issue a summons instead of a warrant upon the request of the prosecuting attorney, or when issuance of a summons appears reasonably calculated to assure the defendant's appearance.

(2) By law enforcement officer with warrant.

In misdemeanor cases where a warrant has been issued to a law enforcement officer, he may, unless the issuing authority includes a prohibition against it in the warrant, issue a summons in lieu of executing the warrant by arrest, when issuance of a summons appears reasonably calculated to assure the defendant's appearance. The officer issuing such summons shall note on the warrant and the return that the warrant was executed by issuing summons, and shall also note the time and place the defendant must appear. No alias warrant shall be issued unless the defendant fails to appear in response to the summons, or unless subsequent to the issuance of summons it appears improbable that the defendant will appear in response thereto.

(3) By law enforcement officer without a warrant.

In misdemeanor cases where a law enforcement officer is empowered to arrest without a warrant, he may issue a summons in lieu of making an arrest, when issuance of a summons appears reasonably calculated to assure the defendant's appearance. The officer issuing such summons shall file, or cause to be filed, a complaint describing the offense. No warrant shall be issued unless the defendant fails to appear in response to the summons, or unless subsequent to the issuance of summons it appears improbable that the defendant will appear in response thereto.

(B) Multiple issuance; sanction.

More than one warrant or summons may issue on the same complaint. If the defendant fails to appear in response to summons, a warrant or alias warrant shall issue.

(C) Warrant and summons: form.

(1) Warrant.

The warrant shall contain the name of the defendant or, if that is unknown, any name or description by which he can be identified with reasonable certainty. It shall describe the offense charged in the complaint, and shall state the numerical designation of the applicable statute or ordinance. A copy of the complaint shall be attached to the warrant. The warrant shall command that the defendant be arrested and brought before the court issuing it without unnecessary delay.

(2) Summons.

The summons shall be in the same form as the warrant, except that it shall not command that the defendant be arrested, but shall order the defendant to appear at a stated time and place and inform him that he may be arrested if he fails to appear at the time and place stated in the summons. A copy of the complaint shall be attached to the summons, except where an officer issues summons in lieu of making an arrest without a warrant, or where an officer issues summons after arrest without a warrant.

(D) Warrant summons: execution or service; return.

(1) By whom.

Warrants shall be executed and summons served by any officer authorized by law.

(2) Territorial limits.

Warrants may be executed or summons may be served at any place within this state.

(3) Manner.

Warrants, except as provided in subsection (A)(2), shall be executed by the arrest of the defendant. The officer need not have the warrant in his possession at the time of the arrest. In such case, he shall inform the defendant of the offense charged and of the fact that the warrant has been issued. A copy of the warrant shall be given to the defendant as soon as possible.

Summons may be served upon a defendant by delivering a copy to him personally, or by leaving it at his usual place of residence with some person of suitable age and discretion then residing therein, or, except when the summons is issued in lieu of executing a warrant by arrest, by mailing it to the defendant's last known address by certified mail with a return receipt requested. When service of summons is made by certified mail it shall be served by the clerk in the manner prescribed by Civil Rule 4.1(1). A summons to a corporation shall be served in the manner provided for service upon corporations in Civil Rules 4 through 4.2 and 4.6(A) and (B), except that the waiver provisions of Civil Rule 4(D) shall not apply. Summons issued under subsection (A)(2) in lieu of executing a warrant by arrest shall be served by personal or residence service. Summons issued under subsection (A)(3) in lieu of arrest and summons issued after arrest under subdivision (F) shall be served by personal service only.

(4) Return.

The officer executing a warrant shall make return thereof to the issuing court before whom the defendant is brought pursuant to Rule 5. At the request of the prosecuting attorney, any unexecuted warrant shall be returned to the issuing court and cancelled by a judge of that court.

When the copy of the summons has been served, the person serving summons shall endorse that fact on the summons and return it to the clerk, who shall make the appropriate entry on the appearance docket.

When the person serving summons is unable to serve a copy of the summons within twenty-eight days of the date of issuance, he shall endorse that fact and the reasons therefore on the summons and return the summons and copies to the clerk, who shall make the appropriate entry on the appearance docket.

At the request of the prosecuting attorney, made while the

complaint is pending, a warrant returned unexecuted and not cancelled, or a summons returned unserved, or a copy of either, may be delivered by the court to an authorized officer for execution or service.

(E) Arrest.

(1) Arrest upon warrant.

Where under a warrant a person is arrested either in the county from which the warrant issued or in an adjoining county, the arresting officer shall, except as provided in Division (F), bring the arrested person without unnecessary delay before the court that issued the warrant. Where the arrest occurs in any other county, the arrested person shall, except as provided in Division (F), be brought without unnecessary delay before a court of record therein, having jurisdiction over such an offense, and he shall not be removed from that county until he has been given an opportunity to consult with an attorney, or another person of his choice, and to post bail to be determined by the judge or magistrate of that court. If he is not released, he shall then be removed from the county and brought before the court issuing the warrant, without unnecessary delay. If he is released, the release shall be on condition that he appear in the issuing court at a time and date certain for an initial appearance under Crim. R. 5.

(2) Arrest without warrant.

Where a person is arrested without a warrant the arresting officer shall, except as provided in Division (F), bring the arrested person without unnecessary delay before a court having jurisdiction of the offense, and shall file or cause to be filed a complaint describing the offense for which the person was arrested. Thereafter the court shall proceed in accordance with Crim. R. 5.

(F) Release after arrest.

In misdemeanor cases where a person has been arrested with or without a warrant, the arresting officer, the officer in charge of the detention facility to which the person is brought or the superior of either officer, without unnecessary delay, may release the arrested person by issuing a summons when issuance of a summons appears reasonably calculated to assure the person's appearance. The officer issuing such summons shall note on the summons the time and place the person must appear and, if the person was arrested without a warrant, shall file or cause to be filed a complaint describing the offense. No warrant or alias warrant shall be issued unless the person fails to appear in response to the summons.

(Amended, eff 7-1-75; 7-1-90)

RULE 4.1

OPTIONAL PROCEDURE IN MINOR MISDEMEANOR CASES

(A) Procedure in minor misdemeanor cases.

Notwithstanding Rule 3, Rule 5(A), Rule 10, Rule 11(A), Rule 11(E), Rule 22, Rule 43(A), and Rule 44, a court may establish the following procedure for all or particular minor misdemeanors other than offenses covered by the Uniform Traffic Rules.

(B) Definition of minor misdemeanor.

A minor misdemeanor is an offense for which the potential penalty does not exceed a fine of fifty dollars. With respect to offenses committed on and after January 1, 1974, a minor misdemeanor is an offense for which the potential penalty does not exceed a fine of one hundred dollars.

(C) Form of citation.

In minor misdemeanor cases a law enforcement officer may issue a citation. The citation shall: contain the name and address of the defendant; describe the offense charged; give the numerical designation of the applicable statute or ordinance; state the name of the law enforcement officer who issued the citation; and order the defendant to appear at a stated time and place.

The citation shall inform the defendant that, in lieu of appearing at the time and place stated, he may, within that stated time, appear personally at the office of the clerk of court and upon signing a plea of guilty and a waiver of trial pay a stated fine and stated costs, if any. The citation shall inform the defendant that, in lieu of appearing at the time and place stated, he may, within a stated time, sign the guilty plea and waiver of trial provision of the citation, and mail the citation and a check or money order for the total amount of the fine and costs to the violations bureau. The citation shall inform the defendant that he may be arrested if he fails to appear either at the clerk's office or at the time and place stated in the citation.

(D) Duty of law enforcement officer.

A law enforcement officer who issues a citation shall complete and sign the citation form, serve a copy of the completed form upon the defendant and, without unnecessary delay, swear to and file the original with the court.

(E) Fine schedule.

The court shall establish a fine schedule which shall list the fine for each minor misdemeanor, and state the court costs. The fine schedule shall be prominently posted in the place where violation fines are paid.

(F) Procedure upon failure to appear.

When a defendant fails to appear, the court may issue a supplemental citation, or a summons or warrant under Rule 4. Supplemental citations shall be in the form prescribed by subdivision (C), but shall be issued and signed by the clerk and served in the same manner as a summons under Rule 4.

(G) Procedure where defendant does not enter a waiver.

Where a defendant appears but does not sign a guilty plea and waiver of trial, the court shall proceed in accordance with Rule 5.

(Amended, eff 7-1-78)

RULE 41

SEARCH AND SEIZURE

(A) Authority to issue warrant.

A search warrant authorized by this rule may be issued by a judge of a court of record to search and seize property located within the court's territorial jurisdiction, upon the request of a prosecuting attorney or a law enforcement officer.

(B) Property which may be seized with a warrant.

A warrant may be issued under this rule to search for and seize any: (1) evidence of the commission of a criminal offense; or (2) contraband, the fruits of crime, or things otherwise criminally possessed; or (3) weapons or other things by means of which a crime has been committed or reasonably appears about to be committed.

(C) Issuance and contents.

A warrant shall issue under this rule only on an affidavit or affidavits sworn to before a judge of a court of record and establishing the grounds for issuing the warrant. The affidavit shall name or describe the person to be searched or particularly describe the place to be searched, name or describe the property to be searched for and seized, state substantially the offense in relation thereto, and state the factual basis for the affiant's belief that such property is there located. If the judge is satisfied that probable cause for the search exists, he shall issue a warrant identifying the property and naming or describing the person or place to be searched. The finding of probable cause may be based upon hearsay in whole or in part, provided there is a substantial basis for believing the source of the hearsay to be credible and for believing that there is a factual basis for the information furnished. Before ruling on a request for a warrant, the judge may require the affiant to appear personally, and may examine under oath the affiant and any witnesses he may produce. Such testimony shall be admissible at a hearing on a motion to suppress if taken down by a court reporter or recording equipment, transcribed and made part of the affidavit. The warrant shall be directed to a law enforcement officer. It shall command the officer to search, within three days, the person or place named for the property specified. The warrant shall be served in the daytime, unless the issuing court, by appropriate provision in the warrant, and for reasonable cause shown, authorizes its execution at times other than daytime. The warrant shall designate a judge to whom it shall be returned.

(D) Execution and return with inventory.

The officer taking property under the warrant shall give to the person from whom or from whose premises the property was taken a copy of the warrant and a receipt for the property taken, or shall leave the copy and receipt at the place from which the property was taken. The return shall be made promptly and shall be accompanied by a written inventory of any property taken. The inventory shall be made in the presence of the applicant for the warrant and the person from whose possession or premises the property was taken, if they are present, or in the presence of at least one credible person other than the applicant for the warrant or the person from whose possession or premises the property was taken, and shall be verified by the officer. The judge shall upon request deliver a copy of the inventory to the person from whom or from whose premises the property was taken and to the applicant for the warrant. Property seized under a warrant shall be kept for use as evidence by the court which issued the warrant or by the law enforcement agency which executed the warrant.

(E) Return of papers to clerk.

The judge before whom the warrant is returned shall attach to the warrant a copy of the return, inventory, and all other papers in connection therewith and shall file them with the clerk.

(F) Definition of property and daytime.

The term "property" is used in this rule to include documents, books, papers and any other tangible objects. The term "daytime" is used in this rule to mean the hours from 7:00 a.m. to 8:00 p.m.

RULE 46

BAIL

(A) Purpose of and right to bail.

The purpose of bail is to insure that the defendant appears at all stages of the criminal proceedings. All persons are entitled to bail, except in capital cases where the proof is evident or the presumption great.

(B) Pretrial release where summons issued.

Where summons has issued and the defendant has appeared, the judge or magistrate shall release the defendant on his personal recognizance, or upon the execution of an unsecured appearance bond.

(C) Preconviction release in serious offense cases.

Any person who is entitled to release under Division (A), shall be released on his personal recognizance or upon the execution of an unsecured appearance bond in an amount specified by the judge or magistrate, unless the judge or magistrate determines that release will not assure the appearance of the person as required. Where a judge or magistrate so determines, he or she, either in lieu of or in addition to the preferred methods of release stated above, shall impose any of the following conditions of release that will reasonably assure the appearance of the person for trial or, if no single condition gives that assurance, any combination of the following conditions:

(1) Place the person in the custody of a designated person or organization agreeing to supervise the person;

(2) Place restrictions on the travel, association, or place of abode of the person during the period of release;

(3) Require the execution of an appearance bond in a specified amount, and the deposit with the clerk of the court before which the proceeding is pending of either $25.00 or a sum of money equal to ten percent of the amount of the bond, whichever is greater. Ninety percent of the deposit shall be returned upon the performance of the conditions of the appearance bond;

(4) Require the execution of a bail bond with sufficient solvent sureties, or the execution of a bond secured by real estate in the county, or the deposit of cash or the securities allowed by law in lieu of a bond;

(5) Impose any other constitutional condition considered reasonably necessary to assure appearance.

(D) Preconviction release in petty offense cases.

A person arrested for a misdemeanor and not released pursuant to Crim. R. 4(F), shall be released by the clerk of court, or if the clerk is not available, the officer in charge of the facility to which the person is brought, on his personal recognizance, or upon the execution of an unsecured appearance bond in the amount specified in the bail schedule established by the court. If the clerk or officer in charge of the facility determines pursuant to Division (F) that such release will not reasonably assure appearance as required, the person shall be eligible for release by doing any of the following, at his option:

(1) Executing an appearance bond in the amount specified in the court's bail schedule, with a deposit of either $25.00 or a sum of money equal to ten percent of the amount of the bond, whichever is greater. Ninety percent of the deposit shall be returned upon the performance of the conditions of the appearance bond;

(2) Posting a bond in the amount specified in the court's bail schedule, which bond is guaranteed to the person as a policyholder of a casualty insurer, or as a member of a bona fide motorists' or travelers' organization;

(3) Executing a bail bond with sufficient solvent sureties, or executing a bond secured by real estate in the county, or depositing cash or the securities allowed by law in lieu thereof in the amount specified in the court's bail schedule.

A person need not be released on his own recognizance or upon the execution of an unsecured appearance bond if he has a history of failure to appear when required in judicial proceedings, or if his physical, mental, or emotional condition appears to be such that he may pose a danger to himself or others if released immediately. When a person is not released because of his physical, mental, or emotional condition, and it appears that his release into the temporary custody of a responsible relative, friend, or other person will obviate the danger to himself or others, he shall be released into such temporary custody on his making bail under Division (D)(1), (2), or (3).

If a person is not released on his own recognizance, or upon the execution of an unsecured appearance bond, or pursuant to Division (D)(1), (2), or (3) he shall be given a hearing without unnecessary delay before a judge or magistrate who shall determine the conditions of his release pursuant to Division (C).

Each court shall establish a bail schedule covering all misdemeanors including traffic offenses, either specifically, or by type, or by potential penalty, or by some other reasonable method of classification. Each court shall, by rule, establish a method whereby a person may make bail under Division (D)(1) or (3) by the use of a credit card. Such rule shall permit only credit cards of recognized and established issuers. No credit card transaction shall be permitted when a service charge is made against the court or clerk.

(E) Release after conviction.

(1) Serious offense cases.

Except when a person has been sentenced to death, a person who has been convicted and is either awaiting sentence or has filed a notice of appeal shall be treated in accordance with the provision of Division (C), unless the judge has reason to believe that no one or more conditions of release will reasonably assure that the person will not flee or pose a danger to any other person or the community. If such a risk of flight or danger is believed to exist, the person may be ordered detained.

(2) Petty offense cases.

A person who has been convicted of a misdemeanor and is either awaiting sentence or has filed a notice of appeal shall be treated in accordance with the provision of Division (C).

(3) Bail or other conditions of release shall not be imposed, amended, or continued by order of a magistrate after conviction.

(F) Conditions of preconviction release; basis.

In determining which conditions of release will reasonably assure appearance, the judge or magistrate shall, on the basis of available information, take into account the nature and circumstances of the offense charged, the weight of the evidence against the accused, the accused's family ties, employment, financial resources, character and mental condition, the length of his residence in the community, his record of convictions, and his record of appearance at court proceedings or of flight to avoid prosecution or of failure to appear at court proceedings.

(G) Order.

The judge, magistrate, clerk, or officer who releases a person under this rule shall make an appropriate written order stating the conditions of release.

(H) Amendments.

Subject to Divisions (C) and (G), a judge or magistrate ordering the release of a person on any condition specified in this rule may at any time amend his or her order to impose additional or different conditions of release.

(I) Information need not be admissible.

Information stated in, or offered in connection with, any order entered pursuant to this rule need not conform to the rules pertaining to the admissibility of evidence in a court of law.

(J) Continuation of bonds.

Unless application is made by the surety for discharge, the same bond shall continue as a matter of right until the return of a verdict or judgment by a jury or by the court on the issue of guilt or innocence. In the discretion of the trial judge, and upon notice to the surety, the same bond may also continue after final disposition in the trial court and pending sentence or pending disposition of the case on review. Any provision of a bond or similar instrument that is contrary to this rule is void.

(K) Sanctions.

Any person released pursuant to any provision of this rule who fails to appear before any court as required, is subject to the punishment provided by law, and any bail given for his release shall be forfeit.

Any person released on his personal recognizance shall, in addition, be deemed to have been released pursuant to R.C. 2937.29.

(L) Justification of sureties.

Every surety, except a corporate surety licensed as provided by law, shall justify by affidavit, and may be required to describe in the affidavit, the property which he proposes as security and the encumbrances on it, the number and amount of other bonds and undertakings for bail entered into by him and remaining undischarged and all his other liabilities. He shall provide such other evidence of financial responsibility as the court or clerk may require. No bail bond shall be approved unless the surety or sureties appear, in the opinion of the court or clerk, to be financially responsible in at least the amount of the bond. No licensed attorney at law shall be a surety.

(M) Forfeiture of bonds.

If there is a breach of condition of a bond, the court shall declare a forfeiture of the bail. Forfeiture proceedings shall be promptly enforced as provided by law.

(N) Exoneration.

The obligor shall be exonerated as provided by law.

(Amended, eff 7-1-90; 7-1-94)

PART IV

GLOSSARY/INDEX

A

ABDUCTION—(a criminal offense—2905.02.) (a lesser offense to kidnapping.)

ABORTION—the purposeful termination of a human pregnancy by any person, including the pregnant woman herself, with an intention other than to produce a live birth or to remove a dead fetus or embryo—see 2919.11 to 2919.14.

ABORTION MANSLAUGHTER—(a criminal offense—2919.13.)

ABORTION TRAFFICKING—(a criminal offense—2919.14.)

ABUSE OF A CORPSE—(a criminal offense—2927.01.)

ABUSING HARMFUL INTOXICANTS—(a criminal offense—2925.31.)

ACCOMPLICE—person conspiring in or abetting an offense—see 2923.01 and 2923.03.

ACTUAL INCARCERATION—an offender is required to be imprisoned for the stated period of time to which he is sentenced that is specified as a term of actual incarceration—2929.01(C).

ADVERTISING DRUG PARAPHERNALIA—(a criminal offense—2925.14.)

AFFIRMATIVE DEFENSE—a defense involving a justification within the knowledge of the accused on which he can induce supporting evidence—see 2901.05(C).

AGGRAVATED ARSON—(a criminal offense—2909.02.)

AGGRAVATED ASSAULT—(a criminal offense—2903.12.)

AGGRAVATED BURGLARY—(a criminal offense—2911.11.)

AGGRAVATED FELONY—any offense classified as an aggravated felony—2901.02.

AGGRAVATED MENACING—(a criminal offense—2903.21.)

AGGRAVATED MURDER—(a capital criminal offense—2903.01.) (For penalty proceedings see 2929.03 and 2929.04.)

AGGRAVATED RIOT—(a criminal offense—2917.02.)

AGGRAVATED ROBBERY—(a criminal offense—2911.01.)

AGGRAVATED TRAFFICKING IN DRUGS—(a criminal offense—2925.03.)

AGGRAVATED TRESPASS—(a criminal offense—2911.21.1.)

AGGRAVATED VEHICULAR ASSAULT—(a criminal offense—2903.08.)

AGGRAVATED VEHICULAR HOMICIDE—(a criminal offense—2903.06.)

AIDING ESCAPE OR RESISTANCE TO AUTHORITY—(a criminal offense—2921.35.)

AIDS—see selling or donating contaminated blood—2927.13.

AIR GUN—any hand pistol or rifle that propels its projectile

GLOSSARY OF TERMS

by means of releasing compressed air, carbon dioxide, or other gas—2909.08(A).

AIRPORT OPERATIONAL SURFACE—any surface of land or water that is developed, posted, or marked so as to give an observer reasonable notice that the surface is designed and developed for the purpose of storing, parking, taxiing, or operating aircraft, or any surface of land or water that is actually being used for any of those purposes—2909.08(A).

ARSON—(a criminal offense—2909.03.)

ASSAULT—(a criminal offense—2903.13.)

ASSAULTING POLICE DOG OR HORSE OR HANDICAPPED ASSISTANCE DOG—(a criminal offense—2921.32.1.)

ASSURED CLEAR DISTANCE—4511.21.

ATTEMPT—(a criminal offense—2923.02.) Purposely or knowingly engage in conduct which if successful would constitute or result in an offense—the penalty is the next lesser degree than the offense attempted.

AUTOMATIC FIREARM—any firearm designed or adapted to fire a succession of cartridges with a single function of the trigger; also any semi-automatic firearm designed or adapted to fire more than 31 cartridges without reloading (other than a firearm chambering only .22 caliber cartridges)—2923.11(E).

B

BALLISTIC KNIFE—a knife with a detachable blade that is propelled by a spring-operated mechanism—2923.11(K).

BET—the hazarding of anything of value upon the result of an event, undertaking or contingency (but not a bona fide business risk)—See 2915.01(B).

BIGAMY—(a criminal offense—2919.01.)

BINGO—a type of gambling offense—see 2915.01 and 2915.07 to 2915.11.

BINGO GAME, CONDUCTING—see 2915.07, 2915.09.

BLOOD, SELLING OR DONATING CONTAMINATED—(a criminal offense—2927.13.)

BODY CAVITY SEARCH—(a criminal offense—2933.32.) An inspection of the anal or vaginal cavity of a person that is conducted visually, manually, by means of any instrument, apparatus, or object, or in any other manner while the person is detained or arrested for the alleged commission of a misdemeanor or traffic offense—2933.32(A).

BOOKMAKING—the business of receiving or paying off bets—see 2915.01(A).

BREAKING AND ENTERING—(a criminal offense—2911.13.)

BRIBERY—(a criminal offense—2921.02.)

BULK AMOUNT—term relating to quantity of a controlled substance—see 2925.01(E).

BURDEN OF PROOF—every person accused of an offense is presumed innocent until proven guilty beyond a reasonable doubt, and the burden of proof is upon the prosecution—see 2901.05(A).

BURGLARY—(a criminal offense—2911.12.)

BURN INJURY—second or third degree burns, burns to the upper respiratory tract or laryngeal edema due to the inhalation of superheated air, or any burn injury or wound that may result in death—2921.22(E)(1).

C

CABLE TELEVISION SERVICE—any services provided by or through the facilities of any cable television system or other similar closed circuit coaxial cable communications system, or any microwave or similar transmission service used in connection with any cable television system or other similar closed circuit coaxial cable communications system—2913.01(S).

CALUMNY—malicious uttering of false charges or misrepresentations calculated to damage another's reputation—see 2905.11 and 2905.12.

CAPITAL OFFENSE—any offense for which death may be imposed as a penalty.

CARE FACILITY—
(1) Any "home" as defined in section 3721.10 or 5111.20 of the Revised Code;
(2) Any "residential facility," "family home," or "group home" as defined in section 5123.19 of the Revised Code;
(3) Any institution or facility operated or provided by the department of mental health or by the department of mental retardation and developmental disabilities pursuant to sections 5119.02 and 5123.03 of the Revised Code;
(4) Any "residential facility" as defined in section 5119.22 of the Revised Code;
(5) Any unit of any hospital, as defined in section 3701.01 of the Revised Code, that provides the same services as a nursing home, as defined

in section 3721.01 of the Revised Code;
- (6) Any institution, residence, or facility that provides, for a period of more than twenty-four hours, whether for a consideration or not, accommodations to one individual or two unrelated individuals who are dependent upon the services of others;
- (7) Any "adult care facility" as defined in section 3722.01 of the Revised Code;
- (8) Any adult foster home certified by a county department of human services under section 5101.531 [5101.53.1] of the Revised Code;
- (9) Any "community alternative home" as defined in section 3724.01 of the Revised Code.

CARE FACILITY, OFFENSES AGAINST RESIDENT OR PATIENT OF—(criminal offenses—2903.34.)

CARETAKER—a person who assumes the duty to provide for the care and protection of a functionally impaired person on a voluntary basis, by contract, through receipt of payment for care and protection, as a result of a family relationship, or by order of a court of competent jurisdiction. "Caretaker" does not include a person who owns, operates, or administers, or who is an agent or employee of, a care facility, as defined in section 2903.33 of the Revised Code—2903.10.

CARRYING CONCEALED WEAPONS—(a criminal offense—2923.12.)

CHARITABLE ORGANIZATION—any tax exempt religious, educational, veterans', fraternal, service nonprofit medical, volunteer rescue service, volunteer firemen's, senior citizens', youth athletic, or youth athletic park organization. An organization is tax exempt if the organization is, and has received from the Internal Revenue Service a determination letter that is currently in effect, stating that the organization is, exempt from federal income taxation under subsection 501(a) and described in subsection 501(c)(3), 501(c)(4), 501(c)(8), 501(c)(10), or 501(c)(19) of the Internal Revenue Code. To qualify as a charitable organization, an organization, except a volunteer rescue service or volunteer firemen's organization, shall have been in continuous existence as such in this state for a period of two years immediately preceding either the making of an application for a bingo license under R.C. § 2915.08 or the conducting of any scheme of chance as provided in R.C. § 2915.02(C).

CHEATING—(a criminal offense—2915.05.)

CHILD ABUSE OR NEGLECT, FALSE REPORT OF—(a criminal offense—2921.14.)

CHILD ENTICEMENT—(a criminal offense—2905.05.)

COERCION—(a criminal offense—2905.12.) (a lesser charge under extortion.)

COIN MACHINE—any mechanical or electronic device designated to receive a coin, bill or token and automatically dispense property, provide a service, or grant a license—see 2913.01(I).

COMPELLING ACCEPTANCE OF OBJECTIONABLE MATERIALS—(a criminal offense—2907.34.)

COMPELLING PROSTITUTION—(a criminal offense—2907.21.)

COMPLICITY—(a criminal offense—2923.03.) (similar to what was formerly known as aiding and abetting.)

COMPOUNDING A CRIME—(a criminal offense—2921.21.)

COMPULSION—forcible inducement to the commission of an act; constraint; objective; necessity; duress.

COMPUTER—an electronic device that performs logical, arithmetic, and memory functions by the manipulation of electronic or magnetic impulses. "Computer" includes, but is not limited to, all input, output, processing, storage, computer program, or communication facilities that are connected, or related, in a computer system or network to such an electronic device—2913.01(M).

COMPUTER NETWORK—a set of related and remotely connected computers and communication facilities that includes more than one computer system that has the capability to transmit among the connected computers and communication facilities through the use of computer facilities—2913.01(O).

COMPUTER PROGRAM—an ordered set of data representing coded instructions or statements that when executed by a computer cause the computer to process data—2913.01(P).

COMPUTER PROPERTY, UNAUTHORIZED USE OF—see 2913.04.

COMPUTER SERVICES—includes, but is not limited to, the use of a computer system, computer network, computer program, data that is prepared for computer use, or data that is contained within a computer system or computer network—2913.01(L).

COMPUTER SOFTWARE—computer programs, procedures, and other documentation associated with the operation of a computer system—2913.01(Q).

COMPUTER SYSTEM—a computer and related devices, whether connected or unconnected, including, but

GLOSSARY OF TERMS

not limited to, data input, output, and storage devices, data communications links, and computer programs and data that make the system capable of performing specified special purpose data processing tasks—2913.01(N).

CONDUCTING BINGO GAME WITHOUT A LICENSE—(a criminal offense—2915.07.)

CONSPIRACY—(a criminal offense—2923.01.)

CONTAINER, OPENED—(a criminal offense—4301.62.)

CONTAMINATING SUBSTANCE FOR HUMAN CONSUMPTION OR USE—(a criminal offense—2927.24.)

CONTRABAND—any property described in the following categories:

(1) Property that in and of itself is unlawful for a person to acquire or possess;

(2) Property that is not in and of itself unlawful for a person to acquire or possess, but that has been determined by a court of this state, in accordance with law, to be contraband because of its use in an unlawful activity or manner, of its nature, or of the circumstances of the person who acquires or possesses it;

(3) Property that is specifically stated to be contraband by a section of the Revised Code or by an ordinance, regulation, or resolution;

(4) Property that is forfeitable pursuant to a section of the Revised Code, or an ordinance, regulation, or resolution, including, but not limited to, forfeitable firearms, dangerous ordnance, and obscene materials;

(5) Any controlled substance, as defined in section 3719.01 of the Revised Code, or any device, paraphernalia, money as defined in section

1301.01 of the Revised Code, or other means of exchange that has been, is being, or is intended to be used in an attempt or conspiracy to violate, or in a violation of, Chapter 2925. or 3719. of the Revised Code;

(6) Any gambling device, paraphernalia, money as defined in section 1301.01 of the Revised Code, or other means of exchange that has been, is being, or is intended to be used in an attempt or conspiracy to violate, or in the violation of, Chapter 2915. of the Revised Code;

(7) Any equipment, machine, device, apparatus, vehicle, vessel, container, liquid, or substance that has been, is being, or is intended to be used in an attempt or conspiracy to violate, or in the violation of, any law of this state relating to alcohol or tobacco;

(8) Any personal property that has been, is being, or is intended to be used in an attempt or conspiracy to commit, or in the commission of, any offense or in the transportation of the fruits of any offense;

(9) Any property that is acquired through the sale or other transfer of contraband or through the proceeds of contraband, other than by a court or a law enforcement agency acting within the scope of its duties;

(10) Any computer, computer system, computer network, or computer software that is used in a conspiracy to commit, an attempt to commit, or in the commission of any offense, if the owner of the computer, computer system, computer network, or computer software is convicted of or pleads guilty to the offense in which it is used.

CONTRABAND, OFFENSES INVOLVING—see 2933.42.

CONTRIBUTING TO UNRULINESS OR DELINQUENCY OF A CHILD—(a criminal offense—2919.24.)

CONTROLLED SUBSTANCE—a drug, compound, mixture, preparation, or substance, included in schedule I, II, III, IV, or V—3719.01(D).

CORRUPT ACTIVITY—engaging in, attempting to engage in, conspiring to engage in, or soliciting, coercing, or intimidating another person to engage in any of the following:
  (1) Conduct defined as "racketeering activity" under the "Organized Crime Control Act of 1970," 84 Stat. 941, 18 U.S.C. Sec. 1961 (1)(B), (1)(C), (1)(D), and (1)(E) as amended;
  (2) Conduct constituting any of the following:
    (a) Any violation of section 2903.01, 2903.02, 2903.03, 2903.04, 2903.11, 2903.12, 2905.01, 2905.02, 2905.11, 2905.22, 2907.322 [2907.32.2], 2907.323 [2907.32.3], 2909.02, 2909.03, 2911.01, 2911.02, 2911.11, 2911.12, 2911.13, 2911.31, 2921.02, 2921.03, 2921.04, 2921.11, 2921.12, 2921.32, 2921.41, 2921.42, 2921.43, 2923.12, 2923.17, 3769.11, 3769.15, 3769.16, or 3769.19, or of Division (A)(1) or (2) of section 1707.042 [1707.04.2], or of Division (B), (C)(4), (D), (E), or (F) of section 1707.44, or of Division (A)(1) or (2) of section 2923.20 of the Revised Code;
    (b) Any violation of section 2907.21, 2907.22, 2907.31, 2913.02, 2913.11, 2913.21, 2913.31, 2913.32, 2913.42, 2913.47, 2913.51, 2915.02, 2915.03, 2915.06,

2925.03, or 2925.37 of the Revised Code when the proceeds of the violation, the amount of a claim for payment or for any other benefit that is false or deceptive and that is involved in the violation, the payments made in the violation, or the value of the contraband or other property illegally possessed, sold, or purchased in the violation exceeds five hundred dollars, or any combination of violations of those sections when the total proceeds of the combination of violations, the payments made in the combination of violations, amount of the claims for payment or for any other benefits that is false or deceptive and that is involved in the combination of violations, or value of the contraband or other property illegally possessed, sold, or purchased in the combination of violations exceeds five hundred dollars;

(c) Any violation of section 5743.112 [5743.-11.2] of the Revised Code when the amount of unpaid tax exceeds one hundred dollars;

(d) Any violation or combination of violations of section 2907.32 of the Revised Code involving any material or performance containing a display of bestiality or of sexual conduct, as defined in section 2907.01 of the Revised Code, that is explicit and depicted with clearly visible penetration of the genitals or clearly visible penetration by the penis of any orifice when the total proceeds of the violation or combination of violations, the payments made in the violation or combination of violations, or the value of the contraband or other property illegally possessed, sold, or purchased in the violation or combination of violations exceeds five hundred dollars;

(e) Any combination of violations of the sections listed in Division (2)(b) above and violations of section 2907.32 of the Revised Code involving any material or performance containing a display of bestiality or of sexual conduct, as defined in section 2907.01 of the Revised Code, that is explicit and depicted with clearly visible penetration of the genitals or clearly visible penetration by the penis of any orifice when the total proceeds of the combination of violations, payments made in the combination of violations, or amount of the claims for payment or for any other benefits that is false or deceptive and that is involved in the combination of violations, or value of the contraband or other property illegally possessed, sold, or purchased in the combination of violations exceeds five hundred dollars.

(3) Conduct constituting a violation of any law of any state other than this state that is substantially similar to the conduct described in Division (2) above, provided the defendant was convicted of such conduct in a criminal proceeding in the other state—2923.31.

CORRUPTING ANOTHER WITH DRUGS—(a criminal offense—2925.02.)

CORRUPTING SPORTS—(a criminal offense—2915.05.)

CORRUPTION OF A MINOR—(a criminal offense—2907.04.) (under sexual assaults.)

COUNTERFEIT CONTROLLED SUBSTANCE—any of the following:

(1) Any drug that bears, or whose container or label bears, a trademark, trade name, or other identifying mark used without authorization of the owner of rights to such trademark, trade name, or identifying mark;

(2) Any unmarked or unlabeled substance that is represented to be a controlled substance manu-

factured, processed, packed, or distributed by a person other than the person that manufactured, processed, packed, or distributed it;
(3) Any substance that is represented to be a controlled substance but is not a controlled substance or is a different controlled substance;
(4) Any substance other than a controlled substance that a reasonable person would believe to be a controlled substance because of its similarity in shape, size, and color, or its markings, labeling, packaging, distribution, or the price for which it is sold or offered for sale—2925.01(P).

CREDIT CARD—includes, but is not limited to, a card, code, device, or other means of access to a customer's account for the purpose of obtaining money, property, labor, or services on credit, or for initiating an electronic fund transfer at a point-of-sale terminal, an automated teller machine, or a cash dispensing machine. "Electronic fund transfer" has the same meaning as in 92 Stat. 3728, 15 U.S.C. 1693a, as amended.

CRIMINAL DAMAGING OR ENDANGERING—(a criminal offense—2909.06.)

CRIMINAL MISCHIEF—(a criminal offense—2909.07.) (a lesser offense in the arson section.)

CRIMINAL SIMULATION—(a criminal offense—2913.32.)

CRIMINAL TRESPASS—(a criminal offense—2911.21.)

CRIMINAL USURY—(a criminal offense—2905.22.) illegally charging, taking, or receiving any money or other property as interest on an extension of credit at a rate exceeding 25% per annum or the equivalent rate for a longer or shorter period, unless the rate of interest is otherwise authorized by law or the creditor and the debtor, or all the creditors and all the debtors are members of the same immediate family.

GLOSSARY OF TERMS

CULPABILITY—any one of the four mental states (purpose, knowledge, recklessness, or negligence) required to impose criminal liability—2901.21, 2901.22.

CULTIVATE—includes planting, watering, fertilizing, or tilling—2925.01(G).

CULTIVATION OF MARIHUANA—(a criminal offense—2925.04.)

D

DAMAGING OR ENDANGERING—see "criminal damaging or endangering"—2909.06.

DANGEROUS DRUG—any drug which, under the "Federal Food Drug and Cosmetic Act," federal narcotic law, sections 3715.01 to 3715.72, or Chapter 3719. of the Revised Code, may be dispensed only upon a prescription; any drug which contains a schedule V narcotic drug and which is exempt from Chapter 3719. of the Revised Code, or to which such chapter does not apply; any drug intended for administration by injection into the human body other than through a natural orifice of the human body—4729.02(D).

DANGEROUS OFFENDER—a person whose history, character and conduct reveal a substantial risk that he will be a danger to others and whose conduct has been characterized by a pattern of repetitive, compulsive or aggressive behavior with heedless indifference to the consequences—see 2929.01(B).

DANGEROUS ORDNANCE—any of the following:
(1) Any automatic or sawed-off firearm, zip-gun, or ballistic knife;
(2) Any explosive device or incendiary device;
(3) Nitroglycerin, nitrocellulose, nitrostarch, PETN, cyclonite, TNT, picric acid, and other high explosives; amatol, tritonal, tetrytol, pentolite, pecretol,

cyclotol, and other high explosive compositions; plastic explosives; dynamite, blasting gelatin, gelatin dynamite, sensitized ammonium nitrate, liquid-oxygen blasting explosives, blasting powder, and other blasting agents; and any other explosive substance having sufficient brisance or power to be particularly suitable for use as a military explosive, or for use in mining, quarrying, excavating, or demolitions;

(4) Any firearm, rocket launcher, mortar, artillery piece, grenade, mine, bomb, torpedo, or similar weapon, designed and manufactured for military purposes, and the ammunition for that weapon;

(5) Any firearm muffler or silencer;

(6) Any combination of parts that is intended by the owner for use in converting any firearm or other device into a dangerous ordnance.

"Dangerous ordnance" does not include any of the following:

(1) Any firearm, including a military weapon and the ammunition for that weapon, and regardless of its actual age, which employs a percussion cap or other obsolete ignition system, or which is designed and safe for use only with black powder;

(2) Any pistol, rifle, or shotgun, designed or suitable for sporting purposes, including a military weapon as issued or as modified, and the ammunition for that weapon, unless the firearm is an automatic or sawed-off firearm;

(3) Any cannon or other artillery piece which, regardless of its actual age, is of a type in accepted use prior to 1887, has no mechanical, hydraulic, pneumatic, or other system for absorbing recoil and returning the tube into battery without displacing the carriage, and is designed and safe for use only with black powder;

(4) Black powder, priming quills, and percussion

caps possessed and lawfully used to fire a canon of a type defined in Division (L)(3) of this section during displays, celebrations, organized matches or shoots, and target practice, and smokeless and black powder, primers, and percussion caps possessed and lawfully used as a propellant or ignition device in small-arms or small-arms ammunition;

(5) Dangerous ordnance which is inoperable or inert and cannot readily be rendered operable or activated, and which is kept as a trophy, souvenir, curio, or museum piece.

(6) Any device which is expressly excepted from the definition of a destructive device pursuant to the "Gun Control Act of 1968," 82 Stat. 1213, 18 U.S.C. 921 (a)(4), as amended, and regulations issued under that act—2923.11.

DATA—a representation of information, knowledge, facts, concepts, or instructions that are being or have been prepared in a formalized manner and that are intended for use in a computer system or computer network—2913.01(R). See 2913.47 for additional definition re: insurance fraud.

DEADLY FORCE—any force which carries a substantial risk that it will proximately result in the death of any person—2901.01(B).

DEADLY WEAPON—any instrument, device, or thing capable of inflicting death, and designed or specifically adapted for use as a weapon, or possessed, carried, or used as a weapon—2923.11(A).

DECEPTION—knowingly deceiving another or causing another to be deceived by any false or misleading representation, by withholding information, by preventing another from acquiring information, or by any other conduct, act, or omission that creates, confirms, or perpetuates a false impression in another, including a false impression as to law, value, state of mind, or other objective or subjective fact—2913.01(A).

DECEPTION TO OBTAIN A DANGEROUS DRUG—(a criminal offense—2925.22.)

DECEPTION TO OBTAIN MATTER HARMFUL TO JUVENILES—(a criminal offense—2907.33.)

DECEPTIVE (re: Insurance Fraud)—see 2913.47.

DEFRAUD—to knowingly obtain by deception some benefit for oneself or another, or to knowingly cause by deception, some detriment to another—2913.01(B).

DEFRAUDING CREDITORS—(a criminal offense—2913.45.)

DEPRIVE—withhold property of another permanently, or for such period as to appropriate a substantial portion of its value or use, or with purpose to restore it only upon payment of a reward or other consideration; or dispose of property so as to make it unlikely that the owner will recover it; or accept, use, or appropriate money, property, or services, with purpose not to give proper consideration in return for the money, property, or services, and without reasonable justification or excuse for not giving proper consideration—2913.01(C).

DERELICTION OF DUTY—(a criminal offense—2921.44.)

DESECRATION—(a criminal offense—2927.11.)

DETENTION—means arrest, or confinement in any facility for custody of persons charged with or convicted of a crime or alleged or found to be delinquent or unruly, or detention for extradition or deportation—2921.01(E).

DETENTION FACILITY—any place used for the confinement of a person charged with or convicted of a crime or alleged or found to be delinquent or unruly—2921.01(F).

GLOSSARY OF TERMS

DISCLOSURE OF CONFIDENTIAL INFORMATION—(a criminal offense—2921.24.)

DISORDERLY CONDUCT—(a criminal offense—2917.11.)

DISPLAYING MATTER HARMFUL TO JUVENILES—(a criminal offense—2907.31.1.)

DISRUPTING PUBLIC SERVICES—(a criminal offense—2909.04.)

DISSEMINATING MATTER HARMFUL TO JUVENILES—(a criminal offense—2907.31.)

DISTURBING A LAWFUL MEETING—(a criminal offense—2917.12.)

DOMESTIC VIOLENCE—(a criminal offense—2919.25.)

DRIVING, RECKLESS—(a criminal offense—4511.20, 4511.20.1.)

DRIVING UNDER IMPLIED CONSENT SUSPENSION—(a criminal offense—4511.19.2.)

DRIVING UNDER THE INFLUENCE—(a criminal offense—4511.19.)

DRIVING WITHOUT REASONABLE CONTROL—(a criminal offense—4511.20.2.)

DRUG ABUSE OFFENSE—a violation of any of the offenses listed in 2925.01(H) or any violation of former or existing law substantially equivalent to those sections; a violation of an existing or former law of this or any other state of the United States, substantially equivalent to any section listed above; an offense under an existing or former law of this or any other state, or of the United States, of which planting, cultivating, harvesting, processing, making, manufacturing, producing, shipping, transporting, delivering, acquiring, possessing, storing, distributing, dispensing, selling, inducing another to use, administering to another, using, or otherwise dealing with a controlled substance is an element; or a conspiracy or attempt to commit, or complicity in committing or attempting to commit any offense herein listed—2925.01(H).

DRUG DEPENDENT PERSON—any person who, by reason of the use of any drug of abuse, is physically, psychologically, or physically and psychologically dependent upon the use of such drug, to the detriment of his health or welfare—3719.01.1.

DRUG OF ABUSE—any controlled substance as defined in R.C. § 3719.01, any harmful intoxicant as defined in R.C. § 2925.01, and any dangerous drug as defined in R.C. §§ 4729.02—3719.01.1.

DRUG PARAPHERNALIA—any equipment, product, or material of any kind that is used by the offender, intended by the offender for use, or designed for use, in propagating, cultivating, growing, harvesting, manufacturing, compounding, converting, producing, processing, preparing, testing, analyzing, packaging, repackaging, storing, containing, concealing, injecting, ingesting, inhaling, or otherwise introducing into the human body, a controlled substance in violation of this chapter. "Drug paraphernalia" includes, but is not limited to, any of the following equipment, products, or materials that are used by the offender, intended by the offender for use, or designed by the offender for use, in any of the following manners:

(1) A kit for propagating, cultivating, growing, or harvesting any species of a plant that is a controlled substance or from which a controlled substance can be derived;

(2) A kit for manufacturing, compounding, converting, producing, processing, or preparing a controlled substance;

(3) An isomerization device for increasing the potency of any species of a plant that is a controlled substance;

(4) Testing equipment for identifying, or analyzing

the strength, effectiveness, or purity of, a controlled substance;
(5) A scale or balance for weighing or measuring a controlled substance;
(6) A diluent or adulterant, such as quinine hydrochloride, mannitol, mannite, dextrose, or lactose, for cutting a controlled substance;
(7) A separation gin or sifter for removing twigs and seeds from, or otherwise cleaning or refining, marihuana;
(8) A blender, bowl, container, spoon, or mixing device for compounding a controlled substance;
(9) A capsule, balloon, envelope, or container for packaging small quantities of a controlled substance;
(10) A container or device for storing or concealing a controlled substance;
(11) A hypodermic syringe, needle, or instrument for parenterally injecting a controlled substance into the human body;
(12) An object, instrument, or device for ingesting, inhaling, or otherwise introducing into the human body, marihuana, cocaine, hashish, or hashish oil, such as a metal, wooden, acrylic, glass, stone, plastic, or ceramic pipe, with or without a screen, permanent screen, hashish head, or punctured metal bowl; water pipe; carburetion tube or device; smoking or carburetion mask; roach chip or similar object used to hold burning material, such as a marihuana cigarette, that has become too small or too short to be held in the hand; miniature cocaine spoon, or cocaine vial; chamber pipe; carburetor pipe; electric pipe; air driver pipe; chillum; bong; or ice pipe or chiller.

In determining if an object is drug paraphernalia, a court or law enforcement officer shall consider in addition to other relevant factors, the following:
(1) Any statement by the owner, or by anyone in

control, of the object, concerning its use;
- (2) The proximity in time or space of the object, or of the act relating to the object, to a violation of any provision of this chapter;
- (3) The proximity of the object to any controlled substance;
- (4) The existence of any residue of a controlled substance on the object;
- (5) Direct or circumstantial evidence of the intent of the owner, or of anyone in control, of the object, to deliver it to any person whom he knows intends to use the object to facilitate a violation of any provision of this chapter. A finding that the owner, or anyone in control, of the object, is not guilty of a violation of any other provision of this chapter, does not prevent a finding that the object was intended or designed by the offender for use as drug paraphernalia;
- (6) Any oral or written instruction provided with the object concerning its use;
- (7) Any descriptive material accompanying the object and explaining or depicting its use;
- (8) National or local advertising concerning the use of the object;
- (9) The manner and circumstances in which the object is displayed for sale;
- (10) Direct or circumstantial evidence of the ratio of the sales of the object to the total sales of the business enterprise;
- (11) The existence and scope of legitimate uses of the object in the community;
- (12) Expert testimony concerning the use of the object.—R.C. § 2925.14.

DRUG PARAPHERNALIA, OFFENSES INVOLVING—see R.C. § 2925.14.

DUTY TO REPORT ESCAPE OF ANIMAL—(a criminal offense—2927.21.)

E

ENDANGERING AIRCRAFT OR AIRPORT OPERATIONS—(a criminal offense—2909.08.)

ENDANGERING CHILDREN—(a criminal offense—2919.22.)

ENGAGING IN PATTERN OF CORRUPT ACTIVITY—(a criminal offense—2923.32.)

ENTERPRISE (re: engaging in pattern of corrupt activity)—any individual, sole proprietorship, partnership, limited partnership, corporation, trust, union, government agency, or other legal entity, or any organization, association, or group of persons associated in fact although not a legal entity. "Enterprise" includes illicit as well as licit enterprises—2923.31(C).

ESCAPE—(a criminal offense—2921.34.)

ETHNIC INTIMIDATION—(a criminal offense—2927.12.)

EXPLOSIVE DEVICE—any device designed or specially adapted to cause physical harm to persons or property by means of an explosion and consisting of an explosive substance and a means to detonate it—2923.11(H).

EXTORTION—(a criminal offense—2905.11.)

EXTORTIONATE EXTENSION OF CREDIT—(a criminal offense—2905.22.) any extension of credit with respect to which it is the understanding of the creditor and the debtor at the time it is made that delay in making repayment or failure to make repayment will result in the use of an extortionate means or if the debtor at a later time learns that failure to make repayment will result in the use of extortionate means—2905.21(F).

EXTORTIONATE MEANS (re: Unlawful Credit Practices)—any means that involves the use, or an express or implicit threat of use, of violence or criminal means to cause harm to the person or property of the debtor or any member of his family—2905.21(G).

F

FAILURE TO AID A LAW ENFORCEMENT OFFICER—(a criminal offense—2921.23.)

FAILURE TO COMPLY WITH ORDER OR SIGNAL OF POLICE OFFICER—(a criminal offense—2921.33.1.)

FAILURE TO DISPERSE—(a criminal offense—2917.04.)

FAILURE TO MAINTAIN BINGO RECORDS FOR THREE YEARS—(a criminal offense—2915.10.)

FAILURE TO PERFORM VIABILITY TESTING—(a criminal offense—2919.18.)

FAILURE TO REPORT A CRIME, KNOWLEDGE OF A DEATH, OR BURN INJURY—(a criminal offense—2921.22.)

FAILURE TO SECURE DANGEROUS ORDNANCE—(a criminal offense—2923.19.)

FAIR MARKET VALUE—money a buyer would give and a seller would receive for property or services provided both are willing and fully informed as to all facts material to the transaction—see 2913.61(D)(3).

FALSE PATIENT ABUSE OR NEGLECT COMPLAINT—(a criminal offense—2903.35.)

GLOSSARY OF TERMS

FALSE REPORT OF CHILD ABUSE OR NEGLECT—(a criminal offense—2921.14.)

FALSIFICATION—(a criminal offense—2921.13.)(under perjury.)

FAMILY, IMMEDIATE—(as used in 2905.21, defining criminal usury) a person's spouse residing in the person's household, brothers and sisters of the whole or of the half blood, and children, including adopted children—2905.21.

FAMILY OR HOUSEHOLD MEMBER—(as used in 2919.25 and 2919.26.) a spouse, person living as a spouse, parent, child, or other person related by consanguinity or affinity, who is residing or has resided with the offender—2919.25.

FELONIOUS ASSAULT—(a criminal offense—2903.11.)

FELONY—any offense classified as a felony—2901.02(D).

FELONY DRUG ABUSE OFFENSE—any drug abuse offense that would constitute a felony under the laws of Ohio except a violation of 2925.11—2925.01(I).

FIREARM—any deadly weapon capable of expelling or propelling one or more projectiles by the action of an explosive or combustible propellant, including an unloaded firearm, and any firearm which is inoperable but which can readily be rendered operable. Circumstantial evidence, including the representations and actions of the person exercising control over the firearm, may be considered—2923.11(B).

FIREARM, ILLEGAL POSSESSION IN LIQUOR PERMIT PREMISES—(a criminal offense—2923.12.1.)

FIREARMS, DISCHARGING—(criminal offenses—2923.16.1, 3773.21, 3773.21.1.)

FOOD, ADULTERATED—(a criminal offense—3716.11.)

FORCE—any violence, compulsion, or constraint physically exerted by any means upon or against a person or thing—2901.01(A).

FORGE—to fabricate or create, in whole or in part and by any means, any spurious writing, or to make, execute, alter, complete, reproduce, or otherwise purport to authenticate any writing, when such writing in fact is not authenticated by that conduct—2913.01(G).

FORGERY—(a criminal offense—2913.31.)

FORGING IDENTIFICATION CARDS; SELLING FORGED IDENTIFICATION CARDS—(a criminal offense—2913.31.)

FUNCTIONALLY IMPAIRED PERSON—any person who has a physical or mental impairment that prevents him from providing for his own care or protection or whose infirmities caused by aging prevent him from providing for his own care or protection—2903.10.

FUNCTIONALLY IMPAIRED PERSON, FAILING TO PROVIDE FOR—(a criminal offense—2903.16.)

FUNDING OF DRUG OR MARIHUANA TRAFFICKING—(a criminal offense—2925.05.)

G

GAIN ACCESS—to approach, instruct, communicate with, store data in, retrieve data from, or otherwise make use of any resources of a computer, computer system, or computer network—2913.01(T).

GAMBLING—(a criminal offense—2915.02.)

GAMBLING DEVICE—any equipment, device, apparatus,

or paraphernalia specifically designed for gambling purposes—2915.01(F).

GAMBLING OFFENSE—any of the offenses listed in 2915.10(G)(1) through (4).

GAME OF CHANCE—any game in which a player gives anything of value in the hope of gain; the outcome of which is determined largely or wholly by chance—2915.01(D).

GROSS PATIENT NEGLECT—(a criminal offense—2903.34.)

GROSS SEXUAL IMPOSITION—(a criminal offense—2907.05.)

H

HANDGUN—any firearm designed to be fired while being held in one hand—2923.11(C).

HARMFUL INTOXICANT—any compound, mixture, preparation, or substance the gas, fumes, or vapor of which when inhaled can induce intoxication, excitement, giddiness, irrational behavior, depression, stupefaction, paralysis, unconsciousness, asphyxiation, or other harmful physiological effects, and includes without limitation any volatile organic solvent, plastic cement, model cement, fingernail polish remover, lacquer thinner, cleaning fluid, gasoline, and any other preparation containing a volatile organic solvent; any aerosol propellant; any fluorocarbon refrigerant; and any anesthetic gas—2925.01(J).

HARMFUL TO JUVENILES—any material or performance if it is offensive to prevailing standards in the adult community with respect to what is suitable for juveniles and one of the seven qualifications apply—2907.01(E).

HAVING AN UNLAWFUL INTEREST IN A PUBLIC CONTRACT—(a criminal offense—2921.42.)

HAVING WEAPONS WHILE UNDER DISABILITY—(a criminal offense—2923.13.)

HAZING—doing any act or coercing another, including the victim, to do any act of initiation into any student or other organization that causes or creates a substantial risk of causing mental or physical harm to any person—2903.31(A).

I

IDENTIFICATION CARD—a card that includes personal information or characteristics of an individual, a purpose of which is to establish the identity of the bearer described on the card, whether the words "identity," "identification," "identification card," or other similar words appear on the card.

ILLEGAL ACTS RE CROWD CONTROL AND SEATING AT LIVE ENTERTAINMENT PERFORMANCES—(a criminal offense—2917.40.)

ILLEGAL ACTS RE INSPECTION OF BINGO GAME OR SCHEME OR GAME OF CHANCE—(a criminal offense—2915.10.)

ILLEGAL ADMINISTRATION OR DISTRIBUTION OF ANABOLIC STEROIDS—(a criminal offense—2925.06.)

ILLEGAL CONVEYANCE OF DEADLY WEAPON OR DANGEROUS ORDNANCE INTO COURTHOUSE; ILLEGAL POSSESSION OR CONTROL IN COURTHOUSE—(a criminal offense—2923.12.3.)

ILLEGAL CONVEYANCE OF WEAPONS OR PROHIBITED ITEMS ONTO DETENTION FACILITY OR INSTITUTION—(a criminal offense—2921.36.)

ILLEGAL CONVEYANCE OR POSSESSION OF DEADLY WEAPONS OR DANGEROUS ORDNANCE ON SCHOOL PREMISES—(a criminal offense—2923.12.2.)

ILLEGAL DISPENSING OF DRUG SAMPLES—(a criminal offense—2925.36.)

ILLEGAL DISPLAY OF LAW ENFORCEMENT EMBLEM—(a criminal offense—2913.44.1).

ILLEGAL DISTRIBUTION OF CIGARETTES OR OTHER TOBACCO PRODUCTS—(a criminal offense—2927.02.)

ILLEGAL MANUFACTURE OF DRUGS—(a criminal offense—2925.04.)

ILLEGAL MANUFACTURE OF DRUGS OR CULTIVATION OF MARIHUANA—(a criminal offense—2925.04.)

ILLEGAL POSSESSION OF AN OBJECT INDISTINGUISHABLE FROM A FIREARM—(a criminal offense—2923.12.2)

ILLEGAL POSSESSION OF FIREARM IN LIQUOR PERMIT PREMISES—(a criminal offense—2923.12.1.)

ILLEGAL PROCESSING OF DRUG DOCUMENTS—(a criminal offense—2925.23.)

ILLEGAL USE OF FOOD STAMPS OR WIC PROGRAM BENEFITS—(a criminal offense—2913.46.)

ILLEGAL USE OF MINOR IN NUDITY-ORIENTED MATERIAL OR PERFORMANCE—(a criminal offense—2907.32.3.)

ILLEGALLY MANUFACTURING OR PROCESSING EXPLOSIVES—(a criminal offense—2923.17.)

IMMEDIATE FAMILY—*see* FAMILY, IMMEDIATE

IMPERSONATING PEACE OFFICER—(a criminal offense—2921.51.)

IMPORTUNING—(a criminal offense—2907.07.) (under sexual assaults.)

IMPROPERLY DISCHARGING FIREARM AT OR INTO HABITATION OR SCHOOL—(a criminal offense—2923.16.1.)

IMPROPERLY DISPENSING OR DISTRIBUTING NITROUS OXIDE—(a criminal offense—2925.32.)

IMPROPERLY FURNISHING FIREARMS TO A MINOR—(a criminal offense—2923.21.)

IMPROPERLY HANDLING FIREARMS IN MOTOR VEHICLE—(a criminal offense—2923.16.)

INCENDIARY DEVICE—any firebomb and any device designed or specially adapted to cause physical harm to persons or property by means of fire, and consisting of an incendiary substance or agency and a means to ignite it—2923.11(I).

INCITING TO VIOLENCE—(a criminal offense—2917.01.)

INDUCING PANIC—(a criminal offense—2917.31.)

INSURANCE FRAUD—(a criminal offense—2913.47.)

INSURER (re: Insurance Fraud)—see 2913.47.

INTERCEPTION OF WIRE OR ORAL COMMUNICATION—(a criminal offense—2933.52.)

INTERFERENCE WITH CUSTODY—(a criminal offense—2919.23.)

GLOSSARY OF TERMS

INTERFERENCE WITH FAIR HOUSING RIGHTS—(a criminal offense—2927.03.)

INTERFERING WITH ACTION TO ISSUE OR MODIFY SUPPORT ORDER—(a criminal offense—2919.23.1.)

INTERFERING WITH CIVIL RIGHTS—(a criminal offense—2921.45.)

INTIMIDATION—(a criminal offense—2921.03.) (under bribery.)

INTIMIDATION, ETHNIC—(a criminal offense—2927.12.)

INTIMIDATION OF ATTORNEY, VICTIM OR WITNESS—(a criminal offense—2921.04.)

INVOLUNTARY ACTS—reflexes, convulsions, body movements during unconsciousness or sleep, and body movements that are not otherwise a product of the actor's volition—2901.21(C)(2).

INVOLUNTARY MANSLAUGHTER—(a criminal offense—2903.04.)

J

JUVENILE—an unmarried person under 18 years—2907.01(I).

JUVENILES, HARMFUL TO—see HARMFUL TO JUVENILES

K

KEY, CAR, MASTER—4549.04.2.

KIDNAPPING—(a criminal offense—2905.01.)

KNOWLEDGE—one of the culpable mental states. A person acts knowingly, regardless of his purpose, when he is aware that his conduct will probably cause a certain result or will probably be of a certain nature. A person has knowledge of circumstances when he is aware that such circumstances probably exist—2901.22(B).

L

LAW ENFORCEMENT OFFICER—the term is defined at 2901.01(K) for the purposes of the Criminal Code.

LIVESTOCK, OFFENSES INVOLVING—see 2925.09.

LOITERING TO ENGAGE IN SOLICITATION AFTER A POSITIVE HIV TEST—(a criminal offense—2907.24.1.)

M

MAINTENANCE OF BINGO RECORDS—(failure constitutes a criminal offense—2915.10.)

MAKING FALSE ALARMS—(a criminal offense—2917.32.)

MAKING OR USING SLUGS—(a criminal offense—2913.33.)

MANUFACTURE—(as related to drug abuse offenses) to plant, cultivate, harvest, process, make, prepare, or otherwise engage in any part of the production of a drug, by propagation, extraction, chemical synthesis, or compounding, or any combination of the same, and includes packaging, repackaging, labeling, and other activities incident to production—2925.01(K).

GLOSSARY OF TERMS

MANUFACTURING DRUG PARAPHERNALIA—(a criminal offense—2925.14.)

MASTER CAR KEYS, OFFENSES INVOLVING—4549.04.2.

MATERIAL—(as used in 2907.01-.37) any book, magazine, newspaper, pamphlet, poster, print, picture, figure, image, description, motion picture film, phonographic record, or tape, or other tangible thing capable of arousing interest through sight, sound, or touch—2907.01.

MEDICAID FRAUD—(a criminal offense—2913.40.)

MENACING—(a criminal offense—2903.22.)

MENACING BY STALKING—(a criminal offense—2903.21.1.)

MINOR—a person under the age of eighteen—2907.01.

MINOR MISDEMEANOR—any offense not specifically classified if the only penalty is a fine not exceeding one hundred dollars—2901.02(G).

MISCONDUCT AT AN EMERGENCY—(a criminal offense—2917.13)

MISCONDUCT INVOLVING A PUBLIC TRANSPORTATION SYSTEM—(a criminal offense—2917.41.)

MISDEMEANOR—any offense classified as a misdemeanor—2901.02(D).

MISSING CHILDREN—(improper solicitation of contributions) (a criminal offense—2901.32.)

MISUSE OF CREDIT CARD—(a criminal offense—2913.21.)

MOTOR VEHICLES, OFFENSES INVOLVING
assured clear distance—4511.21.

> driving, reckless—(a criminal offense—4511.20, 4511.20.1.)
>
> driving under implied consent suspension—(a criminal offense—4511.19.2.)
>
> driving under the influence—(a criminal offense—4511.19.)
>
> driving without reasonable control—(a criminal offense—4511.20.2.)
>
> master car keys, offenses involving—4549.04.2.
>
> speed limits, exceeding—4511.21.

MURDER—(a criminal offense—2903.02.)

N

NEGLIGENT—one of the culpable mental states. Because of substantial lapse from due care, failing to perceive or avoid a risk that conduct may cause a certain result or may be of a certain nature. A person is negligent with respect to circumstances when, because of a substantial lapse from due care, he fails to perceive or avoid a risk that such circumstances may exist—2901.22(D).

NEGLIGENT ASSAULT—(a criminal offense—2903.14.)

NEGLIGENT HOMICIDE—(a criminal offense—2903.05.)

NONSUPPORT OR CONTRIBUTING TO NONSUPPORT OF DEPENDENTS—(a criminal offense—2919.21.)

NUDITY—showing, representation, or depiction of human male or female genitals, pubic area, or buttocks with less than a full, opaque covering, or of a female breast with less than a full, opaque covering of any portion thereof below the top of the nipple, or of covered male genitals in a discernibly turgid state—2907.01(H).

O

OBSCENE—when considered as a whole, and judged with reference to ordinary adults, or if it is designed for sexual deviates or other specially susceptible groups, judged with reference to that group, any material or performance is "obscene" if any of the following apply: (1) Its dominant appeal is to prurient interest; (2) Its dominant tendency is to arouse lust by displaying or depicting sexual activity, masturbation, sexual excitement, or nudity in a way which tends to represent human beings as mere objects of sexual appetite; (3) Its dominant tendency is to arouse lust by displaying or depicting bestiality or extreme or bizarre violence, cruelty, or brutality; (4) Its dominant tendency is to appeal to scatological interest by displaying or depicting human bodily functions of elimination in a way that inspires disgust or revulsion in persons with ordinary sensibilities, without serving any genuine scientific, educational, sociological, moral, or artistic purpose; (5) It contains a series of displays or descriptions of sexual activity, masturbation, sexual excitement, nudity, bestiality, extreme or bizarre violence, cruelty, or brutality, or human bodily functions of elimination, the cumulative effect of which is a dominant tendency to appeal to prurient or scatological interest, when the appeal to such interest is primarily for its own sake or for commercial exploitation, rather than primarily for genuine scientific, educational, sociological, moral, or artistic purpose—2907.01(F).

OBSTRUCTING JUSTICE—(a criminal offense—2921.32.)

OBSTRUCTING OFFICIAL BUSINESS—(a criminal offense—2921.31.)

OCCUPIED STRUCTURE—any house, building, outbuilding, watercraft, aircraft, railroad car, truck, trailer, tent, or other structure, vehicle, or shelter, or any portion thereof, to which any of the following applies: (A) Which is maintained as a permanent or temporary dwelling, even though it is temporarily unoccupied, and whether or not any person is actually present; (B) Which at the time is occupied as the permanent or temporary habitation of any person, whether or not any person is actually present; (C) Which at the time is specially adapted for the overnight accommodation of any person, whether or not any person is actually present; (D) In which at the time any person is present or likely to be present—2909.01.

OFFENSE—when one or more sections of the Revised Code state a positive prohibition or enjoin a specific duty, and provide a penalty for violation of such prohibition or failure to meet such duty—2901.03(B).

OFFENSE OF VIOLENCE—any of the offenses listed in 2901.01(I)(1) through (4), and generally committed purposely or knowingly and involving physical harm to persons or a risk of serious physical harm.

OFFENSES INVOLVING COUNTERFEIT CONTROLLED SUBSTANCES—(a criminal offense—2925.37.)

OFFENSES INVOLVING UNAPPROVED DRUGS; DANGEROUS DRUG OFFENSES INVOLVING LIVESTOCK—(a criminal offense—2925.09.)

OFFICIAL PROCEEDING—any proceeding before a legislative, judicial, administrative, or other governmental agency or official authorized to take evidence under oath, and includes any proceeding before a referee, hearing examiner, commissioner, notary, or other person taking testimony or a deposition in connection with an official proceeding—2921.01(D).

OPENED CONTAINER—(a criminal offense—4301.62.)

OPERATING A GAMBLING HOUSE—(a criminal offense—2915.03.)

OPERATING A MOTOR VEHICLE AFTER UNDER-AGE ALCOHOL CONSUMPTION—(a criminal offense—4511.19(B).)

OPERATION OF BINGO GAME BY A MINOR—(a criminal offense—2915.11.)

OPERATION OF BINGO GAME BY FORMER OFFENDER—(a criminal offense—2915.11.)

ORDER OR SIGNAL OF POLICE OFFICER, FAILURE TO COMPLY WITH—(a criminal offense—2921.33.1.)

ORGANIZATION—a corporation for profit or not for profit, partnership, limited partnership, joint venture, unincorporated association, estate, trust, or other commercial or legal entity. Does not include an entity organized as or by a governmental agency for the execution of a governmental program—2901.23(D).

ORGANIZED CRIME—see CORRUPT ACTIVITY

OWNER—any person, other than the actor, who is the owner of, or who has possession or control of, or any license or interest in property or services, even though the ownership, possession, control, license, or interest is unlawful—2913.01(D).

P

PANDERING OBSCENITY—(a criminal offense—2907.32.)

PANDERING OBSCENITY INVOLVING A MINOR—(a criminal offense—2907.32.1.)

PANDERING SEXUALLY ORIENTED MATTER INVOLVING A MINOR—(a criminal offense—2907.32.2.)

PARAPHERNALIA, DRUG—see DRUG PARAPHERNALIA.

PARENTAL EDUCATION NEGLECT—(a criminal offense—2919.22.2.)

PARTY OFFICIAL—any person who holds an elective or appointive post in a political party in the United States or this state, by virtue of which he directs, conducts, or participates in directing or conducting party affairs at any level of responsibility—see 2921.01(C).

PASSING BAD CHECKS—(a criminal offense—2913.11.)

PATIENT ABUSE—(a criminal offense—2903.34.)

PATIENT NEGLECT—(a criminal offense—2903.34.)

PATTERN OF CORRUPT ACTIVITY—two or more incidents of corrupt activity, whether or not there has been a prior conviction, that are related to the affairs of the same enterprise, are not isolated, and are not so closely related to each other and connected in time and place that they constitute a single event—2923.31(E).

At least one of the incidents forming the pattern shall occur on or after the effective date of this section. Unless any incident was an aggravated murder or murder, the last of the incidents forming the pattern shall occur within six years after the commission of any prior incident forming the pattern, excluding any period of imprisonment served by any person engaging in the corrupt activity.

For the purposes of the criminal penalties that may be imposed pursuant to section 2923.32 of the Revised Code, at least one of the incidents forming the pattern shall constitute a felony under the laws of this state or, if committed in violation of the laws of the United States or of any other state, would constitute a felony under the law of this state if committed in this state.

PEACE OFFICER—includes a sheriff, deputy sheriff, marshal, deputy marshal, member of the organized police department of any municipal corporation, including a member of the organized police department of a municipal corporation in an adjoining state serving in Ohio under a contract pursuant to section 737.04 of the Revised Code, state university law enforcement officer appointed under section 3345.04 of the Revised Code, a police constable of any township, a police officer of a township or joint township police district, and, for the purpose of arrests within those areas, and for the purposes of Chapter 5503. of the Revised Code, and the filing of and service of process relating to those offenses witnessed or investigated by them, includes the superintendent and patrolmen of the state highway patrol—2935.01(B).

PECULATION—embezzlement—2921.41, et seq.

PERFORMANCE—any motion picture, preview, trailer, play, show, skit, dance, or other exhibition performed before an audience—2907.01(K).

PERFORMING UNLAWFUL ABORTION PROCEDURE—(a criminal offense—2919.15.)

PERJURY—(a criminal offense—2921.11.)

PERMITTING DRUG ABUSE—(a criminal offense—2925.13.)

PERSONATING AN OFFICER—(a criminal offense—2913.44.)

PHYSICAL HARM TO PERSONS—any injury, illness, or other physiological impairment, regardless of its gravity or duration—2901.01(C).

PHYSICAL HARM TO PROPERTY—any tangible or intangible damage to property which, in any degree, results in loss to its value or interferes with its use or enjoyment, does not include wear and tear occasioned by normal use—2901.01(D).

POISONS—(offenses involving—3719.32.)

POLICY (re: Insurance Fraud)—see 2913.47.

POSSESS (POSSESSION—as related to drug abuse offenses)—having control over a thing or substance but may not be inferred solely from mere access to the thing or substance through ownership or occupation of the premises upon which the thing or substance is found—2925.01(L).

POSSESSING CRIMINAL TOOLS—(a criminal offense—2923.24.)

POSSESSING DRUG ABUSE INSTRUMENTS—(a criminal offense—2925.12.)

POSSESSING DRUG PARAPHERNALIA—(a criminal offense—2925.14.)

POSSESSING NITROUS OXIDE IN MOTOR VEHICLE—(a criminal offense—2925.33.)

POSSESSION—a voluntary act if the possessor knowingly

procured or received the thing possessed, or was aware of his control thereof for a sufficient time to have ended his possession—2901.21(C)(1).

POSSESSION OF DEADLY WEAPON WHILE UNDER DETENTION—(a criminal offense—2923.13.1.)

POSSESSION OF DRUGS—(a criminal offense—2925.11.)

POSSESSION OR SALE OF UNAUTHORIZED CABLE TELEVISION DEVICE—(a criminal offense—2913.04.1.)

PRESERVING LIFE OF CHILD BORN BY ATTEMPTED ABORTION—(failure constitutes a criminal offense—2919.13.)

PRIVILEGE—an immunity, license, or right conferred by law, or bestowed by express or implied grant, or arising out of status, position, office, or relationship, or growing out of necessity—2901.01(L).

PROCURING—(a criminal offense—2907.23.)

PROMOTING PROSTITUTION—(a criminal offense—2907.22.)

PROPERTY—any property, real or personal, tangible or intangible, and any interest or license in such property. It includes, but is not limited to, cable television service, computer data, computer software, financial instruments associated with computers, and other documents associated with computers—2901.01(J).

PROSTITUTE—a male or female who promiscuously engages in sexual activity for hire, regardless of whether the hire is paid to the prostitute or to another—2907.01(D).

PROSTITUTION; AFTER POSITIVE HIV TEST—(a criminal offense—2907.25.)

PROXIMATE CAUSE—that which, in a natural and continuous sequence, unbroken by any efficient intervening cause, produces the consequence, and without which the result would not have occurred.

PROXIMATE RESULT—one which succeeds naturally in the ordinary course of things.

PUBLIC GAMING—(a criminal offense—2915.04.)

PUBLIC INDECENCY—(a criminal offense—2907.09.)

PUBLIC OFFICIAL—any elected or appointed officer, or employee or agent of the state or any political subdivision thereof, whether in a temporary or permanent capacity, and including without limitation legislators, judges, and law enforcement officers—2921.01(A).

PUBLIC SERVANT—any public official; any person performing ad hoc a governmental function, including without limitation a juror, member of a temporary commission, master, arbitrator, advisor, or consultant; a candidate for public office, whether or not he is elected or appointed to the office for which he is a candidate. A person is a candidate for purposes of this division if he has been nominated according to law for election or appointment to public office, or if he has filed a petition or petitions as required by law to have his name placed on the ballot in a primary, general, or special election, or if he campaigns as a write-in candidate in any primary, general or special election—2921.01(B).

PURPOSELY—one of the culpable mental states required for criminal liability. Specific intention to cause a certain result, or, when the gist of the offense is a prohibition against conduct of a certain nature, regardless of what the offender intends to accomplish thereby, it is specific intention to engage in conduct of that nature—2901.22(A).

R

RACKETEERING—see CORRUPT ACTIVITY

RAPE—(a criminal offense—2907.02.)

REASONABLE DOUBT—is present when the jurors, after they have carefully considered and compared all the evidence, cannot say they are firmly convinced of the truth of the charge. It is a doubt based on reason and common sense. Reasonable doubt is not mere possible doubt, because everything relating to human affairs or depending on moral evidence is open to some possible or imaginary doubt. "Proof beyond a reasonable doubt" is proof of such character that an ordinary person would be willing to rely and act upon it in the most important of his own affairs—2901.05(D).

RECEIVING STOLEN PROPERTY—(a criminal offense—2913.51.)

RECKLESSLY—one of the culpable mental states required for criminal liability. A person acts recklessly when, with heedless indifference to the consequences, he perversely disregards a known risk that his conduct is likely to cause a certain result or is likely to be of a certain nature. A person is reckless with respect to circumstances when, with heedless indifference to the consequences, he perversely disregards a known risk that such circumstances are likely to exist—2901.22(C).

REPEAT OFFENDER—a person who has a history of persistent criminal activity, and whose character and condition reveal a substantial risk that he will commit another offense—2929.10(A).

RESISTING ARREST—(a criminal offense—2921.33.)

RETALIATION—(a criminal offense—2921.05.)

RICO—see CORRUPT ACTIVITY

RIOT—(a criminal offense—2917.03.)

RISK—a significant possibility, as contrasted with a remote possibility, that a certain result may occur or that certain circumstances may exist—2901.01(G).

ROBBERY—(a criminal offense—2911.02.)

RULES FOR CONDUCTING BINGO—(violation constitutes a criminal offense—2915.09.)

S

SAFECRACKING—(a criminal offense—2911.31.)

SAMPLE DRUG—a drug or pharmaceutical preparation that would be hazardous to health or safety if used without the supervision of a practitioner, or a drug of abuse, and that, at one time had been placed in a container plainly marked as a sample by a manufacturer—2925.01(M).

SAWED-OFF FIREARM—a shotgun with a barrel less than 18 inches long, or a rifle with a barrel less than 16 inches long, or a shotgun or rifle less than 26 inches long overall—2931.11(F).

SCHEDULE I, II, III, IV, or V—controlled substance schedules I, II, III, IV or V respectively, established pursuant to R.C. § 3719.41, as amended pursuant to R.C. §§ 3719.44—3719.01(FF).

SCHEME OF CHANCE—a lottery, numbers game, pool or other scheme in which a participant gives a valuable consideration for a chance to win a prize—2915.01(C).

SCHOOL—any school operated by a board of education or any school for which the state board of education prescribes minimum standards under section 3301.07 of the Revised Code, whether or not any instruction, extracurricular activities, or training provided by the school is being conducted at the time a criminal offense is committed—2925.01.

SCHOOL BUILDING—any building in which any of the instruction, extracurricular activities, or training provided by a school is conducted, whether or not any instruction, extracurricular activities, or training provided by the school is being conducted in the school building at the time a criminal offense is committed—2925.01.

SCHOOL PREMISES—either of the following:

(1) The parcel of real property on which any school is situated, whether or not any instruction, extracurricular activities, or training provided by the school is being conducted on the premises at the time a criminal offense is committed;

(2) Any other parcel of real property that is owned or leased by a board of education of a school or the governing body of a school for which the state board of education prescribes minimum standards under section 3301.07 of the Revised Code and on which some of the instruction, extracurricular activities, or training of the school is conducted, whether or not

any instruction, extracurricular activities, or training provided by the school is being conducted on the parcel of real property at the time a criminal offense is committed—2925.01.

SCHOOL ACTIVITIES/SCHOOL PREMISES, WEAPONS OFFENSES CONCERNING—(criminal offenses—2923.12.2.)

SECURING WRITINGS BY DECEPTION—(a criminal offense—2913.43.)

SELLING DRUG PARAPHERNALIA—(a criminal offense—2925.14.)

SELLING OR DONATING CONTAMINATED BLOOD—(a criminal offense—2927.13.)

SEMI-AUTOMATIC FIREARM—any firearm designed or specially adapted to fire a single cartridge and automatically chamber a succeeding cartridge ready to fire, with a single function of the trigger—2923.11(D).

SERIOUS PHYSICAL HARM TO PERSONS—any mental illness or condition of such gravity as would normally require hospitalization or prolonged psychiatric treatment; any physical harm which carries a substantial risk of death; any physical harm which involves some permanent incapacity, whether partial or total, or which involves some temporary, substantial incapacity; any physical harm which involves some permanent disfigurement, or which involves some temporary serious disfigurement; or any physical harm which involves acute pain of such duration as to result in substantial suffering, or which involves any degree of prolonged or intractable pain—2901.01(E).

SERIOUS PHYSICAL HARM TO PROPERTY—any serious physical harm to property which does either of the following: (1) results in substantial loss to the value of the property, or requires a substantial amount of time, effort, or money to repair or replace; or (2) temporarily prevents the use of enjoyment of the property, or substantially interferes with its use or enjoyment for any extended period of time—2901.01(F).

SERVICES—includes labor, personal services, professional services, public utility services, common carrier services, food, drink, transportation, entertainment, and computer services—2913.01(E).

SEXUAL ACTIVITY—sexual conduct or sexual contact, or both—2907.01(C).

SEXUAL BATTERY—(a criminal offense—2907.03.)

SEXUAL CONDUCT—vaginal intercourse between a male and female, and anal intercourse, fellatio, and cunnilingus between persons regardless of sex. Penetration, however slight, is sufficient to complete vaginal or anal intercourse—2907.01(A).

SEXUAL CONTACT—any touching of an errogenous zone of another, including without limitation the thigh, genitals, buttock, pubic region, or, if such person is a female, a breast, for the purpose of sexually arousing or gratifying either person—2907.01(B).

SEXUAL EXCITEMENT—the condition of human male or female genitals when in a state of sexual stimulation or arousal—2907.01(G).

SEXUAL IMPOSITION—(a criminal offense—2907.06.)

SHAM LEGAL PROCESS, USING—see 2921.52.

SIMULATION (CRIMINAL)—(a criminal offense—2913.32.) (under forgery section.)

SLUG—any object that, by virtue of its size, shape, composition, or other quality, is capable of being inserted or deposited in a coin machine as an improper substitute for a genuine coin, bill, or token made for that purpose—2913.01(J).

SOLICITING; AFTER POSITIVE HIV TEST—(a criminal offense—2907.24.)

SOLICITING IMPROPER COMPENSATION—(a criminal offense—2921.43.)

SPEED LIMITS, EXCEEDING—(a criminal offense—4511.21.)

SPOUSE (re: sex offenses [2907.01-2907.37])—a person married to an offender at the time of an alleged offense, except (1) when the parties have entered a written separation agreement per 3103.06, or (2) during the pending of an action for annulment, divorce, dissolution of marriage, or alimony, or (3) in an action for alimony, after the effective date of the judgment for alimony—2907.02.

SPREADING A FALSE REPORT OF CONTAMINATION—(a criminal offense—2927.24.)

SPRING-OPERATED GUN—any hand pistol or rifle that propels a projectile not less than four or more than five millimeters in diameter by means of a spring—2909.08(A).

STALKING, MENACING BY—(a criminal offense—2903.21.1.). Violating an anti-stalking protection order is prohibited by 2903.21.4.

STATEMENT (re: Insurance Fraud)—see 2913.47.

STRIP SEARCH—(a criminal offense—2933.32.) an inspection of the genitalia, buttocks, breasts, or undergarments of a person that is preceded by the removal or rearrangement of some or all of the person's clothing that directly covers the person's genitalia, buttocks, breasts, or undergarments and that is conducted visually, manually, by means of any instrument, apparatus, or object, or in any other manner while the person is detained or arrested for the alleged commission of a misdemeanor or traffic offense. "Strip search" does not mean the visual observation of a person who was afforded a reasonable opportunity to secure release on bail or recognizance, who fails to secure such release, and who is to be integrated with the general population of any detention facility, while the person is changing into clothing that is required to be worn by inmates in the facility—2933.32(A).

SUBSTANTIAL RISK—a strong possibility, as contrasted with a remote or significant possibility, that a certain result may occur or that certain circumstances may exist—2901.01(H).

T

TAMPERING WITH COIN MACHINES—(a criminal offense—2911.32.)

TAMPERING WITH EVIDENCE—(a criminal offense—2921.12.)

TAMPERING WITH RECORDS—(a criminal offense—2913.42.)

TELEPHONE HARASSMENT—(a criminal offense—2917.21.)

TERMINATING OR ATTEMPTING TO TERMINATE HUMAN PREGNANCY AFTER VIABILITY—(a criminal offense—2919.17.)

THEFT—(a criminal offense—2913.02.)

THEFT IN OFFICE—(a criminal offense—2921.41.)

THEFT OFFENSES—any of the following:

(1) A violation of section 2911.01, 2911.02, 2911.11, 2911.12, 2911.13, 2911.31, 2911.32, 2913.02, 2913.03, 2913.04, 2913.11, 2913.21, 2913.31, 2913.32, 2913.33, 2913.40, 2913.41, 2913.42, 2913.43, 2913.44, 2913.45, 2913.47, former section 2913.47 or 2913.48, or section 2913.51, 2913.81, 2915.05, 2915.06, or 2921.41 of the Revised Code;

(2) A violation of an existing or former municipal ordinance or law of this or any other state, or of the United States, substantially equivalent to any section listed in Division (1) above;

(3) An offense under an existing or former municipal ordinance or law of this or any other state, or of the United States, involving robbery, burglary, breaking and entering, theft, embezzlement, wrongful conversion, forgery, counterfeiting, deceit, or fraud;

(4) A conspiracy or attempt to commit, or complicity in committing any offense under Division (1), (2), or (3) above.

TRADEMARK COUNTERFEITING—(a criminal offense—2913.34)

TRAFFICKING IN DRUGS—(a criminal offense—2925.03.)

TRAFFICKING IN HARMFUL INTOXICANTS—(a criminal offense—2925.32.)

TRAFFICKING IN MARIHUANA—(a criminal offense—2925.03.)

U

UNAPPROVED DRUGS, OFFENSES INVOLVING—see 2925.09.

UNAUTHORIZED USE OF A VEHICLE—(a criminal offense—2913.03.)

UNAUTHORIZED USE OF BLOCK PARENT SYMBOL—(a criminal offense—2917.46.)

UNAUTHORIZED USE OF PROPERTY; COMPUTER PROPERTY—(a criminal offense—2913.04.)

UNDERAGE PURCHASE OF FIREARM OR HANDGUN—(a criminal offense—2923.21.1.)

UNEMANCIPATED (re: unlawful abortion)—(a woman) unmarried and under 18 years of age, not having entered the U. S. armed services, not having become employed and self-subsisting, or not otherwise having become independent from the care and control of her parent, guardian, and custodian—2919.12(F).

UNIT DOSE—an amount or unit of a compound, mixture, or preparation containing a controlled substance, such amount or unit being separately identifiable and in such form as to indicate that it is the amount or unit by which the controlled substance is separately administered to or taken by an individual—2925.01(F).

UNLAWFUL ABORTION—(a criminal offense—2919.12.)

UNLAWFUL DEBT (re: engaging in pattern of corrupt activity)—any money or other thing of value constituting principal or interest of a debt that is legally unenforceable in this state in whole or in part because the debt was incurred or contracted in violation of any federal or state law relating to the business of gambling activity or relating to the business of lending money at an usurious rate unless the creditor proves by a preponderance of the evidence that the usurious rate was not intentionally set and that it resulted from a good faith error by the creditor, notwithstanding the maintenance of procedures that were adopted by the creditor to avoid such an error—2923.31(L).

UNLAWFUL POSSESSION OF DANGEROUS ORDNANCE—(a criminal offense—2923.17.)

UNLAWFUL RESTRAINT—(a criminal offense—2905.03.)

UNLAWFUL TRANSACTIONS IN WEAPONS—(a criminal offense—2923.20.)

USE OF DRUG PARAPHERNALIA—(a criminal offense—2925.14.)

USING SHAM LEGAL PROCESS—(a criminal offense—2921.52.)

USING WEAPONS WHILE INTOXICATED—(a criminal offense—2923.15.)

UTTER—to issue, publish, transfer, use, put, or send into circulation, deliver, or display—2913.01(H).

V

VANDALISM—(a criminal offense—2909.05.)

VEHICULAR HOMICIDE—(a criminal offense—2903.07.)

VENDING MACHINE—see COIN MACHINE

VENUE—the trial of a criminal case in this State shall be held in a court having jurisdiction of the subject matter, and in the territory of which the offense or any element was committed. 2901.12 sets forth the requirements for the place of trial.

GLOSSARY OF TERMS

VIOLATING A PROTECTION ORDER, CONSENT AGREEMENT, OR ANTI-STALKING PROTECTION ORDER—(a criminal offense—2919.27.)

VOLUNTARY ACT—by choice, an act done by one's own free will (one of the necessary requisites for criminal liability).

VOLUNTARY MANSLAUGHTER—(a criminal offense—2903.03.)

VOYEURISM—(a criminal offense—2907.08.)

W

WORKERS' COMPENSATION FRAUD—(a criminal offense—2913.48)

WRITING—any computer software document, letter, memorandum, note, paper, plate, data, film, or other thing having in or upon it any written, typewritten, or printed matter, and also any token, stamp, seal, credit card, badge, trademark, label, or other symbol of value, right, privilege, license, or identification—2913.01(F).

Z

ZIP-GUN—any of the following: (1) any firearm of crude and extemporized manufacture; (2) any device, including without limitation a starter's pistol, not designed as a firearm, but which is specially adapted for use as such; or (3) any industrial tool, signalling device, or safety device, not designed as a firearm, but which as designed is capable of use as such, when possessed, carried, or used as a firearm—2923.11(G).